THE MYTHOLOGY OF AMERICAN POLITICS

THE MYTHOLOGY OF AMERICAN POLITICS

A Critical Response to Fundamental Questions

JOHN T. BOOKMAN

POTOMAC BOOKS, INC.
WASHINGTON, D.C.

Library of Congress Cataloging-in-Publication Data
Bookman, John T.
  The mythology of American politics : a critical response to fundamental questions / John T. Bookman. — 1st ed.
    p. cm.
  Includes bibliographical references and index.
  ISBN 978-1-59797-198-0 (hardcover : alk. paper) — ISBN 978-1-59797-199-7 (pbk. : alk. paper)
  1. United States—Politics and government. 2. Public administration—United States—History. 3. Representative government and representation—United States—History. 4. United States. Constitution. I. Title.
  JK411.B66 2008
  320.973—dc22

                                        2008014446

Printed in the United States of America on acid-free paper that meets the American National Standards Institute Z39-48 Standard.

Potomac Books, Inc.
22841 Quicksilver Drive
Dulles, Virginia 20166

First Edition

10 9 8 7 6 5 4 3 2 1

For Andra, Leah, Jessica, and Rachel

CONTENTS

PREFACE

The essays in this book respond to several of the perennial, fundamental questions in American politics. Although the electoral success of today's politicians, the disposition of current legislative proposals, and the consequences of last term's Supreme Court will figure not at all in the pages that follow, the questions taken up by these essays have an enduring currency. Even a casual reading of the daily newspaper attests to the vitality of such ideas as original intent, separation of powers, and tyranny of the majority. These ideas raise questions—the questions addressed here. They also are at the core of those myths that inform the thinking of many Americans about politics. These myths are the popular narratives that impart meaning to the American experience and define for many what it is to be an American. The approach to these myths will be critical, not celebratory. The evidence adduced and the arguments made on their behalf will be carefully examined.

Many books and journal articles have been written in response to each of the questions addressed. My essays can only mine the major seams of evidence and assay the principal arguments relevant to answers to these questions. Much that is said in the essays could be qualified or developed in more detail and thereby more fully disclose the truth of the matter. This would require volumes not essays to accomplish. I have proceeded, nonetheless, despite the limitations of the essay form, out of the recognition that neither the general public nor college undergraduates are likely to read much of the vast literature or to have devoted much time to hard thinking about these fundamental questions. It is for them that this book was written in the hope that they might begin the journey from assertion to argument.

Many others have labored in the fields turned over once again in this book. The lengthy endnotes are the measure of my indebtedness to them. I welcome the opportunity as well to thank my colleagues at the University of Northern Colorado: Brook Blair, John Loftis, and Bill Agan, who read one or another chapter, and particularly Stan Luger and Gail Rowe, who read them all. Thanks are also due to my friends Carl Hunt and Gil Matthijetz, who read the chapter on the market. Their efforts to save me from error are much appreciated. The errors in fact or interpretation that remain are mine alone. Finally, I am grateful to my wife, Andra, for saving me on more than one occasion from sending the manuscript into deepest cyberspace or deleting it altogether, to my editor at Potomac Books, Hilary Claggett, for her interest in and support for the book, and to the staff of the Michener Library, University of Northern Colorado, for help in obtaining materials.

CHAPTER 1

RELIGION AND THE CONSTITUTION

Americans have long sought support for their policy preferences in the intentions of the founders. In the contemporary controversy over the appropriate place of religion in the public sphere, citizens and policymakers invoke once again the names of James Madison, George Washington, Benjamin Franklin, and others among that band who drafted and ratified the Constitution and the Bill of Rights. The U.S. Constitution, of course, does address the matter of religion and politics in Article VI and in the First Amendment. Article VI provides that "no religious Test shall ever be required as a Qualification to any office or public Trust under the United States," and the First Amendment states, "Congress shall make no law respecting an establishment of religion, or prohibiting the free exercise thereof." These few, short clauses, however, do not provide clear answers to many questions.

And so Americans have consulted the historical record to find fuller expression of the intentions that inspired the constitutional provisions relating to religion and politics. The Constitution's provisions on religion, whatever else may have been intended, are generally agreed to have been intended to prohibit the establishment of a national church on the European pattern and to prohibit the imposition of legal disabilities for religious belief. Virtually every other aspect of the founders' thinking about the proper relationship between religion and politics remains in dispute. In what follows I hope to shed light on this subject. The more important question of whether or not we should defer to the founders' views on this, or any other, matter I postpone until the next chapter.

BARRIERS TO UNDERSTANDING THE THINKING OF THE FOUNDERS

Many partisans in the controversy over religion's place in politics have advanced with certainty various claims about the founders and the constitution they adopted. This certainty is misplaced for several reasons. First, the historical record, although voluminous, is not sufficiently complete to support definitive answers to many questions about what this or that group or individual believed or intended. Second, many among the founders about whom much is known, Washington and Madison, for example, were reticent about expressing their religious beliefs. The lesser known could be just as unforthcoming. William Few, a Georgia delegate to the Constitutional Convention, described as a "staunch believer in revealed religion," says not a word in his autobiography about his religious beliefs or experiences.[1] Even if we confine our attention to the Framers—the fifty-five delegates to the Constitutional Convention—we often do not know enough to say that all or most of the Framers held a particular belief. And where the record does permit generalization with some assurance, exceptions usually can be found. The Framers did not think alike. Third, to understand the thinking of the founders, we need to know the assumptions from which they proceeded in saying what they did and acting as they did. To put this another way, it is necessary to understand their worldview or, better, worldviews, for there were at least two that competed for their allegiance.

The clash of two worldviews—the Calvinist and Enlightenment views—largely defined intellectual and religious life in eighteenth-century America. The Calvinist view was the orthodox one, and it informed the tenets of almost all the Protestant churches of the day. The Enlightenment view, as expressed in what Americans called the "New Learning" and associated with the names of Isaac Newton, John Locke, and David Hume, among others, found favor with the better educated, including many clergymen.

Calvinism declared that God had elected from the beginning of time who would be saved—the doctrine of predestination. It declared, too, that Christ's crucifixion assured the salvation of some (the "elect") but not all; that since the Fall in the Garden of Eden humans have been corrupted irretrievably in mind and heart—the doctrine of original sin; that sin makes human beings totally dependent on God for salvation; and that the recipients of God's unmerited grace cannot resist salvation.

The Enlightenment challenged Calvinism in many respects. It subjected to scrutiny the orthodox God who is beyond human comprehension and human criteria of judgment. While retaining God as a First Cause, the

Enlightenment sought to explain the workings of nature, the conduct of the individual, the functioning of society, and the future of humankind by means of secondary causes. Successes in the discovery of natural laws increased confidence in human reason and pushed God into the background in the explanation of the natural order. Those successes served as well to erode belief in the orthodox God who personally and constantly watched over the cosmos and its inhabitants, and they eroded belief in miracles and the effectiveness of petitionary prayer. Furthermore, the Enlightenment's discovery of natural rights brought God within reach of human judgment. Natural rights are rules of right conduct not revealed by God but found out by human reason and attributed to God's ultimate authorship. Instead of the Calvinist portrait of human nature in blackest hue, the Enlightenment rendered several portraits in brighter colors. Seen in this way, individual humans might, under the right conditions, acquire virtue and societies might undergo long-term desirable change. Locke summed up the Enlightenment approach in his contention that "reason must be our last Judge and Guide in every thing."[2]

None of the Framers about whom much is known seem to have given assent wholly to either Calvinism or the Enlightenment.[3] The predominance of one or the other view varied among them and waxed and waned over the lives of each of them. All of the Framers expressed ideas drawn from both these worldviews, but none arrived at a reconciliation of them. Indeed, none of the Framers attempted to work out a reconciliation in an overt, systematic way. Many did attempt to combine elements of Calvinism with Enlightenment ideas in a piecemeal fashion. Perhaps the best example is the Framers' decided tendency to refer to God not as "God" but as the "Supreme Architect," the "Divine Governor," and other expressions reflecting increased acceptance of the Newtonian cosmology. For the most part, the extent to which the Framers regarded the world through Calvinist or Enlightenment eyes is uncertain. It is for this reason, as well as gaps in the record and the reluctance of many to express their religious beliefs, that any inquiry into the religious beliefs of the founders can only reach conclusions hedged about by qualifications.

This inquiry will take up a number of claims that have been made about the beliefs, intentions, and actions of the founding generation of Americans and the Framers in particular. It has been claimed that (1) the Framers of the Constitution were fundamentalist Christians;[4] (2) the Framers subscribed to a Judeo-Christian view of history as heading toward a new kingdom of God;[5] (3) Americans (at any rate, white Americans) at the time of the founding, that is, during the period of the Revolution and the adoption of the

Constitution constituted a "Christian nation";[6] (4) the establishment clause of the First Amendment was intended merely to bar a single national church and national preference of one sect over others;[7] and (5) the establishment clause was intended to protect established churches in the several states from national action.[8] In evaluating these claims, I shall take them up in the order set out above. With regard to the first claim, let us examine a critical time at the Constitutional Convention.

RELIGION AND THE ADOPTION OF THE CONSTITUTION

The Framers came to Philadelphia prepared to take bold measures. Within a week of convening, they had decided to set aside the Articles of Confederation, the constitution under which government had been operating, and to take up a plan proposed by the Virginia delegation. The Virginia (or Randolph) Plan provided for a highly centralized, national government in which representation would be proportional to population or taxes paid by each state. While sympathetic with the creation of a national government with increased authority, the delegates from the smaller states balked at the Virginia formula for representation. They presented an alternative plan.

The New Jersey (or Paterson) Plan, like the Virginia Plan, provided for a national government with expanded powers. But, instead of the proportional representation of the latter, the New Jersey Plan favored the equal representation of states in the national legislature. The presentation of the New Jersey Plan on June 15 shattered the calm that had prevailed for the first several weeks of the Convention. For the next month or so, tempers became frayed and the antagonists on both sides of the representation issue dug in their heels. Prospects looked bleak indeed for a successful outcome for the Convention's deliberations.

At this the darkest hour of the Convention, Benjamin Franklin observed, "The small progress we had made . . . is methinks a melancholy proof of the imperfection of the Human Understanding." Therefore, he moved that prayers "imploring the assistance of Heaven" precede deliberations.[9] Now, according to some, the Framers responded to Franklin's motion by immediately adjourning for three days of prayer and fasting to ask God's help in reconciling their differences; when they reconvened, the bitterness and contention were gone.[10] This report is a fiction.[11] The delegates did not adjourn for three days; they met the next day and the day following. Franklin's motion did not calm the waters; the debate continued to be contentious. The delegates did not fast, and as Franklin himself noted, "The Convention, except three or four persons, thought Prayers unnecessary."[12] The delegates adjourned for the day without taking any action, and no subsequent attempts would be made to seek intercession from on high. Human understanding would have to suffice without divine assistance. The Framers' final draft mentions religion only in Article VI, which expressly forbids the use of religious tests for national office.

None of the proposals made at the Convention made any mention of God or Christianity or any church. The Virginia Plan, although closely reflecting Madison's ideas, was the product of discussion among all the members of the Virginia delegation. The New Jersey Plan too, while often referred to as the Paterson Plan after William Paterson who presented it to the Convention, was a joint endeavor: members of the Connecticut, New York, New Jersey, and Delaware delegations and perhaps Luther Martin of Maryland were all consulted. John Dickinson, Alexander Hamilton, and Charles Pinckney worked alone in the development of their plans. Dickinson's plan, never presented in full to the Convention, did not refer to religion. Hamilton made no reference to religion. It is uncertain whether Pinckney included a prohibition on religious tests for office in his plan as originally submitted to the Convention on May 29. He did later secure the support of his fellow delegates for such a provision. According to Luther Martin, it was "adopted by a great majority of the convention, and without much debate."[13] No other provisions relating to religion were proposed at the Convention.

In the state ratifying conventions, the absence of God and Christianity from the Constitution and particularly the prohibition on religious tests for office provoked criticism. In addition to complaints about the omission of a bill of rights, a powerful executive, and swollen national authority, some Anti-Federalists, as the opponents of ratification were called, decried the secularism of the Framers' draft. They feared that God might withhold his favor from America, that no government without the support of religion could be sustained, and that government officials without religious restraint would become tyrants. The ban on religious tests also drew their ire because, as some pointed out, it would permit Catholics and Jews, pagans and deists to secure office.[14] The attempts of Anti-Federalists to make a state's ratification of the Constitution conditional on the addition of new language in the Constitution recognizing God or Christianity or imposing religious tests for office were unsuccessful. The Constitution proposed by the Framers and ratified by the state conventions declared allegiance to no faith, expressed no devotion to God, embraced no church, and placed itself on no transcendent foundation.[15]

The secular character of the Constitution was, as just noted, a basis of Anti-Federalist objections to ratification. Many ministers joined the Anti-Federalist campaign from the pulpit. Not even the passage of time served to embellish the Constitution for Timothy Dwight. On July 4, 1812, addressing the congregation in the college chapel, the Reverend Dwight, Professor of Divinity and President of Yale, said, "We formed our Constitution without any acknowledgment of God, without any recognition of his mercies to us, as a people, of his government, or even of his existence. The Convention, by which it was formed, never asked, even once, his direction, or his blessing upon their labours. Thus we commenced our national existence under the present system, without God."[16]

Dwight's colleague in the Congregational clergy, Chauncey Lee, made the same appraisal.[17] The Framers themselves regarded the Constitution as a human contrivance issuing from the exercise of human reason. They did not see their work at Philadelphia as divinely inspired. Nothing imperfect would have emerged under divine inspiration and the Framers agreed, as we shall see in the next chapter, that the Constitution was imperfect, although they had somewhat different reasons for thinking so. Three (Elbridge Gerry, George Mason, and Edmund Randolph) thought the Constitution so imperfect that they refused to sign. Four others (Robert Yates, John Lansing Jr., Luther Martin, and John Francis Mercer) left before the signing and went into opposition. None gave religious reasons for his opposition, and only Luther Martin faulted the draft for its secular character. The Framers, then, were not fundamentalist Christians.

THE RELIGIOUS BELIEFS OF THE FRAMERS

The Constitution was not the work of the irreligious, however, although few of the Framers could be described as fervent believers. William Pierce of Georgia wrote a set of character sketches of his fellow delegates in which he singled out only Richard Bassett as a "religious enthusiast." Bassett had undergone a born-again experience and converted to Methodism. Perhaps (the record is murky with respect to many of the Framers) he alone qualifies as a fundamentalist in the modern sense: one who (1) regards the Bible as the inerrant authority, (2) stresses the born-again experience, (3) seeks the moral purification of the individual and society, and (4) emphasizes Christ's redeeming role as the center of Christianity. The religiosity of some of the others, for example, John Blair, William Paterson, Charles Cotesworth Pinckney, Roger Sherman, Richard Dobbs Spaight, and Caleb Strong, was manifest in regular church attendance and financial support of their churches. Indeed almost all the Framers attended church fairly regularly—although, for example, George Washington (an Episcopalian and vestryman in his parish church but a sectarian in neither his beliefs nor his church attendance) did not always attend the same church and William Paterson, a Presbyterian who declined admission to communion, was not an official church member. Almost all had a religious affiliation. Episcopalians were most numerous among the Framers, followed by Congregationalists and Presbyterians. There were two Catholics—Daniel Carroll and Thomas Fitzsimons— and two Methodists—Richard Bassett and William Few. There were also two delegates who had been raised as Quakers—Thomas Mifflin and John Dickinson. Mifflin was expelled from the Quaker church in the course of his rise to the rank of major general in the Continental army. Dickinson, although he remained a religious man throughout his life, was suspicious of all formally organized religious bodies. Absent from the Framers' ranks were any Baptists, who, along with the Methodists, had taken the lead in the evangelical movement.

Few of the Framers set out their religious beliefs at length. Those who did express their beliefs mark out a wide range. On the one hand, Roger Sherman gave voice to quite orthodox Calvinist views in his *A Short Sermon on the Duty of Self Examination Preparatory to Receiving the Lord's Supper*. On the other, Benjamin Franklin in his *Autobiography* and elsewhere was so skeptical about the central claims of Christianity as to place him on the fringes, if not beyond the fringes, of the faith. Despite this diversity of views, most of the Framers occupied common ground in some respects. They believed in a God who created the universe and who rules over it by providence. They did not agree on just how providence manifests itself. Some expressed the orthodox Calvinist teaching that God constantly and personally directs the universe and human affairs. His supervision includes visiting on both the good and the evil calamities like crop failure, disease, or the death of a child but also benefits like a good harvest, relief from pain, and success in business. God might also intervene in response to prayer. Other Framers saw God's superintendence in the laws of nature, laws they understood as both physical regularities (the empirical laws of science) and ethical principles. More particularly, they thought that God had endowed humankind with natural rights. In the words of the Declaration of Independence to which Elbridge Gerry, Roger Sherman, Robert Morris, Benjamin Franklin, George Clymer, James Wilson, George Read, and George Wythe among the Framers were signatories, "We hold these truths to be self-evident, that all men are created equal, that they are endowed by their Creator with certain unalienable Rights." George Mason in his draft of the *Virginia Declaration of Rights* affirmed the same principles as did Madison in the *Memorial and Remonstrance*, James Wilson in his *Lectures on Law*, and Alexander Hamilton in *The Farmer Refuted*.[18]

Hamilton in the same essay affirmed as well that God had "endowed him [man] with rational faculties, by the help of which to discern and pursue such things as were consistent with his duty and interest."[19] John Dickinson made much the same observation: natural rights "are created in us by a decree of Providence which established the laws of our nature. They are founded in the immutable maxims of reason and justice."[20] And James Wilson asked, "How shall we, in particular cases, discover the will of God? We discover it by our conscience, our reason, and by the Holy Scripture. The Law of Nature and the law of revelation are both divine; they flow, though in different channels, from the same adorable source."[21] For Wilson, Hamilton, Dickinson, and the other Framers who spoke on this matter, the law of nature, including that which endows humankind with natural rights, can be known by the exercise of unaided reason—faith is not necessary to discern rights and duties. In sum, many of the Framers believed that people everywhere have the same rights and, as rational beings, have always been able to discern their rights and duties.

For them that part of morality defined by respect for rights is not based on religion. Indeed, at least for several of the Framers, revelation only confirms the moral precepts found out by reason. The same Benjamin Franklin who proposed prayer at the Constitutional Convention wrote in a letter to the Reverend Ezra Stiles, "Revelation had indeed no weight with me, as such; but I entertained an opinion that, though certain actions might not be bad *because* they were forbidden by it, or good *because* it commanded them, yet probably these actions might be forbidden *because* they were bad for us, or commanded *because* they were beneficial to us, in their own natures, all the circumstances of things considered."[22] According to James Wilson, a Pennsylvania delegate, the moral precepts revealed in scripture "generally presuppose a knowledge of the principles of morality; and are employed not so much in teaching new rules on the subject, as in enforcing the practice of those already known. . . . They are addressed to rational and moral agents, capable of previously knowing the rights of man."[23] From this point of view, the significance of religion is as a teacher of morality. Christ's significance too seems for the Framers to be as teacher and exemplar of moral conduct. How many of the Framers shared Franklin's doubts about the divinity of Christ is unknown. It is known that they seldom mentioned Jesus or ascribed to him the role of redeemer.[24] Nevertheless, they accorded to religion an important place in their thinking.

Many Framers believed that, although humans *can* know their rights and duties by reason, many *will not* respect the rights of others or carry out their duties without the support of religion. Madison was a notable exception. He was skeptical at the time about the effectiveness of religion in promoting self-restraint, but in later years he would come around to the view held by most of the other delegates.[25] George Washington expressed the common view when he observed, "Whatever may be conceded to the influence of refined education on minds of peculiar structure, reason and experience both forbid us to expect that National morality can prevail in exclusion of religious principle."[26] For Washington and his fellows, this was critical because they believed, as Montesquieu had taught them, that republican government requires a virtuous citizenry. Madison wrote in *The Federalist* 55, "As there is a degree of depravity in mankind which requires a certain degree of circumspection and distrust, so there are other qualities in human nature which justify a certain portion of esteem and confidence. Republican government presupposes the existence of these qualities in a higher degree than any other form."[27] The necessary qualities constitute "civic virtue" by which the Framers meant a willingness to sacrifice one's private interests to the common good. As James Wilson observed to the Pennsylvania state ratifying convention, "No [republican] government, either single or confederated, can exist, unless private and individual rights are subservient to the public and general happiness of the nation."[28] Pierce Butler, writing to a friend in England, conceded, "Much must depend on the morals and manners of the people at large. . . . Good Order and Obedience must greatly depend on the Patriotism of the Citizen."[29] Civic virtue is manifest in voluntary obedience to the law but more fully in Washington's departure from his beloved Mount Vernon at the risk of everything—home, family, and his own neck—to assume command of the Continental army. Civic virtue is not a Christian virtue, but Christianity, by teaching restraint on private appetite and accountability in the next life for conduct in this, can contribute greatly to the creation of a virtuous citizenry.[30]

Before examining another claim concerning the Framers' religious beliefs, it is worth remarking that these were men who devoted their lives to secular affairs—all of them to politics and many to making money, lots of it. Their worldly concerns did not bar them, of course, from having a religious life, but their religious life seems to have been largely conventional and not very intense for most of them. This would explain in part the almost complete absence of any reference to God, Christ, or scripture at the Convention. Franklin's quotation of scripture and his proposal for prayer marked a rare expression of religious belief in the deliberations. If religion did inform their thinking in the drafting of the Constitution, the Framers did not give voice to the thought. According to Abraham Baldwin, delegate from Georgia and one-time theologian at Yale and chaplain in the Continental army, "They [the Framers] took their principles from that set of political economists and philosophers now generally denominated in the English language Whigs."[31] This appraisal is borne out with respect to Madison and Hamilton in *The Federalist*. In this now famous series of essays, Madison and Hamilton defended the Convention's work.[32] These essays first appeared serially in New York newspapers in an effort to win over delegates to that state's convention where ratification was in jeopardy. In the eighty essays written by Madison and Hamilton, comprising hundreds of pages, scripture is not cited at all and God receives mention in only three essays and then in passing (#20, 37, and 43). When they do invoke authority, and they seldom do, they turn to figures like Montesquieu and Sir William Blackstone.

The Bible, then, would not seem to have been uppermost in the minds of the Framers. Indeed, judging from what they said at the Convention and in the debates over ratification, religion seems to have been consigned to a place well in the background. It is this that makes difficult any evaluation of the claim that the Framers believed that history has a purpose, namely, the realization of a kingdom of God in which Christ would rule in peace and justice. This belief was central to the New England heirs of the Puritan clergy.[33] They saw themselves as party to a covenant between God and His chosen people. From that covenant, they believed, America had developed and only in obedience to that covenant would America survive. And, for them, as a Christian nation, a covenanted people, America had a special role in God's plan for redemption. The Framers, or at any rate some of the Framers, may have held such beliefs, but, unlike the Puritans, they did not accord government an important role in creating the conditions for the Second Coming. The Puritans in contrast invested government with the authority to establish the church and to suppress heretical opinion and practice. The evidence for the Framers having held millennial beliefs, however, is slim and would seem to consist largely in the inference that, since almost all were Christians in some sense, they must have held these beliefs.

It is true that some Framers shared with some other Christians a view that invested history with a new meaning and a direction. History, in this view, is not a recurring tale of rise and decline. Particularly since the Middle Ages, advances in knowledge, scientific and philosophical, had challenged the reign of superstition and ignorance. Increased awareness of natural rights had promoted more liberal government. Increased trade and technological innovations had brought higher standards of living. Over the course of history, then, change had occurred and occurred in a desirable direction. Ideas like these were abroad at the time and could be found in the writings of French thinkers.[34] Certainly the pace of historical change was accelerating, making change more apparent in a person's lifetime. The occurrence of change, desirable change, had not escaped the attention of Washington, who allowed in a letter to Marquis de Lafayette in 1786,

> as a citizen of the great republic of humanity at large; I cannot help turning my attention to this subject. . . . On these occasions I consider how fond, perhaps an enthusiastic idea, that as the world is evidently much less barbarous than it has been, its melioration must still be progressive; that nations are becoming more humanized in their policy, that the subjects of ambition and causes for hostility are daily diminished, and, in fine, that the period is not very remote, when the benefit of a liberal and free commerce will, pretty generally, succeed to the devastations and horrors of war.[35]

In this, there is no imputation of a purpose to history and no assertion that the purpose is realization of a new kingdom of God. If Washington, let alone most of his fellow delegates, had in view a kingdom of God, he (and they) did not say so. The institution of stable republican regimes in which individual rights are respected and the public good promoted and which lived in peace with their neighbors constituted the measures of progress.

It is also true that some of the Framers like some other Christians thought that America had a special role to play in history. The best-known expression of this conviction occurs in *The Federalist*. Hamilton in the first number observed, "It seems to have been reserved to the people of this country, by their conduct and example, to decide the important question, whether societies of men are really capable or not of establishing good government from reflection and choice, or whether they are forever destined to depend for their political constitutions on accident and force."[36] Madison in a later number is no less persuaded of the significance of the American experiment: "Posterity will be indebted for the possession, and the world for the example, of the numerous innovations displayed on the American theater in favor of private rights and public happiness. . . . They [Americans] accomplished a revolution which has no parallel in the annals of human society. They reared the fabrics of governments which have no model on the face of the globe."[37] Hamilton and Madison in seeking to impress on a general audience the importance of the Convention's decision on the proposed constitution were only reaffirming a view expressed earlier at the Convention. Addressing his fellow delegates, Madison had said that they "were now digesting a plan which in its operation wd. decide forever the fate of Republican Govt"—a sentiment with which Hamilton expressly agreed.[38]

Some among their listeners required little persuasion. Elbridge Gerry, delegate from Massachusetts, in the midst of the effort to resolve the dispute over representation said, "Something must be done, or we shall disappoint not only America, but the whole world."[39] And Gouverneur Morris pleaded with his fellows to take a large view of the question. As for himself, "he came here as a Representative of America; he flattered himself he came here in some degree as a Representative of the whole human race; for the whole human race will be affected by the proceedings of this Convention."[40] Franklin believed that, should the Convention fail, "mankind may hereafter from this unfortunate instance, despair of establishing Governments by Human Wisdom and leave it to chance, war and conquest."[41] And Washington in his first inaugural stated, "The preservation of the sacred fire of liberty and the destiny of the republican model of government are justly considered, perhaps, as *deeply*, as *finally*, staked on the experiment intrusted to the hands of the American people."[42] The emphasis in their remarks is not on the distinctive character of Americans as a chosen people of God. Indeed, no such claim is made. What distinguishes Americans is the opportunity to institute a republican government that can endure. If Americans fail to seize this opportunity, the consequence will not be God's wrath but disappointment of humankind.

THE RELIGIOUS BELIEFS OF THE FOUNDING GENERATION

If gaps in the record make it difficult to speak with assurance about the religious beliefs of all the Framers, the record concerning the religious beliefs of those who ratified the Constitution and, more generally, of all Americans at the time of the founding is so thin as to permit only the most tentative conclusions. What of the claim that Americans at the time constituted a "Christian nation"? One answer is provided by The Treaty of Tripoli (1797), to which the Senate gave its unanimous consent and President John Adams affixed his signature. It provided that the United States was "not in any sense founded on the Christian religion." Nevertheless, it is the case that, among the white population, save for a few synagogues, only Christians had erected places of worship in the American colonies. Jews made up a tiny fraction of the population, and Muslims, Hindus, and others immigrated much later. It is also the case that nine of the colonies on the eve of the Revolution maintained established Christian churches. In these respects, Americans constituted, formally, a "Christian nation." Indeed, one could go further and say a Protestant Christian nation because, while they had early established a haven in Maryland, Roman Catholics were few. Something more, however, is surely intended by the claim. To weigh the truth of any more significant meaning of the phrase "Christian nation," let us distinguish between the visible and invisible church. Those who belong to the visible church give outward signs of their devotion. Among these signs are attendance at church, contributions of money and the performance of "good works." They might also make a profession of faith and receive the sacraments. Such behavior may issue from genuine devotion, but it may also be simply customary behavior or come out of a desire for social acceptance, political advancement, and the like. The invisible church is made up of those whose faith is authentic, who have real inward sanctity, who have received God's grace.

Now, if the claim that Americans of the founding generation constituted a Christian nation means that Americans in whole or in part were members of the invisible church, we shall be unable to make a judgment one way or the other. This is not to say that another's mind and heart are completely opaque to us, particularly as we can know someone at close hand, over a long period, and in a variety of situations. It is to acknowledge that these conditions for really knowing someone are not well satisfied with respect to the founders—even the accounts of contemporaries when they are available can be quite unhelpful on this score. It is also to acknowledge that we rely on behavior including speech to inform us of another's inward state, and behavior is only a more or less reliable indicator. Perhaps the fuller meaning of the term "Christian nation" is that most Americans at the founding were members of the visible church or, more specifically, that most Americans were members of a Christian church or regularly attended a Christian church.

The most careful attempt to determine church membership at the time of the founding concluded that roughly 10 percent of white Americans belonged to a congregation.[43] This is, to be sure, an estimate, but even the less well-founded estimates of others fall within the range of 5 to 20 percent. Thus, only a small minority among the founding generation had made a profession of faith and been admitted to communion. It is only this minority about whom we might make inferences concerning their beliefs with any assurance. Their profession of faith would provide a foundation for such inferences. Anecdotal evidence suggests, however, that most Americans were indifferent about doctrinal matters, so even church membership might not imply much in particular, for example, a belief in a new kingdom of God.

Church attendance is a more elusive quarry. There is just not much to go on in arriving at an estimate. Few churches kept records of attendance and, among those that did, it is unknown how church officials counted the number of church-goers. The concept of attendance itself is vague. Did a person (or family) attend regularly—every Sunday, say—or only on the high holidays? Any inferences that we make on the basis of the little we know about the founders' church membership or church attendance are shaky indeed. And this cuts both ways. We can no more claim that most Americans did not believe in Christ's divinity or a new kingdom of God than they did believe in those things. Nevertheless, it can be said that the claim that Americans constituted a Christian nation, except in those respects specified initially, is based on faith and not evidence.

Before we leave the examination of this claim, another body of evidence should be surveyed in the effort to identify the religious beliefs of the founding generation. The period of the founding saw a tremendous outpouring of public commentary in the form of newspaper articles and pamphlets. A study of this literature found that the Bible was the most cited source—34 percent of the total number of citations.[44] Almost three-quarters of these biblical citations came in sermons reprinted for circulation as pamphlets. Except in the pulpit, then, the Bible did not much figure in the thinking of Americans as they debated in the years 1760 to 1805 the course that the country ought to take. In the debate over the Constitution in 1787–1788, Federalist supporters did not refer to the Bible at all and Anti-Federalists only rarely. These indicators offer little support for the idea that the founding generation was particularly pious.

THE STATES' EXPERIENCE WITH ESTABLISHMENT OF RELIGION

By 1787 the Framers, and increasing numbers of Americans generally, had come to rethink the relationship between government and religion. During the colonial period, nine states had established churches that in some respects followed the European pattern: attendance was required and all persons were taxed to build and maintain church buildings and to pay the clergy's salaries. Establishment was typically joined to a regime of persecution and discrimination against those who held unorthodox views.

In Massachusetts and Connecticut, only Congregationalists could vote or hold office. In Virginia and North Carolina, only Anglican ministers could perform marriages. Most states required that ministers be licensed, and in Massachusetts licenses were issued only to those who held college degrees. Outside Pennsylvania and Rhode Island, Catholics risked imprisonment, fines, and banishment if they engaged in public worship or published Catholic views. Until the eighteenth century, Quakers (again outside Pennsylvania and Rhode Island) were nearly everywhere banned, fined, and imprisoned for practicing their religion; in the mid-1600s Massachusetts hanged four Quakers who had the temerity to return to the state after banishment.

Several conditions served to decrease the severity of this oppression. First, the established churches in America, unlike those in Europe, had no centralized church government to define and enforce orthodoxy.[45] This permitted individual congregations to develop their own understandings of church teachings. It also meant that if the purity of worship were to be defended against the unorthodox, then civil authorities would have to do it. And civil authorities might, and often did, see things differently than churchmen. Second, government was weak and clergymen few, particularly in the backcountry and in the more southern states. These circumstances conferred a measure of religious liberty even on those who might not have wanted it.

The eighteenth century saw a relaxation in the grip of the established churches. Nevertheless, on the eve of the Revolution established churches persisted in some form in nine states. And, while the incidence and severity of persecution and discrimination had declined, they too persisted. A young James Madison wrote to a friend in 1774, "There are at this [time?] in the adjacent county not less than 5 or 6 well meaning men in close Goal for publishing their religious sentiments, which in the main are very orthodox."[46] The principles of the Declaration of Independence, the association of the Anglican church with the British imperial government, growing religious diversity, and a new appreciation of the costs of religious intolerance all promoted changes in the relationship between government and religion after independence.

These changes show the extent to which Americans were prepared to abandon inherited systems of church-state relations. Before the close of the century, every state by statute or constitutional provision guaranteed rights of conscience (that is, the free exercise of religion). These provisions were understood to forbid the imposition of criminal penalties for practicing one's religion as long as public order and safety were not disturbed. This freed from molestation the many Baptists, Quakers, Methodists, and others in dissent from established churches. These provisions for free exercise also removed civil disabilities like exclusion from voting, office, giving testimony in court, and the need to marry in the established church. Many of the same legislatures and conventions that had adopted "free exercise" provisions continued, however, to impose civil disabilities on non-Christians (eleven states) and in many cases non-Protestants (seven states). These disabilities took the form of test oaths for office and in some instances the qualification that only Christians (or Protestants) must not be denied civil rights. By 1787 and the convening of the Constitutional Convention, Virginia and Rhode Island alone did not discriminate on religious grounds. South Carolina, Delaware, and Georgia, however, would soon thereafter eliminate their test oaths, and Pennsylvania would modify its test oath to permit Jews to hold office.

The only established churches to survive the early years of the republic were in Massachusetts, Connecticut, and New Hampshire. Disestablishment did not occur at one stroke and in some states required several attempts to accomplish, but by the end of the eighteenth century, six states had cut their ties to the Anglican Church and its successor the Episcopal Church. All six states adopted constitutional provisions banning establishment. Even in the three states where established churches persisted, the form that establishment took was modified. In Massachusetts, the 1780 constitution provided that everyone had to pay taxes for the support of that local Protestant minister designated by the taxpayer. The Congregational ministry was the recipient in the great preponderance of cases. Massachusetts also continued to compel attendance at Protestant services. New Hampshire's constitution of 1784 authorized public support for Protestant ministers but specified that no person of one sect ever be forced to pay toward the support of another sect's ministry. It also did not demand attendance at religious services. The Connecticut legislature adopted a statute in 1784 that relieved dissenters from attendance at Congregational services provided they attended their own churches and from the payment of support for the Congregational ministry. Pennsylvania, New Jersey, Delaware, and Rhode Island, which had never had established churches, continued to forbid them.

The language used to accomplish disestablishment bears examination for the light it may cast on the meaning that Americans of the founding generation attached to the term "establishment of religion."[47] According to Georgia's constitution of 1777, "all persons . . . shall not, unless by consent, support any teacher or teachers [of religion], except those of their own profession."[48] This provision made possible what would later be called "general assessment" or "multiple establishment." On this scheme, everyone is taxed

for the support of religion, but the taxes are distributed to the ministers designated by individual taxpayers. Soon after the Revolution, four other states—
Maryland, Virginia, Massachusetts, and New Hampshire—which had had
established churches in the colonial period, authorized general assessment.[49]
The Massachusetts and New Hampshire legislatures adopted general assessment, although in the former in the face of determined opposition from the
Baptists.[50] General assessment proposals died in Georgia and Maryland for
lack of popular support and in Virginia after a sharply contested struggle.
To prevent any future attempts to provide state support, Georgia in 1798
adopted a constitution that provided, "No one religious society shall ever be
established in this state, in preference to another" and all support for ministers and church buildings must be voluntary.[51] Casting the prohibition in
this form was common. In their constitutions, Delaware (1776 and 1792) and
New Jersey (1776), which had never known established churches, and North
Carolina (1776), which had, all used language like that of Georgia. New York
in 1777 and South Carolina in 1790 guaranteed the "free exercise and enjoyment of religious profession and worship, without discrimination or preference."[52] The struggle in Virginia over general assessment culminated in 1785
in the passage of the Bill for Establishing Religious Freedom, which asserted
that people may not be compelled to "frequent or support" any religious
worship. Pennsylvania, which had never known establishment, had earlier
(1776) adopted a similar prohibition.[53]

Two things should be noted about these state constitutions and statutes and the debate concerning them. First, today's distinction between the
meaning of "free exercise of religion" and "an establishment of religion" was
not a distinction made by many of the founding generation. Today, some
read these two phrases of the First Amendment as defenses against different
threats to freedom of religion. This understanding can be seen in the Supreme
Court's reliance on "free exercise" in striking down what it sees as government interference with an individual's religious beliefs or practices and its
reliance on "establishment" in striking down government aid to religion.
For most Americans of the founding generation, however—insofar as the
record reflects their thinking—an establishment of religion was a violation
of the free exercise of religion. In states where establishment was maintained
or proposed, dissenters invoked the rights of conscience and free exercise
in opposition. Baptists in Massachusetts and New Hampshire, "Separates"
in Connecticut, and Presbyterians and Baptists among others in Virginia all
argued that general assessment constituted state interference in the exercise
of religious freedom. These appeals were unsuccessful in Massachusetts and

New Hampshire. In Connecticut, dissenters won a concession from the legislature in 1784: *An Act for Securing the Rights of Conscience in Matters of Religion, to Christians of Every Denomination* gave exemptions from attendance on the established Congregational Church and from payment of taxes for the support of that church. In Virginia, James Madison rallied opposition to Patrick Henry's 1784 assessment bill by his "Memorial and Remonstrance Against Religious Assessments."[54] This essay, whose conclusion found the proposed establishment a violation of that "free exercise of religion" guaranteed by the state's Declaration of Rights, provided the text for many petitions to the Virginia legislature. The *Bill for Establishing Religious Freedom* brought an end to the campaign for general assessment by declaring establishment to be contrary to the freedom vouchsafed to all "to profess, and by argument to maintain, their opinions in matters of religion."[55] Thus, many Americans regarded an establishment of religion as a violation of the free exercise of religion. It remains to show the meaning they attached to "establishment."

The second thing to note, then, about the religion provisions in the statutes and constitutions adopted by the states after the Revolution is that the founders did not distinguish between two forms of establishment: one established church that alone receives public support for its ministry, on the one hand, and multiple establishment or general assessment schemes under which all (Protestant) churches receive public support for their ministries, on the other. The contention that legislators and others involved in the contest over establishment at the state level did make such a distinction relies on the "no preference" language that they so commonly used. The New Jersey (1776) and Delaware (1776 and 1792) constitutions forbade "the establishment of any one sect . . . in preference to another." The legislators in these states, where no church had received state aid in colonial times, did not intend to begin the practice even on a non-preferential basis. Lest there be any mistake about their intentions, they also forbade the use of any compulsion to attend church or to pay for the support of any church. Under its 1777 constitution, Georgia passed but did not implement general assessment. Georgia's 1798 constitution provided for "no preference" as did the 1776 North Carolina constitution. In neither state was general assessment contemplated as a legal possibility. Both included express prohibitions on laws requiring church attendance or the payment of taxes for the support of churches. New York in 1777 and South Carolina in 1790 used "no preference" language in a somewhat different form. Citizens were assured of the "free exercise and enjoyment of religious profession and worship, without discrimination or preference." Nothing in the record in either of these

states suggests that legislators or citizens thought that this language authorized general assessment. "Without discrimination or preference" was not
regarded as qualifying "free exercise" in such a way as to permit public support for churches in even a nondiscriminatory way.

The opponents of general assessment in those states where it prevailed also used the language of "no preference." The town of Petersham
criticized general assessment in the 1780 Massachusetts constitution as an
"Engine in the Hands of Tyrants" and submitted an amendment providing
that "no subordination of any one Sect or Denomination to another shall
ever be established by law."[56] The Reverend John Leland, a Baptist leader,
who believed that support for religion should be voluntary, proposed an
amendment to the Massachusetts constitution in 1794. It provided that
the state shall never "establish any religion by law, [or] give any one sect
a preference to another."[57] The Reverend Isaac Backus, spokesman for the
Baptists' New England association, who opposed all government financial support for churches, charged that Massachusetts assumed that "the
civil power has a right to set one religious sect up above another."[58] Finally,
Virginia's Baptists opposed Patrick Henry's general assessment proposal in
their petition urging that "all Distinctions in your laws may be done away,
and no order or Denomination of Christians in this Commonwealth have
any separate Privileges allowed them."[59] The idea that "no preference" was
intended only to forbid state aid to one church rests on a misconception
about how the founders were using language. For most of the founders outside Massachusetts, Connecticut, and New Hampshire, state aid to religion
even if nondiscriminatory was impermissible.

Throughout the country, however, people regarded the severing of
church-state ties from a confined point of view. Christian, and more specifically Protestant, perspectives prevailed everywhere. Compulsory attendance laws and taxes for the building and maintenance of churches and
the payment of clergy violated widely held convictions about the rights of
conscience. With some exceptions, conscientious scruples did not extend to
Sabbatarian laws; test oaths for office that demanded belief in Christian doc-
trines and renunciation of allegiance to foreign powers (the papacy); the use
of texts like *The New England Primer*, which contained the Lord's Prayer, and
the Westminster Catechism in public schools; the holding of church services
in public buildings; and the proclamation of days of prayer and thanksgiv-
ing by public officials. In short, some significant ties between church and
state were loosened, even severed after the Revolution, but many remained.

ESTABLISHMENT IN THE DEBATES OVER RATIFICATION

The Framers sent a constitution to the states for ratification whose sole provision relating to religion was a prohibition on test oaths for holding national office. The absence of explicit safeguards for freedom of religion inspired fear among some that the national government might establish a national religion or otherwise violate the rights of conscience. The Federalists believed that the national government had no authority under the Constitution to act with respect to religion, but their arguments failed to persuade some whose support was necessary to secure ratification in several key states.[60] James Madison and other Federalists assured these critics that the new government would move quickly to add a bill of rights. He honored this pledge by proposing a series of amendments in the First Congress. Consideration of these amendments followed months of debate over the Constitution in the states and the recommendation of amendments by several state ratifying conventions. Examination of the record of these events will help in the evaluation of the two remaining claims concerning religion and the founding: that the First Amendment establishment clause was intended to protect established churches in the states against national action and that the establishment clause was intended merely to bar a single national church and national preference of one sect over others but not to prohibit non-preferential state aid to religion.

Many citizens insisted that the rights of conscience must be explicitly protected in the Constitution.[61] Fewer expressed a fear that the national government might impose a national religion.[62] For the most part, there was no elaboration of the meaning of such recurrent phrases as "rights of conscience," "free exercise of religion," and "liberty of conscience." Those who were more specific asserted that no one ought to be compelled to attend any religious worship or to pay taxes for the support of any ministry or be molested for one's religious beliefs or practices.[63] No settled meaning for these phrases was shared throughout the states. Proponents of general assessment, for example, denied that such a system violated rights of conscience. And some proponents of the rights of conscience believed that non-Protestants or non-Christians fell outside their protection.

Let us first take up the claim that the establishment clause was intended to protect established churches in the states from national action. Is this what critics of the Constitution had in mind when they charged that Congress might establish a national religion? It seems unlikely, but the case is not conclusive. "National religion" was a phrase that received no definition in the popular debates or in the proceedings of the state ratifying conventions. Before exploring further, it must be said that there probably was no single meaning shared by all and that one of those meanings may have expressed fear that the national government might take action against established churches in the states. It is worth noticing, however, that the charge that Congress might establish a national religion came not only from Massachusetts and Connecticut, which still had established churches. What might people have had in mind by the expression "national religion"? The imposition of articles of faith? Americans had never known this form of establishment. Compulsory attendance at religious services and taxation for the support of a single ministry? This form of establishment had largely vanished from the law after the Revolution. General assessment? This seems the most likely meaning of "national religion" in most instances. The struggles in the states over establishment from the Revolution forward were provoked by proposals for general assessment. If this is what most Americans feared when they spoke of a "national religion," then New England's established churches were in no jeopardy.

If people in Massachusetts, Connecticut, and New Hampshire feared that their established churches would be in jeopardy under the Constitution, why did they not just say so? They were not reluctant to express other concerns. And yet the record of the debates in the states does not contain any explicit expressions of this fear. Furthermore, none of those states recommended amendments that addressed the matter. Indeed, Connecticut recommended no amendments at all. Massachusetts recommended nine amendments, none of which had to do with religion. New Hampshire proposed that "Congress shall make no law touching religion, or to infringe the rights of Conscience."[64] Such a prohibition would have protected established churches from national action. Its reach, however, is much broader than that—so broad as to make unlikely that the state ratifying convention had established churches in particular in mind.[65] None of this, of course, demonstrates the conclusion that the establishment clause was *not* intended to protect established churches from national action. Neither the general citizenry nor the members of the state ratifying conventions wrote the First Amendment. What can be said is that whatever the establishment clause was intended to accomplish, it was not adopted in response to sentiment in the states that established churches would be in jeopardy under the Constitution.

The second claim about the establishment clause has no support in the record of the debate over the proposed constitution. That claim asserts that the First Amendment establishment clause permits non-preferential aid to religion by government. The only statements from the record of the debate relevant here trumpeted the need to protect rights of conscience. But this argues against the idea that Americans wished to permit non-preferential aid. As we have seen, many Americans regarded even non-preferential aid to churches as a violation of rights of conscience. The amendments recommended by three states seem to lend some support to the idea that non-preferential aid is constitutionally acceptable. This appearance of support, however, is illusory. Virginia, New York, and North Carolina did use the language of "no preference," but as we have seen, "no preference" did not mean that government may give even non-preferential aid to religion. Virginia can hardly be thought to favor such aid in light of its defeat of a non-preferential general assessment bill just a few years earlier. In particular, George Mason, who drafted the Virginia amendment, was a dogged opponent of general assessment. Thus, the claim that non-preferential aid to religion is permissible cannot summon support from the views of Americans expressed at large or in the state ratifying conventions. It is against this background that congressional action on the First Amendment must be seen.

AN ESTABLISHMENT OF RELIGION: THE FIRST AMENDMENT

Madison's proposed amendments were intended to deny explicitly to Congress authority that he and his fellow Federalists never thought Congress had. The critics of the Framers' draft, the Anti-Federalists, also wanted to deny authority over religion that Congress might find in the murkier passages of the Constitution, particularly the "necessary and proper" clause. There was agreement, then, on the end to be secured by an amendment regarding religion—deny authority to the national government. Just what words would best accomplish that result commanded the attention, albeit briefly, of the First Congress and subsequently the state legislatures that ratified the amendments known as the Bill of Rights. Unfortunately, the historical record of these proceedings is so spare as to frustrate the search for clarity about the meaning of the religion provisions of the First Amendment. The only record of the debate in the House of Representatives is unofficial. It is not a verbatim report but a reconstruction by journalists relying on their notes and memories. The House Select Committee (which reported the proposed amendments to the House), the conference committee (convened to resolve House-Senate differences over the amendments), and the state legislatures (which ratified the amendments) failed to leave any record of their discussions. As for the U.S. Senate, its meetings in the early years were held in secret. The Senate's *Journal* of those meetings recorded only motions made and whether they were adopted or rejected. This does not provide a great deal to go on in fleshing out the meaning of First Amendment establishment.

On August 15, 1789, the House took up the report of its Select Committee on amendments. The committee proposed that "no religion shall be established by law, nor shall the equal rights of conscience be infringed." The House devoted a day to consideration of the amendment on religion.[66] At the end of that day, it had adopted Samuel Livermore's formulation: "Congress shall make no laws touching religion, or infringing the rights of conscience." Livermore was one of eight who spoke that day, and like several others, he revealed a certain indifference to the connotations of the words used to accomplish the desired result, namely, to deny Congress authority over religion. Felicity of style seemed to take precedence over the careful articulation of meaning. John Vining of Delaware, commenting on the Select Committee's proposal, suggested "transposing the two members of the sentence." Elbridge Gerry of Massachusetts thought the amendment "would read better if it was, that no religious doctrine shall be established by law." He was here repeating the standard Congregational invective long hurled against the Church of England. Daniel Carroll announced that "he would not contend with gentlemen about phraseology, his object was to secure the substance in such a manner as to satisfy the wishes of the honest part of the community." Livermore thought the language suggested by his state, New Hampshire, was an improvement on the Select Committee's proposal, "but he did not wish to dwell long on the subject." Roger Sherman of Connecticut wished the House to spend no time at all on the matter and moved to strike. Like his fellow Federalists, he believed the amendment unnecessary because the Constitution conferred no authority over religion to Congress. Madison announced himself unwilling to say "whether the words are necessary or not," but he recognized that some insisted on them.

Substance was not slighted altogether. Benjamin Huntington of Connecticut feared that the House Select Committee's version might be understood to make the established church in his state subject to suit for violating freedom of religion. Here at last was an explicit expression of the fear that established churches might be in jeopardy—not in jeopardy under the Constitution as drafted by the Framers and ratified by the states but under an amendment intended to dispel suspicions about national power. Huntington proposed no change in the language of the amendment, and he was not heard from again that day. He would not be chosen as a member of the conference committee. His fear might not have been unique, but it was not widespread. Roger Sherman, his fellow representative from Connecticut and a Congregational stalwart, did not share his concern. Madison sought to reassure Huntington, but he repeated his conviction that citizens feared that Congress might infringe the rights of conscience and establish a national religion. The House, after adopting Livermore's provision on religion, then moved on to the consideration of other amendments.

When the House returned to the amendment on religion several days later, it adopted without debate a proposal by Fisher Ames of Massachusetts that the amendment read, "Congress shall make no law establishing religion, or to prevent the free exercise thereof, or to infringe the rights of conscience." This was the version sent to the Senate. That body rejected three motions to amend the House version in favor of "no preference" language. It adopted a narrower prohibition on congressional authority: "Congress shall make no law establishing articles of faith or a mode of worship, or prohibiting the free exercise of religion." By implication, this would have permitted non-preferential aid to religion. The Senate, however, was not much committed to its language. Even before the conference committee met to resolve House-Senate disagreements over the amendments, the Senate indicated its willingness to yield to the House on the amendment on religion, if the House accepted the Senate version of the others. The amendment that emerged from the bargaining provided that "Congress shall make no law respecting an establishment of religion, or prohibiting the free exercise thereof." This was the language ratified by the states as the First Amendment.

Now, where does this leave us with respect to the two claims about the meaning of the First Amendment? The historical record suggests that the religion provisions were not carefully crafted and that its authors were inattentive to nuances of meaning. It is a mistake, then, to attach great significance to the choice of this word or phrase rather than another. What the First Congress seems to have intended was twofold: First, it wanted to express the perceived popular consensus about what government ought not to do in the religious realm in a brief, felicitous way. And, second, it wanted to apply those prohibitions explicitly to the national government. It was not part of the congressional intention to protect established churches in the states against national action, although, coincidentally, those churches secured such protection under the First Amendment establishment clause. And it was not part of the congressional intention to empower the national government to do anything. In particular, Congress did not intend to authorize non-preferential aid to religion. Keep in mind, however, that when most

Americans spoke of aid to religion what they had in mind was tax support for the building of churches and the payment of ministers' salaries or the use of state power to coerce church attendance or to punish unorthodox beliefs and practices.

In the same session in which Congress wrote the First Amendment, it adopted the Northwest Ordinance. This act provided that "Religion, Morality and knowledge being necessary to good government and the happiness of mankind, Schools and the means of education shall forever be encouraged."[67] The Confederation Congress, which first adopted this provision in 1787, had defeated a proposal that would have provided public funding of churches. Such funding would have run counter to the popular consensus of the 1780s as embodied in the First Amendment. The funding of schools in which religion was taught as part of, or in addition to, secular subjects did not. Nothing like a set of rules for the interpretation of the religion provisions was developed in the early republic. National policymakers, however, often acted on the belief that the national government in the exercise of powers delegated to it by Article I, Section 8 may provide non-preferential aid to religion. Among those who did not share this belief was James Madison, father of the Constitution and of the Bill of Rights. As president in 1811, he vetoed a bill incorporating the Episcopal Church in the District of Columbia. In his veto message, he noted that the bill "enacts into and establishes by law sundry rules and proceedings" for the operation of the Episcopal Church. This constituted an establishment of religion. He objected as well to the bill's provision making the church an agent for the distribution of charity and the education of the poor. This, Madison wrote, "would be a precedent for giving to religious societies as such a legal agency in carrying into effect a public and civil duty."[68]

CONCLUSION

The Framers were not, with perhaps a few exceptions, fundamentalist. Almost all were Christians in some sense, although, owing to their reluctance to express their religious views and the incompleteness of the record, it is not possible to describe the beliefs of most of them in any real detail. They believed in God. They believed that God ruled the universe in general and human affairs in particular. They disagreed about how divine rule is exercised. They believed that religion promoted morality and good citizenship. The Framers did not, insofar as we know, subscribe to the view that history has a purpose, namely, the realization of a kingdom of God, or to the view that America has some central role to play in Christ's reign.

Americans at the time of the founding made up in a nominal sense a "Christian nation." Save for a few synagogues, only Christians had built churches in America by that time. Furthermore, nine colonies on the eve of the Revolution had established churches in some form. Whether or not Americans constituted a Christian nation in any more significant sense cannot be answered conclusively. Certainly only a minority of the general citizenry were members of a church. Estimates of church attendance range widely. The doctrinal beliefs of most will be forever outside our reach.

Neither those who drafted nor those who ratified the First Amendment seem to have intended the establishment clause to protect established churches in the states or to permit even non-preferential, direct aid to churches. In light of their other actions, they did not, however, intend to sever all ties between government and religion. The First Congress by its adoption of the Northwest Ordinance expressed its belief that religion may benefit incidentally from the exercise of congressional authority in pursuit of secular ends.

CHAPTER 2

ORIGINAL INTENT

I n the 1950s and 1960s, the national government embarked on a course, it seemed to many, aimed at realizing ideals too long ignored. *Brown v. Board of Education*, the civil rights acts, *Roe v. Wade*, the school prayer decisions, and *Miranda v. Arizona*, however, embraced policies too secular, egalitarian, and tolerant for many conservatives to swallow. They believed that the federal courts in particular were misinterpreting the Constitution by substituting their own judgment for that of the Framers. From that time down to the present day, conservatives have campaigned for the appointment of judges who they believe would follow the Framers' original intent. What did the Framers intend?

The thirty-nine Framers who signed the Constitution and those who said that they would have signed had they been in Philadelphia on September 17, 1787, intended the words that made up and, for the most part, continue to make up the Constitution. The Framers intended to secure Southerners in their possession of slaves and to permit the continuation of the slave trade until 1808. They intended to provide equal representation of the states in the Senate. These provisions were seen as the price of union. In these and other instances, constitutional provisions clearly express their intentions. There is no need to go beyond the text itself to determine, for example, the length of term for a member of the House, the size of the congressional majorities needed to override a presidential veto, the identity of electors of members of the Senate, or whether the president is eligible for reelection.

All these provisions were controversial at the Constitutional Convention and in the struggle for ratification, and one or another of them would become controversial in later years. The controversies, however, were not over the meaning of the words in a narrow sense of *meaning*. The controversies were over the thing referred to by the words. Thus, in the decades leading up to the Civil War, Americans, with a few exceptions, did not disagree about what the Framers intended by the slavery provisions. They did disagree about the desirability of slavery itself. Similarly, Americans of a later generation did not disagree about what the Framers intended by the provision making the president eligible for reelection. They did disagree about whether the president ought to be perpetually reeligible. Original intent was not at issue in either of these instances. In both of them, resolution of the controversy required the adoption of an amendment changing the words of the Constitution so that intentions different from those of the Framers were expressed.

Other constitutional provisions are not so clear. It is because of vague and ambiguous provisions and the Constitution's silences that questions of meaning arise. During the ratification debate, the Anti-Federalists criticized the Constitution for its lack of clarity. They believed that uncertainty in meaning would permit the abridgment of state authority and individual rights. Their greatest suspicions were aroused by the "necessary and proper" clause of Article I, Section 8 and by the Constitution's failure, with a few exceptions, to provide for individual rights. The latter is an example of constitutional silence. What did this silence mean (in some wider sense of *meaning*)? Did the Framers intend to deny protection to the press or to the free exercise of religion, for example, by not providing protection in the Philadelphia draft? The Bill of Rights allayed the suspicions of many on this score, but it raises questions of meaning too. Just what is an "establishment of religion," "unreasonable search and seizure," or "impartial jury"? Ambiguity and vagueness also occur in those provisions marking out national and state authority and the authority of the three branches of the national government with respect to one another. These provisions raise questions of meaning that make it necessary to go beyond the immediate text for an answer. The proponents of the doctrine of original intent maintain that, in going beyond the passage in question, citizens and officeholders, and particularly judges, should seek to recover the meanings intended by the founders.

THE DOCTRINE OF ORIGINAL INTENT

What is it to appeal to the original intent of the founders? The late Chief Justice William Rehnquist and former federal appellate judge and Yale law professor Robert Bork among other proponents of this doctrine have contended: (1) it is possible to determine what the founders intended by a particular constitutional passage and (2) the intended meaning ought to be authoritative.[1] Before we address these contentions, a few preliminary matters require attention. First, a distinction must be made between the *Framers* and the *founders*. There is no settled usage for either of these terms. As in the preceding chapter, *Framers* will be used here to refer only to the fifty-five delegates to the Constitutional Convention. *Founders* will be used as a far more inclusive term with an open-ended meaning. It includes the Framers but other groups as well. In what follows, I will specify the meaning of *founders* with particular reference to a group. Second, a distinction must be made between *intention* and *understanding*. Only the Framers can be said to have intentions expressed in the Constitution. This is so because *intention* connotes purpose, what something is meant to convey. Since the Framers alone wrote the Constitution, only they can have meant to convey one or another meaning by the choice of this or that word or phrase. All other groups, including the delegates to the state ratifying conventions, can only be said to have *understandings*. Their intentions were not expressed in the Constitution. Their *understandings*, that is, the meaning that they attached to this or that constitutional provision, might or might not have coincided with the Framers' intentions. Those who ratified the Constitution adopted only the text and not the intentions of the Framers.

Finally we must address a preliminary question: Who were the founders? There is vagueness in the doctrine of original intent about just whose intentions or understandings are to be recovered. The Constitution did not have a single author, and it was not ratified by one person alone. When one invokes the founders' authority, does one call upon all fifty-five Framers who attended the Convention however briefly? Just the thirty-nine Framers who signed? Those thirty-nine and the other Framers who said that they would have signed had they been in Philadelphia on September 17, 1789? The delegates to the state ratifying conventions? The electorate that chose the delegates to the state ratifying conventions? The whole generation of Americans alive at the founding, that is, at the time of the proposal and ratification of the Constitution? If we include the Bill of Rights as part of the original constitution, then the intentions or understandings of still others must be sought. James Madison, of course, was the principal author of the Bill of Rights, but he was no more the only author than he was the only author of the Constitution. His recommendations were changed at the hands of his colleagues in the First Congress. Those proposed amendments then had to be ratified by three-quarters of the state legislatures.

THE RECOVERY OF UNDERSTOOD MEANINGS

Substantial difficulties stand in the way of recovering the meanings that any of these people understood by one or another passage in the Constitution or the Bill of Rights. The difficulties are obvious in trying to identify the meanings understood by the founding generation and, more particularly, the electorate that chose the delegates to the state ratifying conventions. Most of these people did not express any views that were recorded. The situation is much the same for the delegates to the state ratifying conventions. Most said nothing. This silence could be eloquent. Few can be found among the delegates, or, for that matter, among the general public, who advocated, say, reunification under the British crown, monarchy or some other nonrepresentative form of government, a national church, or the enfranchisement of women. The delegates to the state ratifying conventions did express by voting their support or opposition to the Constitution as a whole and, in five states, to recommendatory amendments, but this does not advance the cause of constitutional interpretation very far. What the delegates might have understood they were voting for or against in particular remains obscure. Much the same can be said about the state legislators who voted for ratification of the Bill of Rights. Concerning the Constitution, the Federalists worked hard, for the most part successfully, to structure the debate and the vote in the states around one issue: union under the proposed constitution or disunion.

Certainly the record of the debates at the Convention and the debate over ratification of the Constitution is substantial. It consists of pamphlets and newspaper essays, private letters and records of debates at the conventions, and it runs to thousands of pages. If we assume that this record captures the range and variety of American thinking at the time, we can say much about the beliefs that made Americans supporters or opponents of the Constitution. It is not possible, however, to recover those meanings attached to a particular constitutional provision by most Americans, or by most of the electorate, or by most delegates to the state ratifying conventions, or by most of the state legislators who voted for ratification of the Bill of Rights. What any of these groups might have understood by the commerce power or the tax power or freedom of the press, for example, will forever remain outside our reach. To be sure, there were some among the general public and among the delegates who spoke at length about particular provisions or whose actions or statements subsequent to the adoption of the Constitution reveal the meanings they understood by this or that provision. A good deal is known about the meanings understood by some political leaders, for example, Patrick Henry, Melancton Smith, James Iredell, John Marshall, Samuel Chase, and Richard Henry Lee. It is a dubious maneuver, however, to ascribe their views to Americans generally or to their fellow delegates to the state ratifying conventions. This is so, if for no other reason, because they did not hold the same views and there were still other leaders who disagreed with one or another of them. Even among the Federalists, disagreement about particular issues was nearly as pervasive as their agreement on the desirability of the Constitution taken as a whole.

THE RECOVERY OF INTENDED MEANINGS: THE RECORD

What about the Framers? They were after all the authors of the Constitution. And more is known about their views than the views of any other group of fifty-five of their contemporaries. Some of the Framers like Madison, Wilson, Mason, Gouverneur Morris, and Washington left a substantial record. That record permits the recovery in some detail of the meanings they intended by one or another constitutional provision. For many other delegates, the record is thinner. The Constitutional Convention presented the best opportunity for most of them to express their intentions point by point.

The Convention opened on May 25, 1787, and, nearly seventeen weeks later, adjourned sine die on September 17. Never were more than eleven states represented, and average attendance was little more than thirty. Nineteen delegates had absences ranging from two weeks to almost the whole convention: George Wythe of Virginia and William Houston of New Jersey left for their homes after a week; John Francis Mercer of Maryland put in an appearance on August 6, expressed his dislike of the Convention's work, and left less than two weeks later; William Pierce of Georgia left, never to return, on July 1 to take up his seat in the Confederation Congress; John Lansing and Robert Yates, their worst suspicions confirmed, left for New York on July 10 to organize the opposition; Alexander Hamilton's attendance became sporadic at that point because he could not vote as the sole New York delegate; and John Langdon and Nicholas Gilman of New Hampshire did not arrive until July 23 owing to insufficient funds in the state's budget to pay their expenses. Nine delegates were absent altogether after August 5. These last absences were significant because, although the Convention had resolved some major issues, much remained to be settled. And the language that was to express the decisions made and the decisions to be made had yet to be written. Absence reduced the opportunity for many delegates to engage in the debate and thereby to ease the task of recovering intended meanings.[2]

Some of the absent delegates may not have spoken even had they been in attendance. Not all were like Gouverneur Morris, who, despite missing a month, held forth on 173 occasions. No one else was so voluble—not even Madison who never missed a day (he spoke 161 times). Four delegates— John Blair, William Few, Nicholas Gilman, and Richard Bassett—said nothing throughout the Convention. Three others spoke only on the last day: Jared Ingersoll and William Blount to announce their positions on signing, and Washington to support a reduction in the ratio of population to representative. Robert Morris spoke twice, once to nominate Washington as chair of the Convention and once to second a motion. William Livingston presented several committee reports and spoke an additional two times. Alexander Martin and James McClurg each spoke briefly three times. Five other delegates spoke fewer than ten times each: George Clymer, Thomas Mifflin, Thomas Fitzsimons, William Houstoun, and Daniel of St. Thomas Jenifer. All these taciturn delegates were either full-timers or attended for the most part. If their number is added to the number of those who missed two months or more, the sum is twenty-five (better than 45 percent of the whole convention) who contributed little to the debate.

In a few cases—Washington and Hamilton are good examples—it is possible to supplement the record of the Convention with actions taken in office and statements made outside the Convention. Nevertheless, in attempting to recover the meanings intended by the Framers, we must rely on sparse materials for many of them. These obstacles loomed large in Madison's eyes, and from a much closer remove than any more current perspective. On April 6, 1796, Madison observed in the House,

> neither himself nor the other members who had belonged to the Federal Convention, could be under any particular obligation to rise in answer to a few gentlemen, with information, not merely of their own ideas of that period, but of the intention of the whole body; many members of which, too, had probably never entered into the discussions of the subject. . . . There would not be much delicacy in the undertaking, as it appeared that a sense had been put on the Constitution by some who were members of the Convention, different from that which must have been entertained by others.[3]

Madison's notes of the debates had not yet been published and would not be until 1840, but those notes, of course, help not at all in recovering the intentions of those who did not speak. Even for those who joined the debate,

Madison's notes provide only a partial record of what was said—by some estimates no more than 20 percent of the whole.[4]

It might be thought that agreement can be inferred from a delegate's silence. Agreement to what? Those who spoke often took different positions from one another. With which position did the silent delegate agree? Did the delegate agree with any of the positions taken? In most instances there is no way to tell. It is perhaps for this reason that Elbridge Gerry, a delegate to the Convention himself and an outspoken one, insisted on the floor of the House of Representatives in 1791 that "the opinions of the individual members who debated are not to be considered as the opinions of the Convention."[5] Well, one asks, how did the silent delegates vote? This can be a difficult question to answer. Votes at the Convention were taken by state—a procedure that obscures the behavior of individuals. Nevertheless, on some issues Madison or one of the other delegates who took notes recorded the votes of individuals. On some other issues, it is possible to combine what we know about the attendance of delegates with positions taken during debate to infer how the delegates voted. Votes, however, reveal only that a delegate was for or against a particular provision at a particular point in the proceedings. Unless the text is clear, votes rarely reveal a single intended meaning.

THE RECOVERY OF INTENDED MEANINGS: COMPROMISES

Up to this point, the emphasis has been on the incompleteness of the record as a barrier to the recovery of intended meanings. We shall now turn to a difficulty of another kind. The Constitution was the product of compromise. The Great (or Connecticut) Compromise that settled the dispute over representation between the large and small states is surely the best known, but there were many more. The Framers were agreed in principle that: (1) government is instituted to protect individual rights and to promote the common good, (2) the members of the executive and the legislature ought to be chosen directly or indirectly by the people, (3) governmental authority ought to be divided, and (4) a stronger national government is needed. They disagreed about the specific arrangements best designed to realize these ideas. Their disagreements required the Framers to compromise, if they were to draft a constitution that they could support and that could win popular support. Compromise much complicates the problem of recovering intended meanings. There is no group mind of the Framers to consult about the meaning of this or that vague or ambiguous passage. It is only possible to examine the views of individuals.

Such an examination makes clear that the Framers' compromises thwarted in many instances the realization of their individual intentions. Insofar as we know, it seems unlikely that anyone among the Framers had his intentions fully realized. Madison, the "father of the Constitution," fought to the end against equal representation of the states in the Senate. He fought as well for a national veto on state legislation. In both cases, hardly minor ones, his efforts were in vain. Madison's intentions were not fully realized.[6] Gouverneur Morris vowed that "he never would concur in upholding domestic slavery. It was a nefarious institution—It was the curse of heaven on the states where it prevailed."[7] In the end, Morris and some other Northern delegates signed, however reluctantly, a document that upheld slavery. The comments of many of the Framers on the finished draft indicate that their individual intentions were not realized either. Charles Pinckney objected to the "contemptible weakness & dependence of the Executive . . . and to the power of a majority only of Congs over Commerce."[8] Benjamin Franklin objected to the institution of a bicameral legislature.[9] Hamilton signed the Constitution even though, he said, "no man's ideas were more remote from the plan than his own were known to be."[10] Roger Sherman observed, "I do not suppose the Constitution to be perfect. . . . I do not expect any perfection on this side of the grave in the work of man."[11] Many of the Framers acknowledged that they had reservations—some without specifying what they were—and that they believed the Constitution to be imperfect.[12] Most, however, did not regard whatever reservations or objections they had as removing their motive for signing. A few did conclude that the Constitution was so objectionable that they refused to sign. For the great majority of delegates, the desire to institute a stronger national government supplied the motive to compromise their individual views and to support the final document.

Although there is no group mind of the Framers that can be consulted about questions of meaning, the Constitution does express the shared intentions of most of them. That is to say, they agreed on a text and, in many particulars, that text clearly expresses their intentions. When the text does not clearly express their intentions, one can only dig through the record in an attempt to recover them. The record almost always shows that relatively few of the Framers spoke to the matter in question and that the majority's intentions are revealed, if they are revealed at all, only by votes. Votes do reveal something about intended meanings. They do so by eliminating some meanings. Seldom, however, do votes reveal only one meaning. To better appreciate the difficulties so often encountered in any attempt to recover intended meanings, let us briefly examine the record with respect to several vague constitutional provisions.

On August 17, a large majority of the Convention voted twice in favor of investing Congress with the power "to declare war" (Votes 313 and 314).[13] Only eight delegates spoke to the matter, and the discussion occupies less than two pages in Madison's notes.[14] The delegates were responding to a proposal from its Committee of Detail that provided Congress with the power "to make war." Charles Pinckney preferred vesting this power in the Senate rather than in the whole Congress. Pierce Butler thought the power ought to be in the president alone. Both Elbridge Gerry and George Mason objected to that idea, and no one else spoke in favor of it. Madison and Gerry moved to strike "make" in favor of "declare," "leaving to the Executive the power to repel sudden attacks." Roger Sherman, who was concerned about maintaining congressional authority vis-à-vis the president, objected that "declare" reduced congressional authority. "The Executive," he said, "shd. be able to repel and not to commence war." George Mason too thought that "make" is a broader term than "declare." Looking at the matter from a different perspective, he preferred "declare," because "he was for clogging rather than facilitating war." On the motion to substitute "declare" for "make," seven states voted "aye" and two "no" with Massachusetts absent. Rufus King then remarked that "make" war might be construed to include the conduct of war, which is an executive function. This reportedly persuaded Oliver Ellsworth to change his vote, putting Connecticut on the "aye" side of the ledger, and the division at eight states in favor of investing Congress with the power "to declare war" and one state opposed. New Hampshire's opposition must remain a mystery as neither of its delegates expressed a view.

Did that majority intend to permit the national government to wage undeclared war? Did that majority intend to permit the president to commit troops to combat abroad without a congressional declaration of war? In light of the proceedings recounted above, there are no certain answers to these questions. The Convention took other actions that further muddy the waters. On August 27, the Convention adopted, without objection or discussion, a provision making the president commander in chief of the army and navy. On September 7, the Convention enlarged congressional authority over war by adding the power to "grant letters of marque and reprisal." This addition, adopted without objection or discussion, authorized Congress to allow private individuals to prey on the shipping and property of hostile states. Finally, the Convention's Committee of Style placed the restrictions on state war making in Article I, perhaps on the assumption that any such authority in the states would diminish congressional power.

If we look to the state ratifying conventions for clarification, we look in vain. The whole question of war making, declared and undeclared, and the allocation of authority between the president and Congress received superficial attention.[15] *The Federalist* observed that presidential authority "would be nominally the same with that of the king of Great Britain, but in substance much inferior to it. It would amount to nothing more than the supreme command . . . of the military . . . ; while that of the British king extends to the *declaring* of war and to the *raising* and *regulating* of fleets and armies."[16] It was against this background that Madison and Hamilton carried on a lengthy dispute in 1793 over President Washington's proclamation of neutrality with regard to Anglo-French hostilities. Madison and his Republican fellows thought that the 1778 alliance with France was still in force and obligated the United States to defend the French West Indies. Writing as "Helvidius," Madison argued that war making is a legislative function and that any exceptions in favor of the executive—like the commander in chief clause—must be strictly interpreted.[17] Hamilton, writing as "Pacificus," took the contrary position: war making is an executive responsibility and Congress could exercise only those aspects of it specifically granted by the Constitution—and those should be narrowly interpreted.[18]

There are two things worth noticing in this. First, neither Hamilton nor Madison invoked original intent in an attempt to shore up his position. Indeed, few of the Framers seem to have regarded original intent as even relevant to the disposition of constitutional disputes, let alone as providing authoritative resolution.[19] Second, Hamilton and Madison had different ideas about what policies ought to be pursued. Depending on how the Constitution is interpreted, pursuit of a policy might be advantaged or disadvantaged. They could see in 1793 what they could not have seen so well in 1787, namely, how the Constitution, if read in this way rather than that, would inform the resolution of policy differences.

The other Framers who held national office in the new government also seemed to have responded to changed circumstances, or, at any rate, to have come away from the Convention with different ideas about what they had done. In the two great constitutional disputes that occurred during the First Congress, the Framers (eight of whom had been elected to the House, ten to the Senate) disagreed among themselves.[20] Does the Constitution invest the president alone with the authority to remove executive officers? In the absence of an explicit provision, Madison and Roger Sherman took different positions. The votes in the House and Senate divided those who had been delegates to the Convention. Does the Constitution invest Congress with the authority to charter a bank? President Washington and Secretary of the Treasury Hamilton supported the bill. Madison and Attorney General Edmund Randolph opposed it. The Framers in the Senate contributed to a unanimous vote in favor, while their House counterparts divided on the issue. These instances demonstrate the hazards of trying to establish what a Framer intended at the Convention by reference to what he did or said later. More important, when the Framers themselves disagreed about what they had wrought in 1787, could there be much hope for the recovery of original intent more than two hundred years later?

THE AUTHORITY OF THE FRAMERS: THEIR VISION

Why should we defer to the judgment of the Framers or of any group in the founding generation about how government ought to be ordered? This question brings to the fore the second tenet in the doctrine of original intent, namely, that the meaning intended by the Framers (or the understandings of other founders) ought to be authoritative. The Framers themselves acknowledged, as we have seen, that the Constitution as it came from their hands was imperfect. This judgment was in part an admission of human fallibility. But more, it expressed a recognition that the Constitution reflected their experience and their political circumstances. George Washington, writing to his nephew several months after the Convention, observed,

> The warmest friends to and the best supporters of the Constitution, do not contend that it is free from imperfections; . . . And as there is a Constitutional door open for it, I think the people (for it is with them to judge) can, as they will have the aid of experience on their side, decide with as much propriety on the alterations and amendments wch shall be found necessary, as ourselves; for I do not think that we are more inspired—have more wisdom—or possess more virtue than those who will come after us.[21]

For all the praise heaped on them, the Framers were men whose experience bounded their vision and whose interests affected their judgment.

The Framers were men of their times. They drafted a constitution for the society that they knew. That society was largely rural and agrarian, geographically isolated from the major international powers, and thinly populated. While some envisioned the development in the United States of a society continental in extent, far more populous, and in which manufacturing would employ a larger share of the workforce and would produce more of the nation's wealth, none could have anticipated the shape that American society would take as it has developed over the past two hundred years. The society known to the Framers was substantially different from contemporary society, and the differences are significant.

A recital of a few of these differences is revealing.[22] First, the electorate is far larger today than it was in 1787. At the beginning of the republic, the constituency of a House member numbered 30,000; today that constituency numbers over 500,000 even though the size of the House has increased from 65 to 435. The senators of the most populous state in 1789, Virginia, represented some 650,000 people; today the senators from California, the most populous state, represent 34 million. This substantial increase in population weakens the connection between a constituent and his representatives and impedes the expression of popular sentiments. Second, in 1790 (the year of the first census) almost all Americans—3,929,214 including 681,834 slaves—lived in rural areas. Only twenty-four places had more than 2,500 inhabitants and only five cities had more than 10,000. Philadelphia, the largest city, had 45,000. Urbanization has made us all much more dependent on government for the provision of clean water and safe food, sewage and trash disposal, disease control, gas and electricity, streets and traffic control.

Third, farmers made up the bulk of the society known to the Framers. Something close to eight of ten Americans worked the fields, one of ten fished or lumbered for a living, and the rest were merchants or professionals. In contemporary society, well under 5 percent of employed civilians work in farming, forestry, or fishing. The consequences of this development are many. For example, the median household size of that bygone day was larger and included two or more generations.[23] Care of the aged and of children occurred under the farmhouse roof. Today, families are spread out all over the country. The parents drop off the children at the child-care center in suburban St. Louis on the way to work. The grandparents are back in Baltimore in an "independent living" apartment, and when the children are old enough to enter the job market, they might find employment in Portland or Birmingham.

Fourth, Protestantism dominated the religious sphere in the society known to the Framers. On the eve of the revolution, two-thirds of white Americans lived under an established Congregational or Episcopal church. In 1776 the number of Protestant congregations was 3,228 (98.1 percent of the total number of congregations). There were fifty-six Roman Catholic and five Jewish congregations. By 1850 the Methodists and the Baptists had far surpassed the Congregationalists and the Episcopalians in numbers of congregations and adherents. The growth in denominations produced diversity among Protestants. Immigration in the latter part of the nineteenth and throughout the twentieth century brought non-Protestants in increasing numbers—Catholics for the most part, but Muslims, Jews, Eastern Orthodox, Hindus, and Buddhists as well. It is no longer possible to assume that the Westminster Catechism and the Lord's prayer are the common language of worship.

Finally, the twentieth century produced weapons that make the United States vulnerable to devastating, surprise attack by a hostile power or even a few terrorists. The Framers knew enough of war (some had fought in the War of Independence) to make constitutional provision for national defense. The attack on Pearl Harbor that provoked the United States to war in 1941 and the 9/11 attacks on the World Trade Center and the Pentagon, however, would have been unimaginable in the Framers' day. In our own day, the nation must be organized to make war at any time and to defend itself against an imminent blow. Large standing armies, a huge military bureaucracy, whole industries devoted to the production of war matériel, and billions of dollars to pay for it all have distinguished the "peacetime" United States since the end of World War II. In this way also has American society changed since the founding.

The Framers were men of their times too in their perception of government as the principal threat to freedom.[24] Only Alexander Hamilton dissented from the view that both absolute and limited monarchy are an invitation to tyranny. The Framers also thought, however, that even republican government may be tyrannical. For George Mason, delegate to the Convention from Virginia, a government not closely accountable to the people is likely to deny freedom to the whole society. Many Anti-Federalists shared this view. For James Madison, a government would deny freedom when one part of society, the majority, could use the government to oppress the other part of society, the minority. Many Federalists shared this view. The Framers' sensitivity to the threat to freedom posed by government was not misplaced, but they focused their attention exclusively on this threat. They did not see that in a patriarchal society men are a great threat to the freedom of women. Women, even in 1787, were able to see this. Abigail Adams wrote to her husband John during the Revolution, "In the new code of laws which I suppose it will be necessary for you to make, I desire you would Remember the Ladies, and be more favorable to them than your ancestors. Do not put such unlimited power into the hands of Husbands. Remember all Men would be tyrants if they could."[25] Like John Adams and the others who drafted the Articles of Confederation, the Framers did nothing in the Constitution for the ladies.

In a racist society, whites are the principal threat to the freedom of blacks. At the Convention, some expressed opposition to slavery. Madison asserted on June 6, "We have seen the mere distinction of colour made in the most enlightened period of time, a ground of the most oppressive dominion ever exercised by man over man."[26] Others joined John Rutledge of South Carolina who regarded the slaves as simply cheap labor.[27] Still others were indifferent, siding with Rufus King of Massachusetts who "thought the whole subject should be considered in a political light only,"[28] or with Hugh Williamson of North Carolina who announced himself "both in opinion and practice . . . against slavery" but prepared to accede to the demands of South Carolina and Georgia for security for slavery and the slave trade.[29] The Williamson view prevailed. The Constitution as it came from the Framers' hands recognized slavery (although not by name to avoid offending Northern sensibilities) and protected it and the slave trade.

Finally, the Framers were concerned with the threat to freedom posed by the power of employers over employees only in its political consequences. Some saw clearly enough that "a power over a man's support is a power over his will," as Hamilton put it in discussing why the Convention had made the president independent of Congress for his salary.[30] That understanding also provoked proposals at the Convention to impose property qualifications for the vote. Only the economically independent were regarded as having a will of their own. And only the economically independent could live their lives as they saw fit without risk to their livelihood. The Framers were oblivious to this consideration. Many American families of the founding period, however, were the owners of their own farms or small businesses and thus not economically dependent on others.[31] This may have contributed to the Framers' indifference to the matter. Over the course of the nineteenth century, an agrarian society gave way to an industrial one and the yeoman farmer became an employee. The concentration of economic power, particularly in the corporations, permitted a few to decide who was to be hired, fired, or promoted and under what conditions people were to work. This power might be and, of course, often was abused. As blacks after the Civil War and women in still later years were drawn into the labor market, they soon encountered discrimination in a variety of forms. In these ways, then, among others, the Framers' vision was bounded by their experience.

THE AUTHORITY OF THE FRAMERS: THEIR INTERESTS

The Framers appear as demigods in American mythology, but they were not disinterested students of politics. The letter by which the Convention conveyed the Constitution to the Confederation Congress allowed that the Constitution is "the result of a spirit of Amity and of that mutual Deference and Concession which the Peculiarity of our political Situation rendered indispensable."[32] Individual delegates were no less candid in acknowledging that interests had been in play at the Convention. Pierce Butler of South Carolina told a friend shortly after the Convention's close to regard the Constitution "as resulting from a spirit of Accomodation to different Interests, and not the most perfect one that the Deputies cou'd devise for a Country better adapted for the reception of it than America is at this day."[33] Madison's survey in *The Federalist* 37 of the difficulties that had faced the Convention mentions the "interfering pretensions of the larger and smaller states." In addition, "different parts of the United States are distinguished from each other by a variety of circumstances."[34] Madison discusses the "circumstances" of the slave trade in *The Federalist* 42 and slavery in *The Federalist* 54. The constitutional provisions relating to those interests show, according to Madison, that "the convention must have been compelled to sacrifice theoretical propriety to the force of extraneous considerations."[35] The Constitutional Convention was not a seminar in political theory.[36]

This is not to say that the Framers were unprincipled. The Framers did not seek to line their own pockets or to advance their political careers by the adoption of particular constitutional provisions. Those things mattered to them, of course, but any benefits they might have expected, or even enjoyed, as a consequence of the Constitution's ratification were benefits widely enjoyed. Nevertheless, interests affected their judgments about the government to be instituted under a new constitution. This can be seen in several important provisions: the equal representation of the states in the Senate, the slavery provisions, and separation of powers and checks and balances, among others.

SMALL STATES AND LARGE

The Framers were agreed that a stronger national government was needed. Every delegate to the Convention, however, was anxious that his state and section fare well in the new order of things. For this reason, state and sectional interests created the most highly disputed issues at the Convention. One of these issues was representation that pitted the smaller states against the larger. Madison, many years later, recollected, "The threatening contest in the Convention of 1787 did not . . . turn on the degree of power to be granted to the Federal Government, but on the rule by which the States should be represented and vote in the Government."[37] The Virginia Plan, proposed May 29, 1787, in the first days of the Convention, invested broad legislative authority in a national government. The limitation of national authority by the enumeration of powers would come much later, August 6, in the report of the Committee of Detail and appear in the final document as Article I, Section 8. The Virginia Plan also provided for the popular election of representatives to a lower house—representation from each state to be determined by population or tax contributions. The lower house would choose the members of an upper house and the two houses together would select the chief executive and national judges. On this formula, the more populous, wealthier states would have a large voice in national affairs—too large, thought some. The small states proposed an alternative plan on June 15, called the New Jersey or Paterson Plan after its sponsor, William Paterson of New Jersey.

The New Jersey Plan departed from the Virginia Plan in a number of respects, but its provision for equal representation of the states in a one-house legislature provoked the most controversy. On June 19 the Convention voted down the New Jersey Plan. Not so easily thrust aside was the insistence by small state delegates on equal representation in the national legislature. John Dickinson of Delaware remarked, "We would sooner submit to a foreign power, than . . . be deprived of an equality of suffrage, in both branches of the legislature, and thereby be thrown under the domination of the large states."[38] What was the nature of the threat perceived by the small state delegates? Dickinson, Paterson, Gunning Bedford of Delaware, and others who espoused the small state cause were indefinite. They sometimes spoke of the lack of safety under the Virginia Plan as if small state interests would be in jeopardy. But, as Madison never tired of pointing out, the large states shared no interests that distinguished them from the small states and, therefore, they had no motive to gang up on the small states. As evidence of this, he cited the record of the Confederation Congress, which showed no divisions between the large and small states.[39] Bedford saw motives at work of a more general sort. Ambition and avarice, he urged, would inspire the larger states to "aggrandize themselves at the expense of the small."[40] Just how constitutional provision for equal representation of the states would prevent this was never explained. It would seem that, if the larger states were bent on swallowing up the smaller, they would simply ignore the Constitution.

In their defense of the New Jersey Plan, its proponents sometimes invoked the ideas of independence and state sovereignty. This suggests that Paterson and the others wished to preserve the opportunity for state governments to decide for themselves issues that would fall within the national jurisdiction under the Virginia Plan. This understanding of the small states' position, however, flies in the face of what happened after July 16. On that date, the Great Compromise was adopted. This settled the dispute between the large and small states over representation, at least for most delegates. The next day, Bedford moved that the national government have the authority "to legislate in all cases for the general interests of the union."[41] This from the man who, in the heat of the debate over representation, had warned that, if the small states were denied equal representation, they "will find some foreign ally of more honor and good faith, who will take them by the hand and do them justice."[42] His motion was adopted with the support of New Jersey, Delaware, and Maryland, all of which had been prominent in the small state cause. It turned out, as Charles Pinckney had observed a month earlier, "the whole comes to this. . . . Give N. Jersey an equal vote, and she will dismiss her scruples, and concur in the National system."[43]

The objection of the small states to the Virginia Plan came not out of principle, but out of interest—an interest in more power than principle would allow. "What is the true principle of Representation?" asked Paterson on July 9. "It is an expedient by which an assembly of certain individls. chosen by the people is substituted in place of the inconvenient meeting of the people themselves."[44] Madison "reminded Mr Patterson that his doctrine of Representation which was in its principle the genuine one, must for ever silence the pretensions of the small states to an equality of votes with the large ones. They ought to vote in the same proportion in which their citizens would do, if the people of all the states were collectively met."[45] As we have seen, the pretensions of the smaller states were not silenced. They insisted on equal representation in one house of the legislature as a condition of their joining the union. As a consequence, the Convention fastened on the Constitution the most undemocratic feature to have persisted to the present day. Today, as in earlier days, by the mere accident of residence in, say, Wyoming or Vermont, a voter has considerably more weight in the polling booth than a voter in more populous states like California or Texas. This was and remains a blatant violation of the principle of political equality—the principle that underlay the Supreme Court's "one person—one vote" rulings with regard to representation in the House and in the state legislatures.

SLAVERY

The Southern states were no less eager to advance their interests. It was apparent to all that slavery created a significant, even the most significant, division among the states.[46] Throughout the Convention, the Southern delegates sought to secure protection for slavery, the products of slavery, and the slave trade. They sought as well to increase Southern influence in national affairs by maximizing the South's representation. Once the delegates decided to use population, rather than property or tax contributions, as the basis of representation in the lower house, the question of if, and how, to count the slaves came to the fore. If all persons were counted, then Virginia would have by far the largest delegation and the South more representatives than the North. If only free persons were counted, then the North would have a comfortable majority. Gouverneur Morris of Pennsylvania, William Paterson of New Jersey, and Rufus King of Massachusetts demanded to know by what principle the counting of slaves in determining representation could be justified.[47] The only answer they received came from James Wilson of Pennsylvania, who "did not well see on what principle the admission of blacks in the proportion of three-fifths could be explained. Are they admitted as Citizens? then why are they not admitted on an equality with White Citizens? Are they admitted as property? then why is not other property admitted into the computation? These were difficulties however which . . . must be overruled by the necessity of compromise."[48] The North received a stern warning from William Richardson Davie of North Carolina that if the slaves were not counted as at least three-fifths then "the business [of the Convention] is at an end."[49] The Convention adopted the provision to count the slaves at a three-fifths ratio as part of a compromise involving taxation (the same three-fifths rule would apply) and navigation laws (only a simple majority would be required for passage rather than the two-thirds majority preferred by many Southern delegates).

The three-fifths clause not only increased Southern influence in the House of Representatives but increased it as well in the election of the president. The method of electing the chief executive was controversial. Advocates could be found for election by the people, by the national legislature, and by special electors chosen by the state legislatures or governors among other schemes. A variety of considerations informed the debate and its resolution—including the calculation of political advantage. Charles Pinckney of South Carolina, Hugh Williamson of North Carolina, and James Madison of Virginia all expressed their sensitivity to that consideration.[50] For Madison, "The people at large was . . . the fittest in itself. There was one difficulty however of a serious nature attending an immediate choice by the people. The right of suffrage was much more diffusive in the Northern than the Southern States; and the latter could have no influence in the election on the score of the Negroes. The substitution of electors obviated this difficulty."[51] The Electoral College overcame the "difficulty" of more numerous voters in the North by conferring on each state the same number of electors as it had representatives and senators.

This affront to the principle of political equality, however, must pale beside the other constitutional provisions bearing on slavery: Article I, Section 9 prohibited legislation to end the slave trade until 1808; Article IV, Section 2 required that fugitive slaves be returned to their owners; and Article V forbade the adoption of any amendment before 1808 altering those provisions having to do with the slave trade and the levying of direct taxes on the three-fifths rule. All of the preceding, of course, were superseded by the post–Civil War amendments. But still other provisions continue to reflect Southern interests in protecting the products of slave labor, namely, Article I, Section 9, which prohibits Congress from taxing exports, and Article I, Section 10, which prohibits the states from taxing exports. The South's economy was geared to foreign markets, and the South feared the taxation of her rice, tobacco, and indigo. Charles Cotesworth Pinckney, delegate from South Carolina and cousin of fellow-delegate Charles Pinckney, defending the Constitution before the South Carolina House of Representatives, pronounced himself satisfied with what he and his fellows had accomplished. "In short, considering all circumstances, we have made the best terms for the security of this species of property it was in our power to make. We would have made better if we could; but on the whole, I do not think them bad."[52] The Southern delegates had driven a hard bargain backed up by threats to oppose the Constitution were Southern interests not accommodated.[53]

PROPERTY

Before exploring the Framers' interests further, let us take our bearings. The matter presently before us is the second tenet of the doctrine of original intent. That doctrine asserts that the intentions of the Framers (or some other group among the founders) ought to be authoritative. We have seen that experience bounded the Framers' vision. We have seen too that their judgment was affected by their interests and, more particularly, by the interest of the small state delegates in securing more representatives than the principle of political equality would allow and by the interest of the slave-state delegates in securing protection for slavery and the slave trade.

Unlike the state and sectional interests that divided them—like those just identified—the Framers also pursued interests that largely united them. They sought to protect the property created by commercial society. Government under the Articles of Confederation had failed, they believed, to adequately protect property, and many regarded the protection of property as government's principal end.[54] The Framers also sought to ensure the continued political domination of people like themselves: men of education, refinement, and leisure—qualities made possible by commercial society. The first interest was to be achieved principally by the institution of a stronger national government that enforced its laws on individuals directly and that had its own sources of revenue and troops. The Framers also adopted a number of particular provisions to protect property. The second of their interests was to be promoted by enlarging the electoral districts in which national officials would be chosen, by providing for the indirect election of senators and the president, by the appointment of judges, and by the provision of lengthy terms for the president, senators, and judges.[55] By these means, the Framers believed, government would be less subject to popular influence and national officials would be more qualified than had been the case in the state governments.

The Framers' antagonists in this regard were not at Philadelphia but here and there among the general citizenry and disproportionately in the backcountry—away from the coast and navigable rivers and away from centers of population, culture, and wealth. They were small farmers engaged to significant degree in a barter economy. The principal division among Americans over the Constitution, then, was between those who were part of commercial society and those who were not.[56] At issue was who was to rule in the new order of things and how were the burdens of government (principally taxes) to be distributed.

The commercial/noncommercial division coincides only roughly with class. The mechanics and artisans of Boston, New York, Philadelphia, Baltimore, and Charleston, for example, supported ratification. Despite the lower class standing of many of them (as determined by income), they were engaged in commercial society and regarded their interests as better served by joining merchants, professionals, and plantation owners in support of the Constitution. It should be added that commercial society produced far more wealth than noncommercial society and, not surprisingly, all wealthy Americans were creations of commercial society. The commercial/noncommercial division, however, did not pit the propertied against the propertyless. Small farmers had property too. They owned their land, livestock, and tools but produced little surplus beyond the needs of their families. That surplus was given in barter for items that the farmer could not produce like gunpowder, glass, or medicine or sold to pay taxes.

This division too coincides only roughly with the Federalist/Anti-Federalist division. Small farmers were not the only people who opposed ratification. George Mason, Luther Martin, and Elbridge Gerry were leading Anti-Federalists, and they were also firmly enmeshed in commercial society.[57] Mason, Martin, and Gerry seldom gave voice to the particular concerns of their backcountry fellows in the Anti-Federalist cause, and their objections to the Constitution hardly touched on any perceived threat to the particular interests of small farmers. It was also the case that in some places—in backcountry Georgia, in the Shenandoah Valley, and in western Pennsylvania—fear of Indian attacks overrode other concerns and persuaded most small farmers to support a stronger national government.

The commercial/noncommercial division was not a result of the proposal of the Constitution in 1787. It had shown itself with some frequency ever since the Revolution. And while Shays's Rebellion is the best-known expression of backcountry distemper, that distemper was not peculiar to Massachusetts or to the winter of 1786–1787. Up and down the country, disgruntled small farmers had presented petitions to state legislatures, held conventions, defied some state officials and threatened others, and used force to defend their interests.[58] The causes of this agitation were in part political and in part economic.

The political cause of backcountry discontent was unfair representation. At the time of the Revolution, all the states required property ownership as a qualification for the vote (in addition to whatever residency, age, gender, race, or religious qualifications a state might require).[59] Seven states required the possession of a freehold, the size and value of which varied from state to state. In the other six states, the property qualification could be satisfied by paying taxes at some minimum rate or by possessing a prescribed amount of real or personal property. Substantial difficulties stand in the way of determining how many adult white males were disfranchised as a result.[60] Estimates range from 10 to 50 percent depending on the state.[61] In addition to this bar to voting, the states also required that candidates for public office own substantial property. In these ways, then, the states' electoral laws advantaged the better off, all of whom were to be found in commercial society. The electoral laws advantaged the better off in another way as well. In many states, electoral districts were drawn with little attention to population.[62] These malapportioned districts overrepresented commercial society in the legislature. Backcountry farmers sought, in the years leading up to the Constitutional Convention, the reduction of property qualifications for the vote and for the holding of office and the reapportionment of legislative seats to better reflect population.[63] In six states, success in some measure attended their efforts and the efforts of other friends of democracy. The hope of small farmers was to secure the election of representatives more sensitive to their interests—interests that they believed had been ignored.

Those interests were economic and concerned taxation in particular. Throughout the colonies, tax laws imposed disproportionate burdens on the poor. This tendency was most exaggerated in the South. Colonial state legislatures relied on poll taxes (these fell equally on all adult males) and taxes on livestock and improved land (often without regard to value or location) to provide the lion's share of revenue. Taxes on buildings, unimproved land, ships, or stock-in-trade, and on income derived from the practice of a profession or trade or money-at-interest, if they were taxed at all, were nominal. Before the Revolution, backcountry farmers largely suffered these inequities in silence except in North Carolina, where a tax revolt had to be put down by force.[64] Elsewhere, political quiescence was the result of low tax rates. The Revolution upset everything. Prosecution of the war demanded more and more money. State legislatures raised taxes during the War of Independence and after the peace. Two-thirds of every New England state's direct tax revenue in 1786 was devoted to the payment of public creditors.[65] In some states, increases were better than tenfold. Massachusetts, for example, in 1786 imposed direct taxes that consumed some 8 to 11 percent of total personal income as compared to pre-Independence levies that seldom exceeded 2 percent.[66] These taxes were not equally distributed. The poor bore a disproportionate burden. In the western counties of Massachusetts, the sum of overdue and current taxes in 1787 averaged about £10 per adult male.[67] The median income for farmers in that state was £8.[68] For many, then, taxes due exceeded income. Moreover, after the war, Americans experienced a decline in the economy. Britain dumped manufactured goods on the American market, and closed off the British West Indies to American trade and its homeland ports to the products of American fisheries. British and Dutch creditors demanded payment of loans, and in hard currency.

These circumstances bore hard on many but on none so hard as on backcountry farmers, who lived close to subsistence level. In some states, like Massachusetts, small farmers learned that the commodities with which they had earlier paid off taxes and debts would no longer be accepted. Returned veterans were informed that soldiers' pay certificates were also unacceptable. Many faced losing everything—their livestock and tools and even their houses and land—in order to pay taxes to a government created in a revolution against arbitrary and excessive taxes. The irony was not lost on men and women who, in many instances, had fought for independence—Capt. Daniel Shays among them. In an effort to secure relief, these farmers demanded the issuance of paper money, the adoption of laws staying the execution of judgments for unpaid taxes or debts, and legal-tender laws that permitted the payment of taxes and debts with paper money or commodities. They also sought the reform of the tax laws to require those who acquired income from interest or from the practice of a trade or profession and those who held unimproved land on speculation or stock-in-trade to pay their fair share. Successes were won in some states. In others, where the state legislature ignored reformist demands, some Americans turned to violence.

The Framers described backcountry demands and violence and the sympathetic response of some state legislatures in the most sinister terms—as an attack on property itself and prelude to a descent into anarchy.[69] In response to the adoption of tax reforms in New York, Alexander Hamilton wrote in a 1785 letter to Robert Livingston Jr.,

> It is become a serious object of attention to those who are concerned for the security of property or the prosperity of government, to endeavour to put men in the Legislature whose principles are not of the levelling kind. The spirit of the present Legislature is truly alarming, and appears evidently directed to the confusion of all property and principle. . . . All men of respectability, in the city, of whatever party, who have been witnesses of the despotism and iniquity of the Legislature, are convinced, that the principal people in the community must for their own defence, unite to overset the party I alluded to. . . . The safety of all those who have anything to lose calls upon them to take care that the power of government is intrusted to proper hands.[70]

These themes would be sounded again and again at the Convention. The *demos*—the many—had acquired too much power, and property had been placed in jeopardy. In introducing the Virginia Plan, Edmund Randolph observed, "Our chief danger arises from the democratic parts of our Constitutions. . . . None of the constitutions have provided sufficient checks against the democracy."[71] Two days later, Elbridge Gerry asserted that "the evils we experience flow from the excess of democracy. . . . He had been taught by experience the danger of the levilling spirit."[72] And George Mason "admitted that we had been too democratic but was afraid we sd. incautiously run into the opposite extreme."[73] These anti-populist views came from the three delegates who refused to sign the Constitution—two of whom would join the Anti-Federalist opposition. Gerry blamed the extent of the franchise for putting the "worst men" into the Massachusetts legislature.[74] Gouverneur Morris was of the same mind. "The Backmembers," he said, "are always most averse to the best measures."[75] Other delegates, too, expressed their suspicions of popular participation in politics by either opposing popular election of the lower house or by supporting property qualifications for voting.[76] Proposals to adopt these sentiments as constitutional principles, however, were defeated.[77] Some regarded these proposals as contrary to republican principles. Others regarded the proposal to substitute election of the lower house by the state legislatures instead of the people in the context of the large state/small state dispute, and voted on that basis. The proposal to require property qualifications for voting in national elections seems to have been defeated largely for prudential reasons. In particular, the Framers were concerned that requiring stiffer qualifications than required by some states might jeopardize ratification of the Constitution.

Adoption of such measures may have seemed unnecessary in view of Madison's argument that the very institution of an extended republic—like that the Framers were proposing—would thwart popular excesses. He also argued that, even if factional proposals were made at the national level, they could not surmount the barriers imposed by separation of powers and checks and balances. Elaboration of these arguments will be the subject of the next chapter. Suffice it to say here that the aim of many of the Framers in creating a stronger national government and in adopting separation of powers and checks and balances was, in part, to protect property interests that were threatened by the less well off. As for those "unjust laws complained of among ourselves," as Madison described them,[78] that had been adopted by some state legislatures, the Framers made particular provision in Article I, Section 8, which forbids the states from coining money, passing laws that delay the execution of judgment for debt, or allowing payment of debts by anything other than gold or silver.

CONCLUSION

This analysis of the Framers' vision and interests came in response to the question, Why should we defer to the judgment of the Framers or to the judgment of any other group in the founding generation about how government ought to be ordered? The doctrine of original intent holds that the founders' judgment ought to be authoritative. The Framers' vision, however, was bounded by their experience. They drafted a constitution for the society they knew, and they did so in light of their understanding of human capacities and behavior. Significant changes have occurred in the circumstances of American life from their day to ours. The Framers can be of little help in fashioning an appropriate response to those changes because their experience did not include them. We cannot know how they might have responded to those changes. If those changes were, somehow, to be made a part of the Framers' experience, they would be different men.

Furthermore, the Framers were not disinterested stewards of the common good. They may have seen themselves in that way,[79] but the facts suggest otherwise. The interests they pursued were the interests of groups rather than their own individual interests (most of the time anyway) but interests nonetheless: inordinate power for the small states, protection for slavery, and protection for the property of the better off. These interests prejudiced the drafting of the Constitution in ways that much compromise the Framers' authority.

From another perspective, to turn to the Framers as the ultimate authority on the Constitution is to look in the wrong place. According to the principle of popular sovereignty, it is the people who are the ultimate authority. On this principle, it is their understandings that ought to be consulted. This was, by the way, the view of many of the Framers,[80] including James Madison, who said in a speech before the House on April 6, 1796,

> Whatever veneration might be entertained for the body of men who formed our Constitution, the sense of that body could never be regarded as the oracular guide in expounding the Constitution. As the instrument came from them it was nothing more than the draft of a plan, nothing but a dead letter, until life and validity were breathed into it by the voice of the people, speaking through the several State Conventions. If we were to look, therefore, for the meaning of the instrument beyond the face of the instrument, we must look for it, not in the General Convention, which proposed, but in the State Conventions, which accepted and ratified the Constitution.[81]

As a practical matter, however, the meanings understood by the delegates to the state ratifying conventions cannot be known. The record is incomplete. For five states there are records, more or less substantial, of the debates. For the other eight states, the records are sparse to none. In one of those eight (North Carolina), a rather full record is available of the first state ratifying convention, which defeated the motion to ratify, but no record is available of the second, which voted for ratification. Even if we could recover their understandings, the respect to which they are entitled is fundamentally compromised; the state ratifying conventions, after all, were chosen by an electorate that excluded blacks, women, and those unable to satisfy state property qualifications.

Partisans among the general citizenry, on the bench, and in the legislative halls claim for their policy preferences the authority of a group of men shrouded in myth. Part of that myth is that they thought alike and that we can know what they thought. With respect to those constitutional provisions that are not clear on their face, this is rarely true. Part of the myth, too, is that the founders were not bound by time or place or interest. To be sure, the Framers, in particular, were an extraordinary group of men, but they could not foresee the future and they did not stand above the fray. Are we to conclude that we ought to ignore the Framers and others in the founding generation? Not at all.

We can hardly do so if only because that generation gave us a constitution—a constitution serviceable but flawed from a democratic point of view. Americans have, of course, over the life of the Constitution seen fit to amend it to better accord with democratic principles. This essay, however, is not much concerned to identify constitutional shortcomings or to prescribe remedies.[82] Its aim has been to evaluate the doctrine of original intent. The doctrine of original intent falls short in a number of ways but none so significant as misplaced emphasis. That doctrine takes as its central task the determination of *what* the Framers (or founders) thought rather than *why* the Framers thought as they did. Some among the founders not only expressed an opinion but gave reasons for their holding it. We need to evaluate those reasons in deciding how to resolve constitutional disputes.

CHAPTER 3

SEPARATION OF POWERS

The principles of separation of powers and checks and balances have long been held up by Americans as protective of freedom, if not essential to democratic government. Whether these principles are truly protective of those values will not be explored directly here. Comparative analysis suggests that separation of powers may well be protective of freedom and essential to democratic government. Checks and balances, however, at least on the American pattern, seem to be neither protective of freedom nor essential to democratic government. Far more important than these governmental institutions are certain psychological dispositions—like tolerance for the opinions of others—and social structures—like independent families, churches, clubs, interest groups, universities, and trade unions. These will remain only assertions, however, for another question will occupy us here: Why did James Madison advocate constitutional provision for separation of powers and checks and balances? That is, what reasons did he give in support of those principles?

In trying to answer that question, familiarity with constitutional provision for the principles will be helpful.[1] The Constitution, as it came from the Framers' hands, assigned the three governmental functions (powers) to different branches. To Congress, it assigned "all legislative Powers herein granted." This power was to be exercised by two houses, the House of Representatives and the Senate. The "executive Power" is vested in the president, and the "judicial Power" in the Supreme Court and the lower federal courts. This is the separation of powers. In addition, the Constitution imposed limits on each of the branches in the exercise of its assigned function. This was accomplished by so ordering the relationship among the branches and between the two houses of Congress that they would check one another. Thus, both houses of the legislature must agree to all laws. The president can veto measures adopted by Congress. The Supreme Court can hold unconstitutional executive acts and laws adopted by Congress and signed by the president. Parenthetically, the power of judicial review lacked initially the definition it would acquire in later years as the Supreme Court gave shape to the uncertain mandate of Article III. Congress can impeach the president and federal court judges. The array of checks is more elaborate than just described, but these examples indicate the checking aspect of the whole system.

The balancing aspect shows up in the differences among the three branches and between the two houses of Congress in constituency and length of term. Thus, the members of the House were to serve for two years and have as their constituency a district—typically a small fraction of a state. Senators were given a term of six years and a whole state as their constituency. The president was given a four-year term and made indefinitely eligible for reelection, with the whole country as his constituency. Federal court judges, including Supreme Court justices, were given no constituency—no body of voters by whom they can be held electorally accountable. They were to be appointed by the president with the "advice and consent" of the Senate, and they were to serve for life. These differences in constituency and length of term were expected to produce different points of view. It is these different points of view that the Framers sought to balance. All of this remains in place today. Some things have changed from the Framers' day to our own. Senators are now elected by popular vote rather than by the state legislatures. The president is limited to two terms rather than the perpetual reeligibility of the original Constitution, and presidential electors are no longer chosen by the state legislatures but by popular vote. Nevertheless, the effect of checks and balances remains the same. Agreement among many agents who must decide in different political circumstances and with different points of view is required if change is to occur.

The authority attached by most Americans to separation of powers and checks and balances derives, as Madison envisioned, from that "veneration which time bestows on everything, and without which perhaps the wisest and freest governments would not possess the requisite stability."[2] Time, however, may also obscure the meaning of principles, the grounds on which they were founded, and the ends that they were intended to serve. As this occurs, allegiance to principles becomes mere prejudice. In an effort to inform their contemporaries of the meaning and grounds of these principles, generations of scholars have turned to James Madison for illumination. He provided the best-known statement of the theoretical foundations for the principles in *The Federalist* 47–51, and his role in the calling of the Constitutional Convention and in its deliberations was so large as to earn him the title of "father of the Constitution."

No consensus about the Madisonian teaching has emerged among students of American politics. Some regard his support for separation of powers and checks and balances as an attempt to thwart the will of popular majorities and, hence, as an expression of antidemocratic tendencies.[3] Others seek to establish his democratic credentials by arguing that Madison intended these provisions to be a defense of popular sovereignty against governmental usurpation.[4] Where does the truth lie? The following examination of Madison's thinking will not be concerned with the origin of his ideas or with evaluating them but with making clear his position, that is, his position as defined at the time of the Founding.

In rough outline, here is the course that we will take. The essay begins by distinguishing the two principles. They are often lumped together, but while there could be no checks and balances without separate governmental agencies, there could be separation of powers without checks and balances. Although Madison supported both, he advanced one set of reasons for separation of powers and another for checks and balances. As we shall see, separation of powers as Madison conceived it does not offend against the principles of popular sovereignty and majority rule. Checks and balances, however, do run counter to those principles. I contend that Madison adopted checks and balances as a defense against what he called *majority faction*. This contention is controversial. Students of the Founding agree that, for Madison, faction is the great problem to be solved by the institution of a "well-constructed Union." No such consensus exists that he supported checks and balances as a defense against majority faction. Some have argued that *The Federalist* 10 sets out Madison's entire remedy for faction. Such a view, however, ignores *The Federalist* 62 and 63, in which Madison advocates a role for the Senate in checking faction and his remarks at the Convention on the role of the executive and the judiciary in doing the same.

If checks and balances among separated governmental agencies are a defense against faction, a popular phenomenon, then Madison must assume that republican government secures the representation of popular preferences in government. Indeed, he allowed that direct, frequent elections produce the closest bond of sympathy between constituents and representative. In dissent from interpretations of Madison that characterize his republicanism as a politics of *virtue*, I claim that he envisioned a politics of *interest* and, more particularly, that he feared the acquisition of authority at the national level by popular majorities devoted to greater economic equality. I will explain shortly the difference between a politics of virtue and a politics of interest. I conclude that there is tension in Madison's theory between the ends that he wished to realize and the kind of government that he prescribed. The tension is created by his commitment to republican and energetic government and to particular conceptions of private rights and the public good. Separation of powers and checks and balances were aimed at relieving that tension.

SEPARATION OF POWERS AND ITS GROUNDS

There is little discussion in the Framers' writings or in the records of the Constitutional Convention of the grounds for separation of powers. It may be that the Framers regarded such discussion as superfluous in light of the consensus among politically engaged Americans in favor of the principle. Madison himself provided something like a sketch of the case for separation of powers rather than a systematic rationale. We can, nevertheless, discern in his writings two main grounds. Separation of powers is necessary to secure the rule of law and to secure efficient government. Madison set out the first argument in the form of a quotation from Montesquieu: "When the legislative and executive powers are united in the same person or body there can be no liberty, because apprehensions may arise lest *the same* monarch or senate should *enact* tyrannical laws to *execute* them in a tyrannical manner. . . . Were the power of judging joined with the legislative, the life and liberty of the subject would be exposed to arbitrary control, for *the judge* would then be *the legislator*. Were it joined to the executive power, *the judge* might behave with all the violence of *an oppressor*."[5] Liberty, it would seem, consists, at least in part, in the absence of "apprehensions" about what rulers might do if they were to hold several government powers. Thus legislators might enact tyrannical laws if they also possessed executive authority because they could ensure that those laws would not be applied against themselves. If legislators also possessed judicial authority, they could escape the imposition of any penalty for the violation of law. On the other hand, if legislators are subject to the very laws they make because other officials, independent of the legislature, possess executive and judicial authority, the legislature would be more likely to adopt reasonable laws. Madison presupposed this point when he observed that the members of the House "can make no law which will not have its full operation on themselves and their friends, as well as on the great mass of society."[6] The rule of law, on this understanding, does not obtain when rulers can exempt themselves from obedience to laws binding on everyone else. When rulers enjoy such an exemption, government is by men and not of law.

Separation of powers is aimed at allaying apprehensions that the rule of law would be displaced by the rule of men if governmental authority were concentrated. Madison was among those who had such apprehensions. He gave expression to those apprehensions in asserting that *tyranny* is "the accumulation of all powers, legislative, executive, and judiciary, in the same hands, whether of one, a few, or many, and whether hereditary, self-appointed, or elective."[7] This argument for separation of powers has in view a government that uses its power against the rest of society. If government were to use its power in this way, it would be acting against democratic principles. Thus, there is no conflict between this argument for separation of powers and democratic principles.

Madison also argued that separation of powers is necessary to secure "efficiency" in government. The effective performance of the governmental functions—legislative, executive, and judicial—requires different qualities in the agencies to which those functions are assigned. Thus, a numerous body can better represent popular preferences and deliberate than one or a few. In responding to critics of constitutional provision for the House, Madison acknowledged that it "should have an immediate dependence on, and an intimate sympathy with, the people." Elections every two years, he believed, were sufficiently frequent to realize the desired dependence and sympathy.[8] Just as it is not possible to fix precisely how frequent elections ought to be, so is it not possible to fix the optimum number of a representative assembly. Some minimum number is "necessary to secure the benefits of free consultation and discussion, and to guard against too easy a combination for improper purposes; as, on the other hand, the number ought at most to be kept within a certain limit, in order to avoid the confusion and intemperance of a multitude."[9] He regarded the numbers fixed by the Constitution for the House and Senate as falling within the acceptable range.

With respect to the executive, Madison, in the weeks leading up to the Convention, expressed uncertainty about the form it ought to take and the authority to be invested in it. He initially supported Edmund Randolph's proposal for a plural executive, but he was won over to the Constitution's executive during the Convention. In *The Federalist*, Madison asserted that energy in government is essential to security, foreign and domestic, and to "prompt and salutary execution of the laws." Authority in these matters needs to be held for "a certain duration" and executed "by a single hand."[10]

Although it fell to Hamilton to write those numbers of *The Federalist* dealing with the judiciary, Madison did advance an efficiency argument for the separation of the judiciary. He justified the indirect selection of judges on the grounds that members of the bench must possess "peculiar qualifications" that, presumably, would be unknown to the electorate but known to the members of the more permanent branches (federal judges are appointed by the president with the advice and consent of the Senate).[11] Hamilton identified those peculiar qualifications as "knowledge of the laws, acquired by long and laborious study."[12] It is worth noticing that neither the efficiency nor the rule-of-law arguments for separation of powers requires the division of the legislature into two houses or any of the other checks and balances provided by the Constitution.

CHECKS AND BALANCES

Constitutional checks and balances modify separation of powers. It was just this perception that elicited from some critics of the Framers' work the charge that checks and balances constituted a violation of the maxim. Madison responded by arguing that Montesquieu "did not mean that these departments ought to have no partial agency in, or no control over, the acts of each other."[13] Madison thought that checks and balances are necessary to maintain the desired separation because a "mere demarcation on parchment of the constitutional limits of the several departments is not a sufficient guard against those encroachments" that produce a "tyrannical concentration" of governmental power.[14] It is difficult, he asserted, to draw with precision the lines between the several departments, and experience suggests that a popularly elected legislature will not respect limits on its authority.[15] By means of checks and balances, he sought, however, not only to prevent one governmental department from acquiring authority properly exercised only by another. He was concerned not only to prevent, for example, Congress from imposing penalties on individuals for violation of the law (what is properly a judicial function) or the president from appropriating money (what is properly a legislative function).

Madison also sought to diffuse legislative authority itself. "In republican government," he explained, "the legislative authority necessarily predominates."[16] Why did he think this is so? The first reason for legislative predominance is not peculiar to republican government. Whoever holds legislative authority enjoys priority in establishing government control over the governed. The legislative authority gives the law. Until law has been adopted, there can be no execution and no trial in the courts of its application. This hierarchical view of the several governmental functions informed Madison's Virginia Plan, which treated first of the legislative, and it informs the Constitution, which did the same. The second reason is peculiar to republican government. In that species of government, popular elections are used to oblige the government to control itself. Elections, particularly as they are direct and frequent and the seats to be filled are numerous, produce legislators with "an immediate dependence on, and an intimate sympathy with the people."[17] A legislature so composed is inspired by popular support, and it is "sufficiently numerous" to feel popular passions but "not so numerous" as to be incapable of rationally pursuing "the objects of its passions."[18] The executive and the judiciary were, of course, to be chosen by the people, albeit indirectly, but Madison regarded these offices and their incumbents as probable objects of popular suspicion and ignorance.[19] He did not conceive of the executive as an agency for advancing popular preferences, and the judges "are too far removed from the people to share much in their prepossessions."[20] Therefore, in contests between a legislature popularly chosen in direct, frequent elections, and the other branches over the limits of legislative authority, the legislature would probably prevail.[21] Madison did not believe that the legislature ought always to prevail.

In *The Federalist* 51, Madison defended constitutional provision for the division of the legislature into two houses distinguished by different terms, numbers, and constituencies and the investment of the executive and the judiciary with "partial agency" in the making of law. Throughout papers 47 to 51, he was concerned with legislative encroachment on the spheres of the executive or the judiciary. Ostensibly, checks and balances are aimed at reducing the propensity of the legislature to attempt such encroachment and at fortifying the other branches with the means of self-defense should the legislature attempt encroachment. I say *ostensibly* because checks and balances reach not only legislation that encroaches on the rightful spheres of the executive and the judiciary, but legislation that does not encroach on the authority of other branches. Indeed, the Senate (by declining to pass the same legislation as the House has passed), the president (by exercise of the veto), or the courts (in their exercise of judicial review) might defeat the carrying out of the popular will as expressed in legislation adopted by the House. This possibility brought Madison no disquiet because he believed that the popular will ought not to be carried out if it is factional. What is factional legislation? To answer this question, we must examine Madison's understanding of the ends of government because he defines *faction* in terms of those ends.

THE ENDS OF GOVERNMENT

Madison declared that the fundamental ends of government are justice[22] and the public good.[23] He defined neither the *public good* nor *justice*, although he did use alternative expressions for these concepts. The *public good* was variously referred to as "the permanent and aggregate interests of the community,"[24] "national prosperity and happiness,"[25] and "the happiness of the people."[26] *Justice* he used as a synonym for private (that is, individual) rights.[27] In his efforts to fashion a "well-constructed Union," Madison accorded priority to justice for three reasons. First, while both the public good and justice are fundamental ends of government, justice is also "the end of civil society. It ever has been and ever will be pursued until it be obtained, or until liberty be lost in the pursuit."[28] Thus, Madison, following John Locke, thought that individuals agree to form civil society to secure protection for their right to exercise their faculties. On the basis of this agreement government acquires the authority to pursue the public good.[29] Government's primary end, however, remains the protection of those rights whose security all sought in establishing civil society.[30]

Second, protection of private rights contributes to the realization of the public good. When private rights are violated by government, widespread resistance could be stimulated. The lives and property of all are thereby placed in jeopardy.[31] The failure of pure democracies to respect private rights had made them "spectacles of turbulence and contention" and "as short in their lives as they have been violent in their deaths."[32] Safety against domestic violence and invasion[33] and stability in government[34] are in the public good. Third, Madison regarded private rights as more threatened by government than was the public good under the Articles of Confederation. In *Vices of the Political System of the United States*, he declared that the injustice of state government legislation is more alarming than its "multiplicity and mutability." Not only is it "a greater evil in itself," but "it brings more into question the fundamental principle of republican Government, that a majority who rule in such government are the safest Guardians both of the public Good and private rights."[35] At the Convention, he dissented from Roger Sherman's detailing of the ends of union as incomplete by insisting on the "necessity, of providing more effectually for the security of private rights, and the steady dispensation of Justice. Interferences with these were evils which had more perhaps than anything else, produced this convention."[36] Whatever reservation he may have intended to convey by that *perhaps* was absent altogether from his October 24, 1787, letter to Jefferson: the injustice of state legislation "contributed more to that uneasiness which produced the Convention . . . than those [evils] which accrued to our national character and interest from the inadequacy of the Confederation to its immediate objects."[37] For Madison, those evils were an expression of factional impulses, and he sought at the Convention the adoption of checks and balances to guard against their occurrence in the central government.

Madison believed that he had objective knowledge about private rights and the public good. Such knowledge is available only to those few who listen to the "mild voice of reason" and ignore "the clamors of an impatient avidity for immediate and immoderate gain." So he suggested in *The Federalist* 42 in defending the investment of authority over interstate commerce in the national government. "Those who do not view the question through the medium of passion or of interest" will see the wisdom of the Framers' proposal.[38] The distinction between the dispassionate, disinterested few and the passionate, interested many is still more pointed in *The Federalist* 10, in which Madison claimed that a "chosen body of citizens" distinguished by their wisdom, patriotism, and love of justice "may best discern the true interest of their country."[39] Madison did allow that "the people can never willfully betray their own interests"—including presumably their interest in the protection of private rights.[40] They could, however, misperceive their interests "thro' want of information as to their true interests" and "from fickleness and passion"[41] or when they are "stimulated by some irregular passion, or some illicit advantage" or "mislead by the artful representations of interested men."[42] It is from these sources that faction springs.

DEFENSE AGAINST FACTION

For Madison, bicameralism and the other checks and balances provided an important defense against majority faction. In *The Federalist* 10, he identified the problem of popular government as faction, that is, a majority or minority of citizens that pursues some end adverse to private rights or to the public good. Although faction could spring from a variety of passions, opinions, and interests, "the most common and durable source of faction has been the various and unequal distribution of property." The propertied and the propertyless and creditors and debtors have always formed distinct interests.[43] Both at the Convention and in *The Federalist* 10, Madison noted that in "civilized nations" property interests are still further elaborated.[44] But, at the Convention, he added, "There will be particularly the distinction of rich and poor."[45] On his understanding of private rights and the public good, Madison, in *Vices*, condemned state legislation that provided for "paper money, instalments of debts, occlusion of Courts, [and] making property a legal tender."[46] Property interests, in his view, had already inspired factional legislation in some states. And, while he believed that such legislation was unlikely to command national support at the time,[47] he urged his fellow delegates at Philadelphia to recognize that "an increase of population will of necessity increase the proportion of those who will labour under all the hardships of life, & secretly sigh for a more equal distribution of its blessings." Those who so labor may come to outnumber "those who are placed above the feelings of indigence. . . . No agrarian attempts have yet been made in this Country, but symptoms of a leveling spirit, as we have understood, have sufficiently appeared in a certain quarters to give notice of the future danger."[48]

Faction has been the cause of the "mortal diseases" of popular government. Popular government provides the mechanism for defeating minority factions: the majority could vote down a factional minority. Majority factions are not so easily dealt with. Indeed, popular governments of the "pure" type, namely, direct democracies, have always been helpless before the transgressions of factional majorities. A "proper cure" must be found. Therefore, Madison asserted, "the great object to which our inquiries are directed" is "to secure the public good and private rights against the danger of . . . a [majority] faction" while preserving "the spirit and form of popular government." This was for him the principal end to be realized by the Constitution and "the great desideratum by which alone" popular government "can be rescued from the opprobrium under which it has so long labored and be recommended to the esteem and adoption of mankind."[49]

Students of the Founding agree that Madison regarded faction as the great problem to be solved by the institution of a "well-constructed Union." No such consensus exists that he regarded checks and balances as a way to thwart majority faction. Those who object to this understanding point to representative government over an extended sphere as Madison's cure for faction. Their objection relies largely on *The Federalist* 10. There Madison argues that a large republic enjoys two signal advantages over a small republic in curing the mischiefs of faction.[50] First, by comprehending a greater number of citizens divided into a greater variety of parties and interests, a large republic makes it "less probable that a majority . . . will have a common motive to invade the rights of other citizens," and should a common motive exist, "it will be more difficult for all who feel it to discover their own strength and to act in unison." Second, the large republic would have more "fit characters" to serve as representatives, and the increased size of constituencies would discourage the election of unworthy candidates and encourage the election of virtuous ones. Some see *The Federalist* 10 as containing Madison's entire remedy for majority faction. Separation of powers and checks and balances, for them, are aimed at protecting the whole citizenry against the possible tyranny of government officials and not a minority of citizens against the majority.[51]

There are two problems with this position. First, *The Federalist* itself does not support it. Although Madison in *The Federalist* 51 distinguished the purpose of separation of powers (to prevent governmental tyranny) from that of the extended sphere (to prevent majority tyranny), he qualified this distinction in *The Federalist* 62 and 63. Thus, in *The Federalist* 63, he acknowledged that "in a former paper" he had stressed the advantage enjoyed by "a confederated republic" in breaking faction. "At the same time," he continued, "this advantage ought not to be considered as superseding the use of auxiliary precautions."[52] These "auxiliary precautions" are separation of powers and checks and balances. He observed in *The Federalist* 51 that legislative predominance is to be diminished by dividing the legislature into two houses and by giving them "different modes of election and different principles of action."[53] This serves to dampen "the propensity of all single and numerous assemblies to yield to the impulse of sudden and violent passion, and to be seduced by factious leaders into intemperate and pernicious resolutions."[54] Madison did not here specify whether he had in mind resolutions of popular origin or schemes cooked up within the legislature itself. We are told, however, in *The Federalist* 63 that the people "may call for [such] measures" when they are seized by "their own temporary errors and delusions" or are "stimulated by some irregular passion, or some illicit advantage, or mislead by . . . interested men."[55]

If we look outside *The Federalist* for Madison's views on the Senate, we also find deficient the view that the extended republic alone is the Madisonian remedy for faction. At the Convention on June 26, Madison ascribed to the Senate two ends: "first to protect the people agst. their rulers: secondly to protect [the people] agst. the transient impressions into which they themselves might be led."[56] Two weeks later, his fears for the security of property appeared in his assertion that the Senate "had for one of its primary objects the guardianship of property."[57] Those same fears informed his letter of October 15, 1788, to a follower who had sought his advice on a constitution for Kentucky. Madison recommended a property qualification for electors of the state's senators, while the election of representatives could be "left more at large." He continued, "This middle mode reconciles and secures the two cardinal objects of Government; the rights of persons, and the rights of property. The former will be sufficiently guarded by one branch, the latter more particularly by the other. . . . It is now observed that in all populous countries, the smaller part only can be interested in preserving the rights of property. . . . Liberty not less than justice pleads for the policy here recommended."[58] Madison regarded the Senate, which must agree to all legislation, as a check on the House where popular preferences were expected to receive expression.

The second problem with the view that *The Federalist* 10 contains the whole of Madison's remedy for faction is this. It ignores Madison's remarks at the Convention on the role of the executive and the judiciary in checking popular faction. *The Federalist* does not reveal the whole of Madison's position on separation of powers and checks and balances in part because Hamilton assumed responsibility for the writing of the papers on the executive and the judiciary. Madison did say in *The Federalist* 49 that by their mode of selection and terms of office, the president and judges would be less dependent on the people and, therefore, could be expected to hold different views than those of legislators, and in *The Federalist* 51, he asserted the desirability of checks by the other branches on the legislature. The form that such checks ought to take was the subject of much discussion at the Convention. Most delegates, including Madison, assumed that the judiciary had the authority to strike down a law violating the Constitution.[59] Many, again including Madison, believed this was not enough.[60] It must be remembered that the debates concerning the judiciary occurred at a point in the proceedings when the national government was to be invested with the very general powers granted under the Virginia Plan, and therefore, the judiciary would have slight opportunity for judicial review of national legislation. Some delegates favored an absolute veto in the executive. Madison opposed this alternative on the grounds that it would be ineffective and unacceptable to the country.[61]

To create what he believed would be an effective veto, he sought on three occasions to invest the executive and the judiciary acting as a council of revision with a qualified veto.[62] The Framers, of course, decided on a qualified veto invested in the president alone. Parenthetically, Madison voted against the motion that reduced the size of the majority in Congress necessary to override from three-fourths to two-thirds.[63] Whatever its precise form,

Madison said, on no fewer than three occasions, that a veto on the legislature is necessary "for the safety of a minority in Danger of oppression from an unjust and interested majority";[64] "to control the National Legislature, so far as it might be infected with a . . . propensity [for] pernicious measures";[65] and to "prevent popular or factious injustice."[66] It may be that Madison believed that elected officials are capable of acts oppressive of the people and that separation of powers and checks and balances were intended to restrain them. But the threat posed by self-aggrandizing government officials pales beside that posed by self-interested majorities in the citizenry.

This can be seen in Madison's letter to Thomas Jefferson of October 17, 1788, in which he explained, "Wherever the real power in a Government lies, there is the danger of oppression. In our Governments the real power lies in the majority of the Community, and the invasion of private rights is *chiefly* to be apprehended, not from acts of Government contrary to the sense of its constituents, but from acts in which the Government is the mere instrument of the major number of the Constituents."[67] Madison expressed the same view in his remarks to the House on proposing the amendments that would become the Bill of Rights. He urged the adoption of those amendments to win the support of those who believed that the Constitution left individual rights exposed to governmental transgression. His own conviction, he said, was that the "great danger" to liberty lay "in the abuse of the community [rather] than in the Legislative body" because "the highest prerogative of power" resides in the "body of the people, operating by the majority against the minority."[68] Republican government invests real power in the citizenry, and the Framers adopted a government that was "strictly republican." There was to be no "will in the community independent of the majority" in the form of "an hereditary or self-appointed authority." It was primarily by means of popular elections that he intended to control government and thereby avert "acts of Government contrary to the sense of its constituents." Popular elections, however, create a danger of oppression from "acts in which the Government is the mere instrument of the major number of the Constituents."[69] Thus, as legislators adopt laws embracing ends pursued by a popular faction, oppression is the result.

Madison assumed that popularly elected representatives would share, or be responsive to, the interests and passions that motivated their constituents, and that those interests and passions might be factional. This understanding diminishes the importance of virtue as the motive force in the citizenry. Other interpretations have emphasized the importance Madison placed on virtue in the maintenance of republican government. *Virtue,* here, is not the virtue of the ancients or virtue as Christians understand it but civic virtue—devotion to the common good, a willingness to sacrifice one's own good to the good of the community and to participate in community affairs. Civic virtue inspires the people, we are told, to elect representatives who are also devoted to the public good and who are distinguished by their wisdom—the ability to determine the best way to realize the public good. In denying that this was Madison's position, I acknowledge that he said in *The Federalist* 55, "As there is a degree of depravity in mankind which requires a certain degree of circumspection and distrust, so there are other qualities in human nature which justify a certain portion of esteem and confidence. Republican government presupposes the existence of these qualities in a higher degree than any other form."[70] Despite the existence of admirable qualities in people generally, however, Madison thought that passion and personal interest usually overcome reason in individuals and almost always in groups. Thus, in *Vices*, written shortly before the Convention, at the Convention, in *The Federalist*, and in a post-Convention letter to Jefferson, Madison discounted prudence, a concern for reputation, and conscience as restraints on passion and personal interest.[71] Madison did, of course, except some from the reach of this generalization. Dispassionate and disinterested reason can be found, albeit in a few. Would popular elections empower the wise and virtuous?

Madison in *The Federalist* 10 claimed for the extended republic the advantage of "representatives whose enlightened views and virtuous sentiments render them superior to local prejudices and to schemes of injustice."[72] Indeed, when urging the transfer of authority from the state governments to a national government, he compared invidiously the representatives elected to state office with those who would occupy national office. He beseeched the wary to put aside unwarranted suspicions; national officeholders will be disinterested custodians of the public good. When, however, he had the national government in view, his own suspicions came to the fore. Both Madison and Hamilton thought virtue and wisdom to be the only qualifications that should recommend a man to his fellow citizens. But Madison did not believe that the people would elect representatives impartial toward contending interests. This contention only *seems* to contradict an observation in *The Federalist* 55. In this passage, Madison was responding to the question, Is the small number of House members "dangerous to the public liberty"? He wrote, "I am unable to conceive that the people of America, in their present temper, or under any circumstances which can speedily happen, will choose, and every second year repeat the choice of, sixty-five or an hundred men who would be disposed to form and pursue a scheme of tyranny or treachery."[73] These words reveal Madison's trust in the people, although not in the sense that he trusts the people to elect wise and virtuous leaders. *Public liberty* refers to popular control of government—the very liberty that is jeopardized when government adopts policies "contrary to the sense of its constituents." Madison trusted the people to choose representatives who would not attempt to wrest power from them. He was less hopeful that they would not choose representatives to advance their interests.

In responding to the charge that the House would not be sympathetic "with the mass of the people," Madison pointed out that any citizen "whose merit may recommend him to the esteem and confidence of his country" may be a candidate. The Constitution imposes no qualifications "to fetter the judgement or disappoint the inclination of the people."[74] He implicitly acknowledged here that the judgment and inclination of the people about what constitutes "merit" might diverge from his own understanding. Indeed, in *The Federalist* 50 he denied that the people could be expected to decide, even under the most propitious circumstances, the true merits of a question about the division of authority between the legislature and the other branches. Did he expect the people to choose among candidates on the basis of their "true merit"?

Madison argued in *The Federalist* 10 that in an extended republic the "suffrages of the people" would be "more free" and, therefore, "more likely to center on men who possess the most attractive merit and the most diffusive and established characters."[75] Was Madison referring to men of virtue and wisdom who could impartially adjudicate among contending interests? Madison's use of the term *merit* is ambiguous. Although he might have meant virtue and wisdom, he might also have recognized that the merit "most attractive" to the electorate included qualities other than virtue and wisdom. To be sure, the large constituencies required by an extended republic would make more likely the election of candidates of "the most diffusive and established characters," that is, candidates not tied to local and narrow interests. But making "the suffrages of the people . . . more free" from local and narrow interests does not necessarily free them from interest in favor of virtue and wisdom. The electorate might choose representatives on the basis of more general and widely held interests such as those identified in *The Federalist* 10: the propertied and the unpropertied, creditors and debtors, a landed interest and so on.

This was what Madison expected. He regarded Americans as divided along a number of lines. Different opinions concerning religion had produced

a multiplicity of sects. This circumstance permitted a depoliticization of religion through a policy of toleration and disestablishment—already much
advanced by the time of the Convention. The North and the South were
divided "principally from [the effects of] their having or not having slaves."[76]
For Madison, slavery itself was not the politically significant issue; it did
not figure in his recital at the Convention of "those unjust laws complained
of among ourselves."[77] The slave-holding South and the non-slave-hold-
ing North had different property interests. During his June 30 speech at the
Convention, he spoke of interest, not of virtue and wisdom.[78] Interest, he
assumed, would inform electoral choice and secure representation in the
legislature. Just as the Northern and Southern states were divided by the possession of different kinds of property, so Americans generally were divided
by the "possession of different degrees and kinds of property." The "regulation" of property interests "forms the principal task of modern legislation
and involves the spirit of party and factions in the necessary and ordinary
operations of government."[79]

One or another property interest might be subjected to factional legislation. And, Madison said, "whenever there is danger of attack there ought
to be given a constitutional power of defense." This proposition holds with
respect to "every peculiar interest whether in any class of citizens, or any
description of states." Madison did not invoke here the extended sphere as
affording protection, let alone the only protection, "against the mischiefs of
faction." He proposed "a constitutional power of defense." With respect to
the North-South division, he allowed that the defense that had occurred to
him was an "arrangement" conferring an advantage in representatives to the
South in one chamber of the legislature and to the North in the other.[80]
Such an arrangement would suggest itself to someone, like Madison, who
expected legislators to defend the peculiar interests of their constituents.
The same expectation informed his comments on equality of representation
in the Senate in The Federalist 62. There he observed that the defense afforded
to the small states "would be more rational if any interests common to them
and distinct from those of the other states would otherwise be exposed to
peculiar danger."[81] Madison, of course, fought doggedly throughout the
Convention against equal representation of the states, and he did not let pass
this opportunity to express a jibe at its proponents. He did not think that
interests were divided along large-state, small-state lines. He did think that,
if they were, the insistence of the small states on equal representation would
be more rational. It would be more rational only on the assumption that representatives would defend the distinct interests of their constituents.

CONCLUSION

Can this view of Madison's position on separation of powers and checks and balances be reconciled with other positions that he held concerning the structure and function of the proposed government? This essay concludes that not only is such reconciliation possible but that his position on separation of powers and checks and balances as described here is integral to his whole scheme.

Madison declared that the fundamental ends of government are justice (private rights) and the public good. How, according to him, can we ensure, insofar as that is possible, that government will respect and protect private rights and pursue the public good rather than exercise its power to advance the interests or gratify the passions of its own members or of some group in society at everybody else's expense? Madison's answer was government that is republican, national, energetic, and constrained by separation of powers and checks and balances.

Government must be republican. It must derive "all its powers directly or indirectly from the great body of the people" and be administered by "persons . . . appointed, either directly or indirectly, by the people."[82] No other form of government is defensible. Madison rejected not only absolute monarchy[83] but also a limited monarchy like that of England.[84] While a government with one popularly chosen branch is preferable to absolute monarchy—it "tempers the evils of an absolute one"— it, too, is defective.[85] The apparent advantage of a government with self-appointed or hereditary officials is largely illusory. It offers "but a precarious security" for private rights and the public good. This is so because "a power independent of the society may as well espouse the unjust views of the major as the rightful interests of the minor party, and may possibly be turned against both parties."[86] Although Madison thought that a republic, properly qualified, was that government best formed to realize justice and the public good, he was a republican not for this reason alone. He also believed that people ought to enjoy that liberty afforded by republican government to engage in "political life."[87]

Compared with "the most respectable theoretical sources of its time (Locke and Montesquieu)" or "the most respectable actual regime of its time (Great Britain)," the regime defended by *The Federalist* was a long step toward the democratization of politics.[88] Many Americans of the Founding period, however, did not regard the British government or the regimes favored by Locke or Montesquieu as the standard against which the Constitution ought to be measured. They already lived under (state) governments far more republican than those regimes, and it was to their own state governments that many, some unfavorably, compared the Constitution. Although Madison was critical of many of the specific arrangements found in one or another state government, his principal objection was that they were too small.

For him, government must be national. His Virginia Plan looked toward a government in which the states would have been largely reduced to administrative units of the national government. The Constitution, of course, fell considerably short of doing any such thing—to Madison's grave disappointment.[89] It did not include the national veto on state legislation or the general grant of legislative authority to the national government provided by the Virginia Plan. Nevertheless, the Constitution did provide for government far more national than government had been under the Articles. Madison of *The Federalist* 10 thought that, by extending the sphere in which democratic politics would occur, the Constitution offered a "republican remedy for the diseases most incident to republican government." Those diseases, he thought, were most virulent in direct democracies, but small republics, like those of the states, suffered them as well. In both, justice and public good were in jeopardy from factions that could more readily unite and carry out their schemes of oppression than could a large republic. *The Federalist* 10 argued that the extended republic "rendered factious combinations less to be dreaded" at the national level. They were not precluded even there, however, and factions would almost certainly continue to plague state politics. It was this latter expectation that principally recommended to Madison an energetic government of national compass.

Not only must government be republican and national, it must be energetic.[90] By *energy* Madison meant authority and power. To secure justice, government itself must refrain from committing injustice, and it must protect the individual's rights against violation from within and without the society. Government does not require energy to refrain from committing injustice, but if it is to protect private rights, it does need energy. Pursuit of the public good also requires that government possess energy. In *Vices*, Madison detailed the failings of government under the Articles.[91] The Confederation Congress had failed to realize the ends of government in part because it lacked energy. The state governments, on the other hand, had too often abused the authority and power that they possessed. This analysis led him to conclude that the authority and power of the states had to be diminished and the energy of the national government augmented.

Madison's support for energetic government at the national level might well have expressed his profound distrust of the state governments rather than a commitment to some ambitious legislative program like that later advanced by Hamilton. He did think, however, that provision needed to be made for national protection against external attack and domestic convulsion and for national regulation of commerce among the states and between the United States and other nations.[92] These, along with taxation, he expected to be "the principal objects of federal legislation."[93] In the exercise of the authority to do these things, he also allowed considerable discretion in the selection of means.[94] The Constitution, then, by investing substantial authority in the national government so that it might realize desired ends also created ample opportunity for abuse.[95]

There is tension in Madison's theory between the ends that he wished to realize and the kind of government that he prescribed. The tension is created by his commitment to republican and energetic government, on the one hand, and to particular conceptions of private rights and the public good as the ends of government, on the other. Madison recognized that many Americans did not share his views on private rights and the public good. He regarded them as wrong and their views as factional. With the liberty afforded by republican government to act on their views, citizens had formed, in his view, factional combinations and won successes in state politics. On the argument of *The Federalist* 10, national government will make majority faction less likely. Nevertheless, Madison was unwilling to rest his hopes for government in the service of private rights and the public good on the efficacy of the extended sphere as a remedy for faction. Separation of powers and checks and balances offered additional protection and thereby served to relieve the tension between republican and energetic government and the realization of justice and the public good as Madison understood them.

CHAPTER 4

TYRANNY OF THE MAJORITY

I n the late eighteenth and nineteenth centuries, the practice of democracy underwent a profound transformation. The extension of the suffrage and the elimination of property qualifications for office, first in the United States and then in Europe, made modern democracies far more inclusive than their historic predecessors. The democracies of ancient Greece and Renaissance Italy had confined participation in politics to small minorities of their populations. Not only did the practice of democracy change, but so did our understanding of it. On this modern understanding, earlier claimants to the title were not democracies at all. James Madison, for example, insisted in *The Federalist* 39 that a democracy derives "all its powers directly or indirectly from the great body of the people . . . not from an inconsiderable proportion or a favored class of it."[1] This popularization of democracy created a problem, or so it seemed to some of democracy's early observers.

The problem perceived by these observers was that a popular majority may oppress the minority. This is the problem of tyranny of the majority. The fear aroused among Americans by this problem has inspired the adoption of constitutional measures and legislative rules aimed at thwarting tyrannical majorities. The Framers justified constitutional provision for a bicameral legislature, separation of powers and checks and balances, equal representation of the states in the Senate, and the extended republic as defenses against tyranny of the majority.[2] In subsequent years, the cloture rule in the Senate has been justified on the same grounds.[3] Have these remedies been effective in preventing tyranny in the United States? Before this essay is concluded, I shall seek to answer this question as well as others suggested by the subject:

What distinguishes tyranny of the majority from other forms of tyranny? What is the likelihood of tyranny of the majority? What is tyranny? What remedies ought to be adopted against tyranny of the majority?

In answering these questions, frequent reference will be made to James Madison (1751–1836), Alexis de Tocqueville (1805–1859), and John Stuart Mill (1806–1873). They first recognized the symptoms, diagnosed the problem, and prescribed remedies.[4] Later observers of democracy are in their debt. While we will follow their lead, the principal task to be undertaken will not be the explication of their understanding of tyranny of the majority but coming to grips with the problem itself.

THE SEVERAL FACES OF TYRANNY

For Madison, tyranny of the majority occurs when a democratically elected government adopts a law, supported by a popular majority, that oppresses the minority. Such a law might be aimed at either opinion or conduct. In either case, government would compel observance of the law by attaching sanctions like fines, imprisonment, or death for its violation. Tocqueville and Mill agreed that tyranny of the majority might take this form, but they also regarded as tyrannical the application of social sanctions like ridicule, ostracism, and milder expressions of disapproval against those who dissent from majority-held views or who act contrary to the majority's sense of right.

Against the threat of tyrannical laws, Madison and Mill recommended the adoption of constitutional measures. Madison, as we have seen, argued at the Constitutional Convention and in *The Federalist* on behalf of separation of powers and checks and balances. Mill favored plural voting for the educated and proportional representation. Madison and Mill did not dismiss altogether the role that moral and social constraints might play in reducing the threat from tyranny of the majority. Tocqueville, however, gave almost exclusive emphasis to these kinds of constraint. He urged, for example, the encouragement of voluntary associations of all descriptions. Such associations can serve as centers of resistance to the concentration of power in a domineering majority. We can see in this the same sort of thinking to which Madison gave expression in *The Federalist* 10 about religious diversity. Tocqueville also sought to foster recognition of the benefits to all of diversity.

Before taking up the matter of tyrannical laws imposed by popular majority, let us first examine the idea of a social tyranny as propounded by Tocqueville and Mill. They believed that aristocratic society had permitted, even promoted, the influence of scientific and philosophical learning and artistic and spiritual sensibilities on public life. They did not oppose the passing of the old regime, but they thought the sensibilities and learning of the aristocracy deserved to be respected and cultivated. The rise of the middle and lower classes to social ascendancy would, they feared, bring an end to the influence of those sensibilities and that learning. Mass society and mediocrity would displace individuality and excellence. So great was their fear that they characterized these expected developments as *tyranny of the majority*. This was a tyranny, remember, that would be enforced by social sanctions—"a tyranny not over the body, but over the mind," as Mill put it.[5] The remedy that Tocqueville and Mill proposed for tyranny of the majority in this form was education. Tocqueville's *Democracy in America* and Mill's *On Liberty* constitute their attempts to persuade us to be open-minded and sympathetic.

Few, I suppose, would deny the dominance today of mass culture in public life: in the media, in legislative chambers and community centers, and in coffeehouses, for example. I also suppose that few would deny the difficulty of resisting social pressures to conform, although to speak about this in terms of resistance and pressure is seldom appropriate. From birth on, subtle processes are at work in the family, among friends, and in churches and schools that make for willing and unquestioning adoption of the reigning views. Tocqueville and Mill, with respect to this point, tell us nothing new. Judging from Plato's observations in *The Republic*, ancients found it no less difficult than moderns to question the authority of the gods, the government, and parents and to think for themselves.

This is to deal with the idea of a social tyranny in a summary way. I do so for several reasons. First, that form of tyranny of the majority referred to here as *social tyranny* is no less interesting or troubling than the other form, but it is not the form that has concerned most Americans. They have been concerned about the use of governmental power by popular majorities to tyrannize over the minority. Second, what Tocqueville and Mill called *social tyranny*, however lamentable, is not tyranny. In making this assertion I beg, for the moment, the question, What is tyranny? Whatever else tyranny may be, it is something to be condemned and resisted if possible. We may agree, in the spirit of Mill, that it is unfortunate that in some communities the majority scorns homosexuals, shuns blacks, or ridicules the Amish but deny that such behavior is tyrannical. Following Tocqueville, we may agree that it is unfortunate that an intellectual cannot be elected president of the United States but deny that the intellectual's exclusion constitutes tyranny.

Those who suffer only reproach or isolation for their views, lifestyles, or personal qualities are the victims of tyranny only in hyperbolic speech. People ought to be free to associate with whomever they want, to criticize those whom they disapprove, and to vote for candidates whom they favor. So valuable are these freedoms and so vulnerable are they to attack that Americans have accorded them the status of rights. There can be no assurances that people will exercise these rights in a civil, let alone sympathetic, way. The ridicule and shunning of racial and ethnic minorities are examples of the uncivil and unsympathetic exercise of rights. Contrary to the old saw that "words will never hurt me," such behavior does cause hurt. Moreover, these rights are limited. One's reproach of another must not perpetrate slander or libel. One's association must not be a criminal conspiracy. One's vote must not be offered to the highest bidder and so on. These observations made, it remains the case that in doing what they ought to be able to do, people cannot tyrannize. People can, however, tyrannize in the exercise of rights because some rights have been understood to permit people to do what they ought not to be able to do. Rights of property have been so understood for example.

In denying that the application of social sanctions by a popular majority to secure conformity to its will is tyranny, I do not say that only government can tyrannize. While only government may legitimately use or permit the use of violence to secure observance of its will, still other sanctions are available to some to secure observance of their will. Mill pointed to the tremendous power held by employers over their employees.[6] This power, although somewhat confined since Mill's day, includes the power to hire and fire, to grant or withhold increases in pay and benefits, to confer or deny promotion, and, in general, to dictate the conditions of employment. This power might be, and of course has been, abused. Perhaps the clearest instances of such abuse in the American experience were the long-standing restrictions adopted by many employers against the employment of blacks and women in any but the most lowly positions, and the subjection of them to the rule of last hired, first fired. Formally, employees are free to find more congenial employment, but such employment may not be available or the employee may, for a variety of reasons, be unable to seek employment elsewhere. As Mill pointed out, "men might as well be imprisoned as excluded from the means of earning their bread."[7]

The abuse of employer power might be tyrannical. Nevertheless, however severe the tyranny established by some employers, unless that employer is government itself, it is not tyranny of the majority. We may, therefore, exclude employer tyranny from further consideration here. We took tyranny of the majority as our subject and not tyranny in general. The tyranny exercised by monarchs and oligarchs of the past or by the authoritarian generals and totalitarian parties of modern day is also no part of our concern. We are concerned with a form of tyranny peculiar to democracy and, in particular, to mass democracy. Furthermore, for the reasons stated, so-called tyranny of the majority in its social form is excluded from consideration. In what follows, we shall be concerned solely with tyranny of the majority as it may be imposed by democratic government.

ASSUMPTIONS UNDERLYING THE IDEA

Madison, Tocqueville, and Mill in raising the alarm about tyranny of the majority made several assumptions, First, they assumed that there are ethical criteria independent of the majority's will by which policies pursued by democratic government can be judged. It is on the basis of this assumption that they can hold that the popular majority is not always right, indeed, that the popular majority may be tyrannical. All supporters of democracy must acknowledge the existence of such criteria. Only if there are such criteria, can the democratic process itself be adjudged superior to its alternatives. One such criterion might be respect for certain fundamental interests. On this criterion, if a law, even a law adopted by democratic processes, harmed one or another of those fundamental interests, then that law would be tyrannical. On this criterion, a justification for the democratic process itself would consist in showing that democracy is more likely to respect those fundamental interests than alternative decision-making processes.

Another implication of the assumption that there are ethical criteria independent of the majority's will is that among the fundamental interests that must be respected by government are interests not essential to the operation of the democratic process. Democracy does by definition rule out many forms that tyranny might take. For example, democracy requires that people have a right to express their beliefs, including criticism of public policy and political leaders. Denial of this right is tyranny. Democracy requires that people have a right to form and join autonomous political organizations like political parties and interest groups. Denial of this right is tyranny. Democracy requires that virtually all adults have the right to vote for government officials. Denial of this right is tyranny—and so on through the whole list of rights essential to democracy. Madison, Tocqueville, and Mill assume that those rights do not exhaust the list of fundamental interests that must be respected lest tyranny occur.

Second, they assumed that many people harbor tyrannical beliefs that they might seek to enact into law. Religion, education, and social pluralism, then, cannot be relied on even in a democracy to teach sufficient restraint to prevent tyranny. In part, their suspicions concerned religion. Madison and Mill worried that democratic government under the influence of the religiously intolerant would persecute dissenters. Tocqueville, with an eye to his own country, feared that an anticlerical majority would attack religious institutions. Much more prominent in Madison's thinking, and only somewhat less prominent in the thinking of the others, was property. They all accused the lower classes of having designs on the property of the wealthy. We have already seen how Madison castigated the state legislatures of the Confederation period for their passage of stay laws, and paper currency and legal tender laws.

Whether Madison and the others were right to attribute tyrannical thoughts to a majority depends in part on the meaning of *tyranny*. They were certainly right in identifying religion and property as enduring sources of political division and conflict. Many other qualities that distinguish one group from another have also been politically divisive: language, geographic section, social status, ideology, race, and ethnicity, among others. Differences among people along these lines have inspired intense emotions. Were tyranny to be imposed by a popular majority in a democracy, one or another of those differences would probably mark the division between the tyrants and the tyrannized.

Third, Madison, Tocqueville, and Mill believed that tyranny of the majority posed a threat because they assumed that the democratic process created a close relationship between the people and their elected representatives. In their view, elected representatives share or are responsive to the policy preferences of the majority of their constituents. For some at the Constitutional Convention, such a relationship was the ideal to be realized. In the words of George Mason, delegate from Virginia, "The requisites in actual representation are that the Reps. should sympathize with their constituents; shd. think as they think, & feel as they feel; and that for these purposes shd. even be resident among them."[8] Realization of the ideal, Mason thought, would ensure that the policy preferences of the popular majority would be adopted into law. Madison rejected such a relationship as the ideal, but he too believed that frequent elections and short terms would create such a relationship, particularly in small constituencies.

Modern observers of democracy have found the relationship between constituents and representatives to be more remote than Madison, Tocqueville, and Mill supposed. Instead of congruence between the policy preferences of a majority and the laws adopted by popularly elected representatives, modern democracies are characterized by incongruence more or less great over many policy areas.[9] National policy on Cuba and gun control and certain state educational policies, for example, do not accord with the policy preferences of the majority.[10] In the United States, this incongruence can be explained in part by constitutional arrangements like equal representation of the states in the Senate and separation of powers and checks and balances. But, in all modern democracies, many voters are ignorant of the issues and unaware of policy alternatives. Voters also support candidates even though they oppose them on some issues. And, voters have different priorities—they feel more intensely about some issues than others.[11] As a consequence, elections usually produce a clear expression of voter preferences about candidates. They rarely produce a clear expression of voter preferences about policies.[12] Under these circumstances, even those officeholders who feel most bound to do their constituents' bidding must exercise discretion. Furthermore, most voters do not pay attention to politics after the elections, when policy is made. And, of course, there are great inequalities in resources, opportunities, and motivation that create inequality in influence over the policymaking process.[13] Some minorities, particularly the corporations, are advantaged in these respects.

Must we conclude that the popular majority never rules and, therefore, that tyranny of the majority is impossible? We need reach that conclusion if rule by the popular majority occurs only on the satisfaction of two conditions: (1) there is close coincidence between a policy preference of a popular majority and a public policy and (2) the public policy was adopted because the popular majority preferred it.[14] Reality does not satisfy so stringent a test. Nevertheless, we may continue to think that Madison, Tocqueville, and Mill were on to something. Even though it fails to produce close coincidence between the policy preferences of the majority and public policy, democracy produces closer coincidence than any other decision-making process. I propose to relax the conditions under which tyranny of the majority may be said to exist. The effect of this move will be to bring closer the real world of popular influence on policy in a democracy.

Democratic elections do not express the specific policy preferences of popular majorities. Democratic elections do, however, enforce limits that representatives must respect in the making of public policy.[15] Representatives learn what those limits are by listening to activists like political party officials

and interest group spokesmen, by talking to members of the general electorate, by reading the public opinion polls, and by the results of elections. These
limits are broader or narrower depending on the policy area and vary from
one constituency to another.[16] When representatives exceed these limits, they
risk losing their seats. They may, of course, lose their seats for other reasons
as well. Within these limits, representatives may exercise discretion in choosing among policy alternatives. On some occasions, those alternatives may
include a tyrannical policy. If such a policy, falling within the limits established by the popular majority, were adopted, then tyranny of the majority
would exist.

On this view, the popular majority becomes complicit in the adoption of
any tyrannical law that persists over two election cycles. The popular majority is also complicit in the tyranny worked by any administrative official,
the president or a governor, for example, whom it returns to office. Such
complicity is incurred, it must be emphasized, only when the citizenry has
had an adequate opportunity to learn of the law or administrative act, and
democratic rights of participation can be exercised without fear of retri-
bution. These qualifications are aimed at relieving citizens of any duty to
acquire obscure information or to risk punishment in order to avoid joining the ranks of a tyranny of the majority. Citizens do need to be politically
conscious and active; they do need to exercise their participatory rights in
an effort to defeat tyranny. In taking this position, I depart from Madison,
Tocqueville, and Mill. They thought that tyranny of the majority would issue
from the pursuit of tyrannical ends by a popular majority—and it might. It
might also, however, be a consequence of political ignorance and passivity.

Fourth, Madison, Tocqueville, and Mill assumed that the democratic
process does not preclude tyranny of the majority. This sounds much like
the first assumption. There, however, we were concerned with uncovering
certain logical implications of their position. Here, we are concerned with
a matter of fact, namely, the practice of democratic politics. Democracy, it
might be contended, makes unlikely the adoption of tyrannical laws by the
majority in this way: In order for political leaders to assemble the majorities
needed to make law, they must forge coalitions among diverse groups. This
requires compromise among these groups all of whom have (to some extent)
competing interests. Such compromise may so moderate the narrow (and
perhaps tyrannical) interests of the several groups making up a coalition
as to eliminate the threat of tyranny. Madison remarked on the moderating
effect of coalition-building in mass democracy in *The Federalist* 10:

The smaller the society, the fewer probably will be the distinct parties and interests composing it; the fewer the distinct parties and interests, the more frequently will a majority be found of the same party; and the smaller the number of individuals composing a majority, and the smaller the compass within which they are placed, the more easily will they concert and execute their plans of oppression. Extend the sphere and you take in a greater variety of parties and interests; you make it less probable that a majority of the whole will have a common motive to invade the rights of other citizens; or if such a common motive exists, it will be more difficult for all who feel it to discover their own strength and to act in unison with each other.[17]

Coalition-building does not, of course, occur once and for all. From election to election, candidates and parties must to some extent forge new coalitions. And, from issue to issue, legislators must to some extent forge new coalitions. Now, if one needs to find allies on the next issue among one's opponents on the current issue, then one will not want to foreclose the possibility of finding such allies by tyrannizing. Such *shifting majorities* as they are sometimes called reduce the threat of tyranny. Nevertheless, however unlikely democracy makes tyranny of the majority in this or other ways, it remains a distinct possibility.

TYRANNY DEFINED

Up to this point, *tyranny* has remained undefined. I have assumed, to be sure, an understanding of tyranny. More particularly, I have assumed that a definition of tyranny would comprehend the denial of those participatory rights that characterize modern democracies like the rights of free speech and association and the right to vote. I have also assumed that a definition of tyranny would comprehend interests beyond those rights such as one's physical safety and welfare and one's freedom of movement. It is now time to redeem the earlier promise to define the term. *Tyranny* is the severe deprivation of fundamental interests. *Tyranny of the majority*, then, is tyranny imposed by public policy acquiesced in or supported by a popular majority. This definition of tyranny needs qualification in four ways. First, it is not tyranny when severe deprivation of fundamental interests is imposed as punishment for acts that severely deprive another of fundamental interests. Second, it is not tyranny if no alternative policy is available that would not impose severe deprivation of fundamental interests.[18] Third, it is not tyranny if one *consents* to a policy that results in a severe deprivation of one's fundamental interests. Fourth, it is not tyranny when democratic government demands of its citizens that they contribute to the operation and defense of the state.

The first qualification acknowledges that government rightly imposes severe deprivations on many for the violation of statutes against homicide, rape, armed robbery, and so on. Our fellows in society often deprive us of fundamental interests. In proceeding against those who deprive others of fundamental interests, government is not a tyrant. Rather, it seeks to discharge one of its principal responsibilities, namely, the protection of fundamental interests. One may not, then, cry "tyranny" as one languishes in a prison cell after conviction for murder in a fair trial. Of course, some acts made criminal by government ought not to be, and some punishments imposed by government are disproportionate to the crime. In such instances tyranny raises its head. Nevertheless, tyranny is not all severe deprivations of fundamental interests. It is not tyranny to impose such deprivations as punishment for acts that severely deprive others of fundamental interests.

The second qualification recognizes that circumstances might exist in which there are no policy alternatives open to government that do not impose severe deprivation of fundamental interests. This is the case in the following hypothetical example: In response to the anticipated spread of a deadly influenza virus, the government distributes all available vaccine to those most vulnerable. For reasons beyond the control of the government, there is insufficient vaccine to inoculate everyone. As a consequence, some will die after contraction of the flu. The government's policy imposes severe deprivation of fundamental interests on those who do not fall in the "most vulnerable" group and who contract the flu and die as a result. Nevertheless, the government's policy is not tyrannical because all alternative policies would also impose severe deprivation. Such alternative policies for the distribution of the available vaccine like "first come/first served" and "only those who can pay" would also impose severe deprivation, and they have an additional quality: they are unfair.

The third qualification allows consent to a severe deprivation of fundamental interests. One might, for example, volunteer for a government study of an experimental drug and subsequently die sometime after the administration of the drug. Let's say that this drug has shown promise in animal studies as a cure for some debilitating disease. The risks and side effects for humans are, however, largely unknown. The government informs the prospective subjects of all this, and it uses no coercion in the recruitment of subjects. It does offer modest cash payment. Furthermore, no one's choice to become a subject is unduly burdened—the choice is not between taking the government's money and going hungry, for example. On these conditions, one's consent to participate was given knowingly and willingly. Therefore, the government did *not* act tyrannically in administering the drug that caused one's death.

The absence of consent given knowingly and willingly made the government policy in the Tuskegee syphilis experiment tyrannical.[19] In 1932 the U.S. Public Health Service began a study of the effects of syphilis when left untreated. The subject population consisted in part of 399 African-American men diagnosed with syphilis. The Public Health Service recruited these poor and mostly illiterate men in Macon County, Alabama, by offering free medical exams, free meals on examination days, and free burial insurance. The subjects were told that they had *bad blood*. By the time the study was closed down in 1972, twenty-eight had died of syphilis, one hundred others had died of syphilis-related diseases, forty wives had become infected, and nineteen children had been born with congenital syphilis. During World War II some two hundred of the infected subjects were drafted or volunteered for service in the military. At the behest of the assistant surgeon general, the local draft board waived the usual requirement that inductees with venereal disease be treated. Even after the introduction of penicillin in 1947 as the standard cure, the test subjects were denied treatment and were not informed of their real illness or of its consequences. This was tyranny, although not tyranny of the majority. Until a Public Health Service investigator broke the story to the *Washington Evening Star* in 1972, few outside of official circles had ever heard of the study.

The fourth qualification assumes that citizens of a modern democratic state owe a good deal to one another. Much of the affluence, security, and freedom that they enjoy is a consequence of their association in a stable, effective, and democratic state. Government is not a tyrant in requiring citizens to contribute to the operation and defense of such a state. The obligations of democratic citizenship are not absolute, but such obligations do exist, and they arise at least in part from the benefits conferred by the democratic state.

In the absence of some compelling reason to the contrary, democratic government may, without working tyranny, require citizens to serve on juries, to pay taxes, and to help defend the state against its enemies. It may even require citizens to vote, as Belgium now does, without overstepping the line beyond which government becomes tyrannical. These are burdens, it must be emphasized, that are to be borne by all citizens (children except-ed), although not necessarily in the same way. The policies whereby government imposes these demands can result in the severe deprivation of fundamental interests. Indeed, military conscription always does so. At best, one's freedom of movement is constrained, and, at worst, one suffers death on some battlefield. Nevertheless, no tyranny is worked if the conscription policy is fair.

It might be objected here that an alternative policy is available that imposes no severe deprivation of fundamental interests on anyone. A military force can be raised by soliciting the consent of prospective recruits. The American "all-volunteer" force is an instance of this kind. Certainly one or another member of such a force might suffer grave injury or death as many Americans have in Iraq. These severe deprivations were not imposed, how-ever, because those members consented knowingly and willingly to a service that poses those risks. Therefore, no tyranny has occurred. But government is not necessarily tyrannical in adopting a conscription policy. A military force made up of consenting members might, after all, be insufficient. It might be necessary in some circumstances to adopt conscription in order to defend the state.

SOME APPLICATIONS

Whatever consensus these definitions so qualified may command will, I suspect, be challenged as they are applied to concrete cases. It is to that task that I now turn. Consider the following cases drawn from the American experience:

- the prohibition on same-sex marriage
- the internment of Japanese Americans during World War II
- the segregation by race of schools, transportation facilities, and other institutions in the South after Reconstruction
- forbidding women to vote and to hold and dispose of property on an equal basis with men
- requiring the teaching of creationism in the public schools
- the loss of some thirteen hundred lives in New Orleans in Hurricane Katrina

In each of these cases, ask yourself "Is it tyranny?" and, more particularly, "Is it tyranny of the majority?" With respect to several of these cases, one might well contend that the laws in question are tyrannical, but they are not tyranny of the majority. The Jim Crow laws and the exclusion of women from the suffrage are cases of this kind.

What casts into doubt the status of these cases as tyranny of the majority is the character of American government at the time. Tyranny of the majority by definition can be worked only by a democracy. Was American government democratic in, say, 1890? In trying to answer this question, it will be helpful to distinguish between criteria and standards. The distinction will be familiar to college students in the following example. The criteria for a well-written essay include a clearly stated thesis, the absence of errors in grammar and diction, and so on. Professors may agree on the criteria, but they disagree about standards. Professor Smith is a generous grader, prepared to overlook major shortfalls from the criteria. Professor Rowe, on the other hand, is death itself on any paper that fails to well satisfy the criteria. The distinction here comes to this: What qualities must a government have in order to be a democracy?

Democracy requires that (1) throughout the decision-making process, citizens have an adequate and equal opportunity to express their preferences for public policy; (2) citizens have an equal opportunity to express a choice that will be counted as equal in weight to the choice expressed by any other citizen; (3) each citizen has adequate and equal opportunities for acquiring an informed understanding of his or her interests and of the policies that will best serve those interests; (4) the citizens have the final say on what matters are to be placed on the agenda for collective decision; and (5) with the exception of the mentally challenged and children, all who are subject to the law are citizens.[20] This ideal has never been realized in practice. In moving toward the ideal, the United States has instituted the election of public officials in free and fair elections, a free press, freedom of speech and assembly, and the extension of the right to vote and the right to run for office to virtually all adults. These institutions are necessary, but not sufficient, conditions for democracy.[21] Nevertheless, governments that employ these processes and respect those rights are customarily referred to as democracies.

On either set of criteria—the five qualities first described or the institutions just named—every government falls short in one respect or another. This fact raises the question of standards. To what extent must a government possess democratic qualities in order to be properly called *democratic*? In 1890 American government was perhaps more democratic than any other, but it too failed to fully satisfy the criteria for democracy. In particular, American government was not very inclusive. It denied the vote to all women (until 1920) and, until 1965, to virtually all black men and women in the South.

Furthermore, blacks were denied other participatory rights. However much disagreement there might be about the standards to be applied in making a judgment about its overall character in 1890, American government was certainly not democratic with respect to women and blacks. Therefore, the tyranny imposed on women and blacks in the cases above was not tyranny of the majority.

Another of the cases—the Hurricane Katrina deaths—points to another facet of the problem worth considering, namely, tyranny as an act of omission. In all the other cases government did something. It imprisoned, prohibited, conscripted, or required. In response to Hurricane Katrina, national, state, and local government did nothing or, more accurately, acted tardily and ineffectually. Can a government tyrannize in this way? Consider this hypothetical case (like the preceding one, it departs only a little from actual events): An authoritarian government stands by passively as an armed militia in an orgy of violence slaughters and rapes an ethnic minority. The government could intervene effectively to stop the killing and rape but chooses not to do so because it is indifferent to the interests of the ethnic minority. If the policy of nonintervention pursued by that government is tyrannical, then governments can tyrannize by doing nothing. Was the response of American government to Hurricane Katrina similar to the response of the government in the hypothetical case?

There are, of course, major differences between the two. Katrina was a natural event; the attacks of the armed militia are a result of human will. The government in the hypothetical case is a nondemocracy; in the United States, government is more or less democratic. The significance of the latter difference for present concerns is that the killing and rape of the ethnic minority, while tyranny, is not tyranny of the majority. Some of the deaths suffered in New Orleans as a result of Hurricane Katrina, however, might be tyranny of the majority. The significance of the former difference (natural event versus acts of human will) is slight. Whatever the cause, circumstances had developed that jeopardized fundamental interests. The common feature is the truly significant one—great loss of life. We stipulated in the hypothetical case that the government could intervene effectively to stop the killing or, at any rate, to greatly reduce the level of violence.

Could American government have acted in response to Katrina to greatly reduce the loss of life?[22] This is a factual question, and facts must provide the answer. An affirmative answer to the question must show that the government's failure to act or to act effectively was a consequence not of impotence or incompetence but of malice or careless disregard for the victims' interests. If the national government were found to have not acted in a timely and vigorous way to save lives, then tyranny makes its appearance. It would not, however, be tyranny of the majority. The initial response to the hurricane was an administrative responsibility. The voters who elected Bush in 2004 could not have anticipated the occurrence of the hurricane or what response his administration would make to it. The national popular majority, therefore, cannot be complicit in any failure on the part of the Bush administration in responding to Katrina. I do not propose to attempt to answer the factual questions and to determine the culpability, if any, of the several governments involved in the loss of life in New Orleans.[23] I am concerned only with advancing the idea that governments can tyrannize by omission.

Some school boards have required the teaching of creationism in public schools as part of the science curriculum. This doctrine contends that the account of the origins of life as given in Genesis is the correct one—contrary to the prevailing view in the scientific community. Let us assume that this requirement wherever adopted has the support of the popular majority in the school district. Is this an instance of tyranny of the majority imposed on the minority that holds to evolution as the explanation for the origins of life? In the course of answering this question, it will not be necessary to examine the theories of evolution and creationism or the evidence for them. It will be necessary to explore further the meaning of *fundamental interests* as that phrase is to be understood in the definition of *tyranny* specified earlier.

A distinction between privately oriented and publicly oriented interests will be helpful here.[24] *Privately oriented interests* are those that have oneself or one's family as their object. For example, one's want to worship in one's own way is a privately oriented interest, and so is one's want to not be excluded from an education on the basis of one's gender. *Publicly oriented interests* are those that have everyone or some large group as their object. For example, one's want that no one should be permitted to worship false gods is a publicly oriented interest. One's want that no one should be permitted to consume alcoholic beverages is also a publicly oriented interest. The *fundamental interests* referred to in the definition of tyranny above and whose severe deprivation constitutes tyranny include only privately oriented interests. Why should the meaning of *fundamental interests* be confined in this way? Were publicly oriented interests to be included among those fundamental interests that must not be denied, then the individual would be able to claim "tyranny" anytime his publicly oriented interests did not prevail. Thus, my (or your) interest in excluding creationism from the high school biology curriculum, in forbidding same-sex marriage, or in barring the consumption of alcoholic beverages must be public policy lest tyranny be imposed. Such an understanding of tyranny would render illegitimate any policymaking process that did not make me (or you) the absolute ruler. This principle would destroy any kind of authority and make most forms of social relations impossible. This is not a promising road to travel. As long as one's participatory rights in the making of public policy are not violated, then no tyranny occurs if your publicly oriented interests do not prevail; there has been no severe deprivation of fundamental interests.

Although there is no tyranny in the defeat of one's publicly oriented interests, one does suffer tyranny if the policy adopted imposes severe deprivation of fundamental interests, that is, privately oriented interests. This occurred in the case of Japanese Americans during World War II. Following the Japanese attack on Pearl Harbor, President Franklin Roosevelt in February 1942 issued an executive order directing the secretary of war to create military areas from which any and all persons might be excluded.[25] A month later Congress made it a federal crime for anyone ordered to leave a military area to refuse to do so. Military authorities designated the West Coast as a military area and ordered the exclusion, removal, and detention of all persons of Japanese ancestry. This policy was executed against some 120,000 people of whom the great majority were American citizens. During the removal phase, which took many months, no test of loyalty was used except race. The evacuees were permitted to take with them only what they could carry. Consequently, most were dispossessed in addition to suffering loss of freedom. The internment camps to which the Japanese Americans were moved were surrounded by barbed wire and patrolled by armed guards. Most spent the duration of the war within their confines. The press and radio, particularly on the West Coast, gave considerable publicity to these events.[26]

A society should be able to protect itself against espionage, sabotage, and other acts that aid an aggressor. But "not a single documented act of espionage, sabotage or fifth column activity was committed by an American citizen of Japanese ancestry or by a resident Japanese alien on the West Coast."[27] President Gerald Ford stated in a proclamation in the bicentennial year 1976, "We now know what we should have known then—not only was the evacuation wrong, but Japanese-Americans were and are loyal Americans."[28] There were those who knew then that virtually all Japanese Americans were loyal and that exclusion and internment were unnecessary. Attorney General Francis Biddle and FBI Director J. Edgar Hoover among others expressed these views directly to the president.[29] Roosevelt chose to ignore them and to respond instead to a racism virulent among some and to groups glad to be rid of their Japanese-American competitors.[30] The executive order and its implementation were a case of tyranny of the majority.

A more contemporary example is the prohibition on same-sex marriage. Surely marriage is a fundamental interest, and prohibition is a severe deprivation. Furthermore, same-sex relationships are morally unobjectionable. They are consensual, and they are legal. (The behavior characteristic of some same-sex relationships is no longer criminal. The U.S. Supreme Court declared sodomy laws unconstitutional in *Lawrence v. Texas* in 2002.[31]) The Court, by the way, has long recognized marriage as a constitutionally protected right. As early as 1923 the Court stated that marriage is a component of 14th Amendment "liberty" that must not be denied without due process of law.[32] Since then, the Court has held laws prohibiting marriage between persons of different races to be an unconstitutional violation of "one of the vital personal rights."[33] Not even prison inmates, who rightly suffer severe deprivation of their fundamental interests in other respects, can be denied the right to marry.[34] Despite these precedents, the Court is unlikely anytime soon to rule that same-sex marriage enjoys constitutional protection.

The majority, of course, ought to be able to express its disapproval of homosexuality and lesbianism. Many do express their disapproval time and again in conversation, in the media and in a multitude of other places—living rooms, churches, shops, and playing fields. When the majority expresses its disapproval, however, in laws forbidding same-sex marriage, it imposes tyranny. The majority's publicly oriented interest in confining marriage to heterosexual couples deprives same-sex couples of their privately oriented interest in marriage. Permitting same-sex couples to marry deprives no one of privately oriented interests and, therefore, imposes no tyranny.

In reaching this conclusion, I have treated the consequences of marriage as inseparable. This need not be the case. What are those consequences? Marriage confers a new status. A man becomes a husband, and a woman a wife. In its traditional practice, a woman even assumes a new name, that of her husband. Together they are said to be married. Marriage also confers many rights and obligations—legal, financial, and medical. The state, by issuing a marriage license, legitimizes the new status and enforces the rights and obligations. Some have urged that these consequences be separated and another status created—the civil union. On this arrangement, the state accords same-sex couples the rights and obligations of marriage but withholds the name. The withholding of the name preserves the expression of the majority's disapproval in the law. Withholding the name is hurtful.

It demeans the lives of homosexuals and lesbians.[35] Nevertheless, same-sex couples cannot claim tyranny because they do not have the approval of a majority of their fellow citizens. Civil unions conferring all the rights and obligations of marriage enjoyed by heterosexual couples would eliminate the tyranny of current practice.

REMEDIES

Faced with the threat of tyranny of the majority, some have recoiled from the adoption of simple majority rule as the principle for the making of collective decisions. Madison and Mill were among them, and they prescribed constitutional restraints on the majority. There is no disagreement among democrats that a simple majority, that is, 50 percent plus 1, ought to be necessary to adopt legislation. The dispute over possible remedies for tyranny of the majority begins with the question: Should a simple majority be enough? In the absence of a strong argument to the contrary, it would seem that a simple majority ought to be enough. This is *not* because in a test of strength the majority would win, as some have contended. As a matter of fact, minorities have been besting majorities in most places most of the time throughout history. These contests for control have rarely been straightforward tests of physical strength. Organization, knowledge, and motivation have usually counted for more than a strong arm. The popular majority gains control over government only under special circumstances. Most people, and particularly elites, must believe that authority (at least ultimately) ought to reside in the popular majority, and a whole set of institutions must be in place to permit the expression and adoption of popular preferences. These are all empirical matters, however, and the contention before us is that the simple majority *ought* to prevail—not that it *does* prevail.

The simple majority ought to prevail for three reasons.[36] First, simple majority rule maximizes the number of people who can live under laws of their own choosing. The assumption here is that people want to control their own lives but recognize that at least some collective decisions are necessary and desirable. This rationale emphasizes the moral autonomy of the individual who lives in a world in which at least some common rules must be observed. Second, simple majority rule maximizes the number of people who can advance their interests (as they understand them) by means of the law. This rationale emphasizes the individual in another way—as a claimant to a share of public goods, both material and symbolic. Third, simple majority rule is most consistent with democratic principles. Democrats (small d) reject the idea that some one or a few, unaccountable to everyone else, have a special competence to govern. Democracy is founded on the principle of political equality as can be seen in the criteria identified earlier. Once political equality is acknowledged, it is difficult to avoid the conclusion that not only should a simple majority be necessary to pass legislation but it ought to be enough. If a minority is permitted to block the majority, then the members of the minority count for more than one. They become political unequals.

One common form that proposed remedies for tyranny of the majority has taken is in the requirement of extraordinary majorities. The possibilities range from 50 percent plus 2 to unanimity with two-thirds and three-fourths as popular way-stations in between. The U.S. Constitution requires extraordinary majorities for Congress to override a presidential veto and for Congress to propose and for state legislatures or state ratifying conventions to ratify a constitutional amendment. The Equal Rights Amendment was a recent casualty of the requirement for more than a simple majority. Senate rules require an extraordinary majority to cut off debate. Senate opponents of proposed action have often used the filibuster to prevent taking action. Southern senators were able in this way to block for decades the passage of civil rights legislation.

Another form of defense is the creation of a second legislative body with a basis of representation different from that of the other chamber. This was the course taken by the Framers of the U.S. Constitution in response to the demand by small-state delegates for equal representation to protect themselves against tyranny imposed by the large states. The threat of such tyranny, Madison argued at the time, was fanciful, and it proved to be fanciful. Madison had the best of the argument, but interest won out over logic and experience. Consequently, the residents of the less populous states continue to enjoy inordinately great voting power as a result of the Connecticut Compromise.

Still another remedy adopted in the United States is judicial review. Whatever the Framers' intentions might have been regarding judicial review, its development has enabled a small, unelected group of men and women who serve lifetime terms to decide significant questions of public policy. Many have defended the practice from Chief Justice John Marshall's day to the present as a defense against tyranny of the majority and, in particular, as a defense against violations of civil liberties. The record is at best mixed. In cases like *Dred Scott*, *Plessy v. Ferguson*, *Minersville v. Gobitis*, *Korematsu v. United States*, and *Dennis v. United States*, the Supreme Court upheld restrictions on civil liberties that had been imposed by majorities.[37] The list could be considerably lengthened.

The remedies identified above have not averted tyranny in the United States. Separation of powers and checks and balances did not prevent the internment of Japanese Americans during World War II. The president issued his executive order, Congress passed supporting legislation, and the Supreme Court ruled the policy constitutional. Nor have restraints on majority rule at either the national or state level prevented the adoption of prohibitions on same-sex marriage. Parenthetically, the national government has no constitutional authority over marriage. In 1996 Congress did pass the Defense of Marriage Act, which defines marriage as between a man and a woman for the purposes of national law and relieves the states from recognizing same-sex marriages that might be permitted in other states. Restraints on majority rule did not prevent the economic ruin of many for alleged ties to the Communist Party or other leftist groups during the Red Scare of 1919–1920 and during the McCarthy period of the mid-twentieth century. Those periods also saw some of those same people subjected to deportation, police beatings, seizure of property, and imprisonment without charge.[38]

The lesson in this is that the fundamental interests of the minority are only as safe as the respect that the majority has for those interests. If the majority is hostile, or even indifferent, to minority interests, constitutional provisions and legislative rules are a weak barrier to tyranny. Ironically, the very restraints intended to avert tyranny of the majority thwarted the majority's efforts early in the twentieth century to eliminate child labor. And only after the passage of decades was the national majority able to bring an end to state-imposed segregation and discrimination. As these examples show, when tyranny is part of the status quo, the minority that benefits from that tyranny is advantaged by restraints on majority rule. Why should the defenders of the status quo enjoy such an advantage? They usually do not need such an advantage because they are the powerful. They are typically distinguished by wealth, education, status, and other sources of political power. Their power has allowed them to shape the status quo as they have preferred it. The defenders of the status quo do not deserve the advantage provided by restraints on majority rule because they are distinguished by no virtue or accomplishment that entitles them to count, as individuals, for more than one.

Up to this point, I have assumed that the unit within which collective decisions are to be made is not in dispute. In practice, this is sometimes not the case. Democratic theory, however, provides no answer to the question: What is the appropriate unit within which the preferences of the majority ought to prevail over those of the minority?[39] The problem can be clearly seen in the example of Northern Ireland. Who is to decide on the laws that all must obey? The "simple majority" one might respond, but the simple majority of what unit? The whole of Great Britain (England, Scotland, Wales, and Northern Ireland)? Only the Irish (Eire and Northern Ireland)? Only Northern Ireland? Each county in Northern Ireland? There have been times in the recent past when rather different results would have been secured in elections in those several units.

Simple majority rule is most consistent with democratic principles. Adoption of that rule, however, has been prevented in some countries by language, religious, ethnic, or other divisions that have impeded the formation of coalitions that attract members from every group in the society. As a consequence, a minority has often felt itself to be a *permanent minority*—the persistent loser in decisions on issues affecting its cultural life and standing in the community—and a victim of tyranny of the majority. Many among the French-speaking minority in Canada and Belgium, for example, have felt this way. Whether such cultural minorities are justified in their conviction that they are the victims of tyranny of the majority is not the question. The question here is whether their claims for justice can be satisfied in order to avoid insurrection.

When a minority has felt itself to be a permanent minority, appeal to the principle of majority rule has failed to persuade that minority to accept its deserts. Indeed, the minority has rejected the principle and insisted on arrangements to better protect its interests. Accommodation of such demands is eased when the minority is geographically concentrated. A federal scheme can be used to grant autonomy over cultural issues to the more homogenous provinces. This is in part the course that Canada has pursued in an effort to head off a separatist movement in Quebec. As this suggests, a geographically concentrated minority might attempt by insurrection or negotiation to establish a state of its own. The latter was the course successfully taken by leaders of the Slovak minority in the former Czechoslovakia just a few years ago.

If the permanent minority is not geographically concentrated, boundary-drawing of another kind may be used. It may in some instances be possible to place certain contentious issues beyond collective decision. The effect of this restriction is to allow individuals and nongovernmental groups to decide for themselves. This is just what the First Amendment accomplishes with respect to religion. Instead of the state-imposed churches of the colonial period, Americans became able to worship when and how they wanted (or not at all) free of legal disability. The First Amendment, of course, has not taken all the heat out of the issue of religion, but it has dampened down the fires. Such boundary-drawing has its limitations. It affords protection to a minority whose interests are threatened by governmental action. In this, it is like extraordinary majorities and other arrangements that permit a minority to veto governmental action. For a minority that experiences deprivation of interests by nongovernmental groups and individuals, governmental action is necessary.[40]

CONCLUSION

No decision-making process can ensure that no one will suffer the severe deprivation of fundamental interests. Democracy can offer no such assurances. The practice of American democracy in particular testifies to the persistent threat of tyranny. Madison, Tocqueville, and Mill were right to alert us to the danger of tyranny of the majority. It is a persistent threat, albeit a threat much diminished by democracy itself. Democracy diminishes the threat of tyranny by requiring that people be able to exercise certain participatory rights like free speech and assembly and the right to vote. Democracy also diminishes the threat of tyranny by motivating political leaders to seek support from diverse groups in their relentless search for majorities. This tendency in democratic politics is shown by the behavior of Governor George Wallace of Alabama. An ardent segregationist in his successful gubernatorial campaigns and in a failed bid for the presidency in 1968, he later reversed course. Once blacks had secured the vote, Wallace sought their support, and he did so in the usual way—by promising to serve their interests.

Madison and others who followed in his train were wrong to think that tyranny of the majority could be averted by extraordinary majorities or other constitutional or legislative hurdles for the passage of legislation. Small minorities under such a regime remain vulnerable to the severe deprivation of fundamental interests as the example of the Japanese Americans shows. Only a requirement of unanimity offers complete protection against the deprivation of fundamental interests by governmental action. The principal beneficiaries of any requirement for more than a simple majority are the advantaged whose interests are served under the status quo. They are thereby enabled to more easily block any change in the status quo. Any requirement for more than a simple majority, however, exposes the interests of the disadvantaged to continued damage by nongovernmental action and in the United States by state governments. As long as Southern senators could filibuster civil rights legislation, the fundamental interests of black Americans were subject to severe deprivation at the hands of state governments and private employers, for example. And, as earlier remarked, requirements for more than a simple majority run counter to the principle of political equality.

CHAPTER 5

WHY NO SOCIALISM?

Is the United States different from other countries, even unique among the nations of the world? President George W. Bush has often referred to a God-given mission to spread freedom across the world in justification of the invasion and occupation of Iraq. But he is only one among the more recent exponents of an idea long expressed by Americans. From the first immigrants on New England's shores to our contemporaries across the country have come claims that America is exceptional.[1] These claims range from the sacred (God has made Americans a chosen people) to the profane (the United States has the most productive economy), from the sublime (the United States was the first new nation) to the ridiculous (Americans have invented everything or, if not everything, everything worthwhile). Such claims have not been confined to Americans. Indeed, the perspective provided by foreign birth and upbringing has often enabled foreigners to see what Americans have not seen, or seen so well, about their own country. Alexis de Tocqueville, whose *Democracy in America* (1835 and 1840) is still invoked to illuminate the American experience, is the best-known, but not the only, foreign observer to have advanced the idea that America is exceptional.[2]

THEORIES: TWO TYPES, FOUR QUESTIONS

We shall begin by distinguishing between two types of theories of American exceptionalism and then take up each of them in turn. One type is descriptive; the other is moral. The descriptive type makes wholly factual claims. These claims come in part out of close-up observation of the United States at a particular moment. For example, the United States today has the most productive economy in the world. Such claims also come out of reflection on the whole course of American history. For example, the absence of a feudal past has produced a consensus on fundamental political principles among Americans. The moral theories of American exceptionalism claim some superiority or advantage for the United States and ascribe a mission to Americans. This type of theory will be taken up in the next chapter. Last thoughts about the whole subject will be found at the end of the next chapter.

Of any theory of American exceptionalism, we need to ask four questions:

1. What is the difference that distinguishes the United States from other countries?
2. What is the significance of that difference?
3. How can that difference be explained?
4. Is the theory true?

The first question recognizes that unless the difference said to distinguish the United States from other countries is specified with some particularity, it is not possible to answer any of the other questions with any confidence. For example, among the claims made are that American society is more egalitarian than societies elsewhere and that politics is more populist than in other countries. Any attempt to determine the significance of these alleged differences, to explain them, or to adjudge their truth requires greater precision in meaning. Meaning must be sufficiently precise to permit determination of the relevant evidence for and against the claim. The second question demands to know why some difference, however real, is worthy of our attention. It has often been pointed out, for example, that the United States is the outlier with respect to soccer. In most other countries, soccer has mass appeal—played and watched by millions. In the United States, the popularity of other sports has consigned soccer to distinctly minor-league status. So what? Is this a difference that makes a difference in the lives of Americans or to the understanding of the American experience? Most who have asserted claims of American exceptionalism have responded to the third question (how can the difference be explained?) by reference to a variety of factors—social, economic, political, and cultural. The weight to be assigned to these several factors is usually indeterminate. Finally, the fourth question asks: (1) Does the alleged difference really exist? (2) Are the effects or implications of that difference as claimed? And (3) are the links between the explanatory factors and the alleged difference adequately shown?

DESCRIPTIVE THEORIES: AMERICA AT CLOSE RANGE

Let us begin by examining those theories of American exceptionalism that, at least explicitly, ascribe no religious, moral, or political superiority and no mission to the United States. Many social scientists and historians have undertaken comparative analysis of societies at various levels of generality. Typically, the subject of analysis has been the nation-state and the universe of analysis has been either industrialized states, members of the Organization for Economic Cooperation and Development (OECD), or the United States and members of the European Union.[3] Studies undertaken at close range, that is, with respect to particular social, political, economic, or cultural qualities, have found differences among nations.

Seymour Martin Lipset, the late American political sociologist, brings together much of this research in his recent work *American Exceptionalism* (1996). He claims that in light of this research "America continues to be qualitatively different. . . . Exceptionalism . . . does not mean better. This country is an outlier."[4] Let us see. With respect to political qualities, Lipset notes the "greater strength of populism in the United States" as compared to other countries.[5] This populism is manifest in the greater frequency of elections; the availability of the initiative and referendum in some states; the weakness of political party hierarchies in controlling membership, nominating candidates, and determining the party's legislative program; and the election of many state officials like judges, district attorneys and coroners who would be appointed in other nations.[6] All this may be conceded, but this is a case where specification of the alleged difference requires elaboration. One might infer that Americans exercise more control over their governments than peoples elsewhere. That would be a dubious inference. For all the apparent sovereignty afforded to the general populace, there are cultural and legal factors that depress popular participation in politics. This can be seen in the low voter turnout in recent decades in the United States relative to other democratic countries. Furthermore, structural features like separation of powers and checks and balances and the Supreme Court limit the exercise of popular sovereignty.

Among these structural features, the U.S. Supreme Court remains unique.[7] Several European countries instituted more powerful judiciaries after World War II. Nevertheless, only in the United States is an unelected body made up of judges who serve for life permitted to decide fundamental questions of public policy.[8] In its exercise of judicial review, the Court has struck down many state and national statutes and interpreted statutes in ways unintended by legislative majorities. The Court, of course, claims that it is upholding limits imposed by the Constitution. What about those limits?

Is it the case that "no other elected national government apart from the Swiss is as limited in its powers"?[9] Once again questions of meaning must be answered. Is it the power of the national government that is so limited or its authority or both? Distinction between the concepts of authority and power is necessary because different evidence must be brought to bear to demonstrate their presence. Authority is what government *may* legitimately do. In the United States, the authority of government is provided by the Constitution, and it has its ultimate origins in the people. Power is what government *can* do, given the popular support and the resources (police, information, and the like) it has. Authority and power coincide only more or less. Thus, the national government has the authority under the Constitution to levy an income tax. Its power to enforce the tax laws does not match its authority. The tendency to cheat is widespread, and the numbers of IRS officials are few.

Certainly the authority of the U.S. national government is limited. Federalism (by dividing governmental authority between the national and state governments) and the Bill of Rights are the most important among those limits. Federalism, however, is less restrictive than it once was, and the Bill of Rights imposes no more severe restrictions than those under which other democratic governments operate. The Supreme Court has given such an expansive reading to the Constitution's "necessary and proper," "tax and spend," interstate and foreign commerce, and war powers provisions as to much reduce the significance of federalism as a limitation. The Supreme Court too has displayed its readiness on a number of occasions to acquiesce in congressional and presidential restrictions on civil liberties—the Espionage Act of 1917, the Sedition Act of 1918, the Smith Act, Roosevelt's Japanese internment orders during World War II, and the Communist Control Act of 1954, for example. Reference, then, to federalism and the Bill of Rights is insufficient to corroborate the claim that the authority of the U.S. national government is especially limited.

What about its power? Can the national government exercise the authority that it has? Certainly the separation of powers and checks and balances, the weakness of the political parties, and antigovernment attitudes held by the general citizenry limit the power of the national government to act: separation of powers and checks and balances provide many opportunities for minorities to block change; the weakness of the parties makes difficult the mobilization of popular majorities to support action; and antigovernment attitudes discourage government activity.[10] But the Great Depression and World War II brought into being a large standing army, a large bureaucracy, and a government authorized to act throughout the society—institutions characteristic of a powerful state. It would seem rather difficult to maintain as Lipset does that the United States is "relative[ly] stateless" in the face of state legislation banning same-sex marriage, smoking in public places, and the consumption of alcohol by those under eighteen and national legislation that permits government access to the library records of individuals, requires elementary and secondary students to pass standardized exams, and provides health care to the poor.[11]

In addition to these structural differences, American public policy is different from that of other countries. In particular, the United States has devoted a lesser share of its gross domestic product (GDP) to improve the living conditions of the poor than other industrialized countries, and Americans are the least taxed among industrialized countries. It is the welfare state outlier.[12] Currently, total governmental expenditure in the United States (national, state, and local) consumes 35.7 percent of GDP. Only in Ireland, Korea, and Switzerland among thirty OECD countries, does government spend a lesser share of GDP than the United States does.[13] Governments in the United States also collect a smaller percentage of GDP in taxes than other OECD countries. The U.S. percentage (28.9 percent) falls well below the European Union average of 41 percent and even further below the average of the Scandinavian countries.[14] Only Japan, Korea, and Mexico collect less. Nevertheless, owing to the extraordinary size of the U.S. economy, governmental expenditure per capita in the United States ranks among the upper third of OECD countries.[15] A significant fraction of this expenditure is devoted to defense and the payment of interest on the debt.[16] The priorities of American governments are different from the OECD average. In general, American governments spend a lesser share of GDP on major domestic programs—health, pensions, unemployment compensation, and family assistance—than most other OECD countries. Even spending on public education, which had long exceeded the OECD average, has now dipped below that average.[17] The United States, however, is not alone as a rich society with a relatively small domestic outlay—as measured by government expenditure as percent of gross domestic product. Canada, Japan, and Australia, among others, also fall below the OECD average in this regard and in spending on domestic programs.[18]

None of the above should be understood to deny the contention that the United States is different politically from other nations. Indeed, the particular combination of institutions (like the separation of powers and checks and balances, federalism, and the Supreme Court), the particular distribution of political resources (like wealth, education, and motivation), and the particular cultural characteristics (like race and ethnicity, and antigovernment attitudes) that distinguish the United States from other countries makes its politics unique—unique but not exceptional. This is so because the politics of every other nation when examined close-up is also unique. Therefore, the United States cannot be an exception to a rule—a generalization that comprehends all the rest.[19]

Explanations of the differences that distinguish American politics invoke a variety of causes: the early enfranchisement of the lower classes, the availability of cheap land, the immigrant experience, the Puritan heritage of Congregationalism and limited government, and state government autonomy during the colonial and Confederation periods are among those causes. The explanations proffered are more or less satisfactory. None of these explanations, of course, manifests the rigor of explanation in the natural sciences, but many are informed by sensitive, wide-ranging review of the evidence. Specification of the particular variables advanced in explanation of this or that alleged difference would require more space than is available here. Even a cursory review of these explanations makes clear the peculiar character of American society. How could American politics not be different? It is also the case, however, that every country has won independence under different circumstances, experienced industrialization at a different time and pace, suffered the devastation of wars, foreign and domestic, served as home to a different mix of ethnic groups and on and on. Is it any wonder that the politics of one country differ from that of another?

In addition to political differences, close-up analysis has also identified many economic differences that set off the United States from other nations. For example, in the early 1870s, the United States surpassed Britain in gross domestic product and remains today the most productive economy in the world.[20] Other countries are catching up however. European countries, recovering from the ravages of World War II, experienced growth in their economies that, at times, outstripped that of the United States. More recently, countries on the Pacific Rim like Japan, Korea, Singapore, and China have seen great spurts of growth. As a consequence, American dominance in the world economy has declined. As much as 40 percent of the world's production of goods and services was "made in U.S.A." in 1950.[21] That figure had declined to about 30 percent in 1970 and to about 25 percent by 1989.[22] In several areas, the United States has lost leadership (consumer electronics, shoes and clothing, and textiles, for example), and in several others its leadership is under challenge (automobiles and commercial aircraft). Still another indicator of the extent to which other countries have become rich is GDP per capita (adjusted to reflect national differences in purchasing power). On this measure, Norway and Ireland have eclipsed the United States (as have a handful of sparsely populated tax havens and oil-rich emirates).[23]

All rich nations spend large sums on health and education, but none exceeds the United States in its expenditures. If government spending (as a percentage of GDP) alone is considered, the United States ranks low with respect to health and about average with respect to education among industrialized countries. If private spending is taken into account, however, the United States soars to the top. Americans spend a greater percentage of GDP on health (14.6 percent) and education (6.97 percent) than the peoples of other OECD nations, and Americans spend more per capita.[24] Neither figure, of course, implies anything about the distribution of education or health care, that is, who enjoys the benefits of these expenditures. In all societies, the enjoyment of goods such as these depends to some extent on the possession of money. And the United States is "the least egalitarian among developed nations with respect to income distribution."[25] Among twenty-one OECD countries, the United States is tied with Italy for second as the most unequal. Only Turkey, which has relatively little industry, is more unequal in the distribution of income.[26] Income inequality can also be seen in poverty rates when poverty is defined as income less than half of the median disposable income of the whole population (after transfer payments, like Social Security and housing assistance, and taxes). On this measure, 17.4 percent of Americans live in poverty. Mexico has an even greater share of its people living in poverty (20.3 percent), while many European countries have poverty rates below 10 percent.[27]

In mitigation of substantial income inequality, some have argued that society is more mobile in the United States than elsewhere and that those willing to expend the effort can significantly improve their station—even rise to the top. Certainly many more Americans than Europeans believe their society to be open to individual advance, and, more particularly, to afford the poor a good chance of escaping poverty.[28] The fact of the matter appears not to corroborate these beliefs, although more comparative research needs to be done and controversy continues to attend the whole effort to get at the truth.[29]

Social mobility has several facets that are related to one another but are not wholly determined by one another. Among those facets are income, occupation, and educational attainment. Income is closely associated with occupation and educational attainment. Occupation is indicative of income. Income significantly affects educational opportunity and so on. What do we know about the relative rates of social mobility in Europe and the United States? The most ambitious (and cautious) survey of the evidence available fifty years ago concluded, "Industrial societies possess similar rates of social mobility."[30] A growing body of evidence since that day has done nothing to cast doubt on the truth of that conclusion.[31] In all industrialized nations, including the United States, there is mobility upward and downward in income, occupations, and educational attainment of families. Nevertheless, large transitions are unusual over the course of a person's working life or over the course of several generations of a family.[32] The poor are likely to remain poor, and the children of poor parents are likely to be poor as adults. The sons of fathers who work in manual occupations are very likely to work in manual occupations themselves.[33] Furthermore, the income and occupational status of parents largely determines the amount and quality of their children's education. Poor parents send their children off to schools that will ill-prepare them to compete for college acceptance.[34] The children of the wealthy and powerful, on the other hand, are assured of admission to elite colleges.[35]

The United States is different in the social and cultural realms. In making this assertion, we must rely on public opinion surveys. This is so because the only way we can discover the beliefs, feelings, and values of most people is by asking them about their beliefs, feelings, and values. Before the advent of public opinion polling some sixty years ago, the beliefs, feelings, and values of the man-in-the-street were largely the subject of anecdote and inference. Comparisons across national borders were often little more than conjecture. Students of politics can now draw on surveys conducted in recent years in some eighty countries comprising 85 percent of the world's population. Something approximating a representative sample responded to the same, large battery of questions in each of these states. These surveys provide the best evidence available for the existence of cross-national differences and the magnitude and variety of those differences. Nevertheless, the "best evidence" must be treated with caution. Political and cultural differences among nations can produce ambiguous responses.

That said, the findings of these surveys lend support to claims that the United States is the "most religious country in Christendom," "the most . . .

patriotic" in the industrialized world, and has the "highest rate of participation in voluntary organizations."[36] According to the World Values Survey of 1999–2002, some 60 percent of the Americans in the survey reported that they attended religious services once or more a month, and 57 percent reported that they regarded religion as "very" or "rather important" in their lives. Most Americans said that they believed in God (96 percent), in life after death (81 percent), and in heaven (88 percent).[37] On these measures of religiosity, the United States was exceeded by many Muslim countries but also by a number of South American states. It is not quite true, then, that the United States is the most religious in Christendom. Among industrialized nations, excepting Poland, the United States leads on every measure of religiosity.[38] The American response to two questions expressed patriotism. Some 72 percent said that they were "very proud" to be Americans—a figure exceeded only by the Australians' 73 percent among developed countries. In response to the question, "would you be willing to fight in a war for your country?" 73 percent of Americans said that they would. In this regard too, the United States ranks higher than most, although not all, modern nations.[39]

Americans have long been a nation of joiners. Tocqueville, writing during the 1830s, remarked, "Americans of all ages, all stations in life, and all types of disposition are forever forming associations."[40] The World Values Surveys found that Americans continue to join voluntary associations in numbers that outstrip most other countries.[41] Among industrialized countries, only the Netherlands shows comparable numbers. Tanzania, Bangladesh, and Vietnam in the developing world post higher percentages of joiners than the United States does. For Americans, as well as other nationals, "belonging" may be no more than sending in a check. Certainly far fewer report that they do unpaid voluntary work on behalf of these associations.[42] More Americans, however, report doing voluntary work than Europeans. This distinction promises to disappear as the generation born in the first third of the twentieth-century passes from the scene.[43]

The United States also leads the world in energy consumption, traffic accidents involving injury, and CO_2 emissions, and it is tied with Iceland for the amount of municipal waste generated per capita.[44] These distinctions are, in part, a reflection of the enormous wealth of the economy. To conclude this recital of social and cultural differences that distinguish America from other nations, mention must be made of education. In keeping with the principle of equality of opportunity, Americans have long supported public education for the many. A greater percentage of Americans have graduated from secondary schools and colleges than have citizens of other countries.[45]

Do the differences identified above demonstrate that America is exceptional, i.e., "qualitatively different"? There is much to be said against the claim. First, many of the differences that do exist are differences of degree and not of kind. As long as the United States can be ranked on the same scale as other nations, it is not qualitatively different.[46] Second, it might be contended that American exceptionalism consists in the location of the United States at the extremes of a cluster of measures. This understanding, however, cannot be sustained because it assumes that a norm exists. You will recognize this as the same objection raised to the claims made for the exceptionalism of American politics.

The qualities that make up American politics are different to be sure. And, as seen above, the United States also differs from other nations socially, economically, and culturally. But, not only does the United States differ from all the rest, so do all the rest differ from one another. The United States, then, is not an exception to a rule. Third, almost all the qualities—political, social, economic, and cultural—examined above are persistent qualities of every country. Thus, every country has had, for example, a gross domestic product, education expenditures, and believers in God. In principle, values could be assigned to these factors over many decades, even centuries. Alas, in practice this cannot be done. Adequate records were often not kept. Some that were kept have been lost or destroyed or are not comparable with one another. Furthermore, states have changed boundaries; others have come into existence or passed from the scene. Nevertheless, enough data are available over sufficiently long periods of time to see that when cross-national comparisons are made, nations change rank. The United States, for example, no longer leads the world in gross domestic product per capita. How long must a country occupy the extreme on some ranking to qualify as exceptional? *Exceptionalism* would seem to be an inappropriate term for a transitory event.

Finally, it remains to examine the significance of the differences identified. It is a common failing of theories of American exceptionalism that pursue close-up analysis to not assess the significance of any differences discovered. Perhaps the significance of some of these differences between the United States and other nations is obvious enough, but with respect to others it is not at all clear. For example, what is the significance of American religiosity?[47] From a religious point of view, no quality could be of greater significance. Humankind, indeed the whole universe, the believer holds, was created for the greater glory of God. By believing in God, praying, and attending church, Americans pay homage to God's glory. From a secular point of view, American religiosity introduces a moralism into politics greater than that found in European countries. Issues like abortion and same-sex marriage, while not unknown elsewhere, divide American political activists into bitter, opposing camps. It should be noted too that religiosity has contributed much to the American sense of a national mission—a matter that will occupy us in the next chapter. What else can be said on this score? Does religious conviction make Americans happier, more at peace with themselves and the world? Does that religiosity reduce the incidence of suicide, divorce, domestic violence, or crime?

And what are we to make of the well-founded proposition that the United States has been the richest country in the world absolutely and, until recently, relative to population? From one perspective, the significance of this is clear: these are resources that might be expended to realize desired ends. But whose ends? What ends have been chosen? What have been the costs of American productivity? These are all questions that deserve answers. We might ask as well, Significant for whom? All the differences identified above are descriptive of the nation as a whole. One must, therefore, be careful in making inferences from these national qualities to the experience of any subnational unit—person, group, or section of the country. The great wealth of the United States, for example, did not extend to the South for decades. Blacks continue to suffer from shoddy education and poor health care despite government spending on schools and health care. In short, the American experience has not been the same for all.

AGAINST EXCEPTIONALISM: THE IDEA OF CONVERGENCE

Up to this point, we have examined theories of American exceptionalism that have issued from a close-up view of the United States and other industrialized countries. From this perspective, differences among nations are brought sharply into view. The differences are many and varied. What comes into view if we step back? Looked at from a distance, individual differences are obscured and similarities become more prominent. We can now see that the United States and the members of the European Community are industrialized and urbanized. They have all undergone the popularization of politics—a process in which, among other things, mass parties (not necessarily democratic in nature) have developed to mobilize popular support for public ends and elections (not necessarily competitive) are used to grant authority to political leaders. Government in them all has greater authority and power than ever in the past. And their peoples have higher standards of living, longer life expectancy, and higher rates of literacy than their counterparts in less developed nations. From this vantage point, America does not appear exceptional at all.

It was just this vantage point that Tocqueville took up in the writing of *Democracy in America*, a book about the young American republic but written, he said, with France always in his mind. For all that he tells us about the exceptional nature of America, Tocqueville believed that societies (or, at any rate, those in view "wherever one looks . . . throughout the Christian world") had a common destiny. The United States was of particular interest to him because by the 1830s it had advanced farther along the course of development that France, indeed all Europe, would take. In Europe, many forces were at work that would bring about the democratization of society: the increasing affluence of the common man, increased literacy and the dissemination of knowledge, the availability of firearms, Protestantism, and secularization. In democratic society, an "equality of conditions" prevails. Tocqueville observed, "The more I studied American society, the more clearly I saw equality of conditions as the creative element from which each particular fact derived."[48]

"Equality of conditions" meant several things to him, and his emphasis was always on the difference between feudal and democratic society. First, he meant that people are presumed to be equal. This equality was in part social—no more deferring to one's betters—and in part legal. One was equal before the law as a subject of it and equal as a citizen in voting for representatives. Any distinctions made between persons must be on the basis of merit. In contrast stood the inequality of feudal society in which nobility of birth determined one's dress, proper deportment, occupation, and political status. Second, by "equality of conditions" he meant that power had become more widely distributed. No longer could the knight in full armor mounted on a huge horse (the medieval version of the modern tank) command the field. Tocqueville had seen and felt the power of the Parisian many. Popular sovereignty, one of the defining principles of democracy (understood as a form of government), was for him not only an assertion about where ultimate political authority ought to lie but also where ultimate political power did lie. The exercise of that power, he thought, would bring equal political rights.

Karl Marx never visited the United States, but he did keep track of American developments. What's more, in 1851, he began an eleven-year period as a regular contributor to the *New York Daily Tribune*. The *Tribune's* editor, Horace Greeley, was in general sympathy with Marx's views and provided this forum for their expression. Marx thought that large historical processes were at work pushing societies toward a common end. In particular, capitalism, the system of ownership under which industrialization occurred in Europe and North America, created the conditions for the emergence of a new society. In this new society, men and women would no longer exploit one another, or punish themselves, or work under the yoke of necessity. Capitalism developed the productive forces and created unprecedented riches, and it created an industrial working class (the *proletariat*) that would, he thought, grow larger, poorer, and more class-conscious. Capitalism thereby created its own grave diggers. Like Tocqueville, Marx expected that his new society would, at least typically, be instituted by means of revolution.

After the premature declarations of the *Communist Manifesto* (1848), Marx consigned the proletarian revolution to a certain but indeterminate future. Conditions had, after all, not been ripe for such a revolution in 1848 and might not be for some time to come. Nowhere was this more evident than in the United States. Marx observed in 1852 that working-class consciousness was low among American workers because "though classes, indeed, already exist, they have not yet become fixed, but continually change and interchange their elements in a constant state of flux."[49] Marx believed that social mobility was greater in the United States than in other industrializing societies and that social mobility impeded working-class formation. Friedrich Engels, Marx's longtime collaborator and patron, later wrote, "Only when the land—the public lands—is completely in the hands of speculators, and settlement on the land becomes more and more difficult or falls prey to gouging—only then, I think, will the time come, with peaceful development, for a third [that is, socialist] party."[50] Engels, like so many other observers of American society, saw the frontier as a safety valve for the relief of pent-up social pressures and, therefore, an impediment to the organization of the working class. The conditions identified by Marx and Engels were believed to postpone but not avert the triumph of the proletariat. Even here, however, Marx allowed in a speech in 1872 that the proletariat in America might institute socialism by "peaceful means."[51] In contrast to many European societies, workers in America could organize politically and they could vote.

In retrospect, we can see that Tocqueville was the better prophet. Marx's socialist society is nowhere to be seen (and never has been), and Tocqueville's democratic society can be found across the West. The ideas of these two thinkers, both of whom predicted the convergence of societies, have inspired the major descriptive theories of American exceptionalism with the whole of American history in view. It is to them that we now turn.

DESCRIPTIVE THEORIES: THE COURSE OF
AMERICAN HISTORY—CONSENSUS

The democratization of society would culminate in equal political rights for all. While this was for Tocqueville the fundamental fact of modern life for societies across the West, he recognized that the means by which equal political rights might be secured and the course of development that democratic society might take could differ in significant respects from country to country. In France, for example, the defenders of the old order had sought to deny equal political rights to the many, and the many had revolted in 1789 to secure them. Americans, in contrast, acquired equal political rights without revolution. For Tocqueville, the American Revolution was neither political nor social; it was a revolution of national liberation against the imperial power. As a consequence, political differences in the United States are not, Tocqueville contended, fundamental—"differences of view are only matters of nuance."[52]

Writing in 1955, Louis Hartz, a Harvard political scientist, seized on Tocqueville's insight that Americans were "born equal." This idea provided the basis for his claim that American exceptionalism consists in the inheritance of a liberal society (what Tocqueville called a *democratic* society)—a society free from the constraints of priests, aristocrats, and monarchs. Americans did not have to fight for the institution of liberal society; they did not need to overthrow feudalism in a revolution. There was no feudal order in America to overthrow.

From the beginning, then, Americans have enjoyed "the reality of atomistic social freedom."[53] This fact is significant on two counts. It has imparted a distinctive trajectory to American history. And it has inspired an enduring consensus on a set of principles that Hartz characterizes as Lockean or liberal in the classical sense: egalitarianism, natural rights, representative government, least government, and individualism. Americans have regarded these principles as self-evident. Now, self-evidence is not a warrant permitted by an opposition. An opposition would demand arguments. But, Hartz explains, these principles have known no opposition in the United States. Therefore, they have been adopted without reflection, without any felt need to justify them, and without consideration of the alternatives, that is, "irrationally."

The absence of feudalism in America has much shaped its history. Because there was no feudal order, there was no dispossessed class of aristocrats and clerics to argue and fight for the reinstitution of the old regime. Traditional society in the European sense has had no advocates. To appeal to tradition in the United States is to appeal to Jefferson—certainly a liberal in good standing. The liberal character of American society also explains why there has been no socialist movement and no socialist thought of any significance. American liberals have not had to make exaggerated promises that could not be fulfilled within a liberal society in order to mobilize the populace against feudalism. Nor did American liberals need to compromise with the defenders of feudal privilege. Thus, socialists have been denied grounds on which to mount an attack on the liberal order. The absence of conflict over fundamental political questions is reflected in the stability and continuity of American political institutions and public policy. The Constitution continues to command widespread adherence and remains much as it was written two hundred years ago. The U.S. Supreme Court, an unelected body, appointed for life, continues to be accepted as the Constitution's interpreter. And public policy, with rare exceptions, is changed only incrementally.

Hartz does not stand alone in claiming that there has been a consensus among Americans on principles and that American political life has been characterized by continuity and stability.[54] Elaboration of these other theories, however, is unnecessary because the facts do not sustain the claim. The consensus that has supposedly prevailed on principles like egalitarianism and individualism dissolves on closer examination. Now, it is the case that few have called for the replacement of those principles by others, for example, the divine right of kings or communist centralism. But, Americans have disagreed about the meaning of their principles from the beginning.[55]

Many who have given voice to these principles have implicitly attached qualifications excluding women, the poor, and racial and ethnic minorities from their reach. A black tenant farmer in nineteenth-century Alabama could hardly have been less free had he lived under Louis XIV in seventeenth-century France or in Stalin's Soviet Union—ruled by force, denied equality before the law, and required to humble himself before the man. Like that tenant farmer, others excluded from the reach of American principles have disagreed with the principles as understood by the powerful while appealing to the very principles under which they have suffered. Disagreement about the meaning of shared principles can, then, have consequences as significant as the absence of agreement on principles. And, consensus on principles—differently understood, of course—did not preclude the fighting of the Civil War, the bloodiest in American history.

The exhibit in chief for continuity in American political life is the Constitution. It is true that the letter of the Constitution remains much as it was adopted in 1788 and that it has served as the fundamental law for two hundred years. We cannot pass over as insignificant, however, that break in continuity created by the attempted secession of the Southern states. For four years, nearly half the country was ruled under the constitution of the Confederate States of America. Only by force of arms was the union effected by the Constitution restored. It will not do either to discount the changes that have been made to the Constitution by amendment and by interpretation. They have been profound. The Constitution is more democratic than it was when it came from the Framers' hands as a result of amendments providing for the popular election of senators and the enfranchisement of women and blacks. Legislation has provided protection for the exercise of that franchise and for the popular election of presidential electors. The meaning of the Bill of Rights has also changed greatly over the years as the Supreme Court has applied its provisions to particular cases. The rights of political dissenters are far more generous today than in any earlier day. No change, however, has been as great as that marked by the passage of black Americans from slaves to second-class citizens to legal equals. These changes, moreover, do not represent the inevitable working out of American principles. Violence has attended virtually all of them. The discontinuities in American political life, then, have been several and profound.

Stability is the persistence of some order. The stability of the public order is upset by ordinary criminality. It is shattered when people engage in violence to realize their aims. This is not to say that violence is always undesirable. The order that some wish to preserve may not be worth preserving. Far more common in the United States than violent challenge to the existing order has been violence used to uphold it.[56] When the advantaged use violence in defense of the existing order, they pose no threat to political stability. And until the 1930s, the national government was not the principal battleground for the contending forces in society. These circumstances have produced a combination of social instability and political stability. With the exception of Lee's armies after the first and second battles of Bull Run (a large exception, indeed), none of the contending forces has threatened in word or deed to overthrow the national government or any of the state governments. The action has occurred elsewhere—in the society at-large. It was there that the battles occurred between whites and Indians, blacks and whites, and labor and management. These battles were, or are, long-standing, and they have been violent.

The character of white-Indian relations is perhaps sufficiently well-known to require no extended comment here. Broken treaties, unkept promises, and the relentless expansion westward of white settlers provoked many

Indian tribes from colonial days to the late nineteenth century to violence. White settlers and army troops responded in kind with no quarter given on either side. Sand Creek, the Little Big Horn, and Wounded Knee are the names of terrible massacres, but they are just the best known among many.

Relations between blacks and whites have, until recently, scarcely been less violent. Some 3,440 blacks were lynched between 1882 (the first year for which data are available) and 1956, 512 of those since 1918.[57] Following the Civil War, hundreds more died and thousands were wounded in riots that, at least until World War II, had something of the character of the pogrom. In the Reconstruction period alone, eighty-two riots occurred as white Southerners sought to reestablish control over the newly freed slaves. In Memphis, forty-six blacks and one white died in a riot in May 1866. The local paper, the Memphis *Avalanche*, commented after the riot, "Thank heaven the white race are once more rulers of Memphis." At the end of July of that year, an estimated thirty-four to fifty blacks died and some two hundred were wounded in a New Orleans riot that the Union general Phil Sheridan called "an absolute massacre by the police . . . a murder which the mayor and police perpetrated without the shadow of necessity."[58] The incidence of riots has declined since that period, and none has matched the severity of the so-called draft riots in New York in July 1863 (twelve to fifteen hundred white deaths and many more black). Nevertheless, there were scores of riots during the twentieth century and many claimed lives.[59]

As for labor-management relations, the United States is distinguished by a long history of violence. Whether the measure is the number or duration of strikes, the use of deadly force (firearms, dynamite, and the like), the frequency with which troops were called in, or the number of lives lost, the battles between labor and management have been longer and more violent than in any European country.[60] This recitation might be much prolonged. It is enough to show that the stability of the social order in the United States has been shaky on many occasions.

DESCRIPTIVE THEORIES: THE COURSE OF AMERICAN HISTORY—WHY NO SOCIALISM?

Marx, like Tocqueville, believed that modernizing societies had a common end. Nevertheless, he too advanced a theory of American exceptionalism and inspired others to do so. These theories have come in response to the question, Why is there no socialism in the United States? Among those who have responded to this question, the best known is Werner Sombart, a German sociologist and Marxist. After a visit to the United States in 1904, he sought to explain why the United States seemed to stand in defiance of history or, at any rate, Marxist history. He set out the orthodox position as follows: "If . . . modern socialism follows as a necessary reaction to capitalism, the country with the most advanced capitalist development, namely, the United States, would at the same time be the one providing the classic case of socialism, and its working class would be supporters of the most radical of socialist movements."[61] But reality fell short of theoretical expectation, and this made America exceptional. He wrote *Why Is There No Socialism in the United States?* in explanation.

The United States, Sombart said, is characterized by a working class with a capitalist mentality, early enfranchisement of the lower classes, a high standard of living, the availability of cheap land, and a widespread belief in opportunities for upward mobility. He concluded, however, much as Marx and Engels had, that the effect of these conditions would be overcome in the course of continued capitalist development. The United States would not remain exceptional. It would assume the lead on the path to socialism, or so his Marxist ideology assured him.

During the nineteenth and early twentieth centuries, countries in Europe and North America were still industrializing. For Sombart and others writing at the time, the question, Why is there no socialism in the United States? was understood to ask, Why is the United States an exception to the laws of history as set out by Marx?[62] As the most developed capitalist economy, the United States should have had the largest, most class-conscious and radical proletariat. In fact it did not, and, for Marxists, this constituted a fundamental challenge to doctrine. A century later, if we take up the same theoretical perspective and look at the world through a Marxist lens, we see many mature capitalist economies and no socialist societies. The question that raises the fundamental challenge to Marxist theory today is, Why has no socialist transformation occurred anywhere? The United States is not exceptional in this regard. All countries have defied Marx's laws of history. Convergence impinges once again on our inquiries as a macroview is taken. We have not, however, finished examination of the responses to Sombart's question.

The question came to be given a different twist with the maturation of capitalist economies over the course of the twentieth century. Socialists and academic scholars have sought to explain why no socialist party of consequence emerged in the United States even though such a party was a common feature in other industrialized nations.[63] Their responses provide a long list of explanatory factors. There is general agreement that the existence of democracy induced a reformist rather than revolutionary posture among workers in the United States. Revolutions are risky and their outcomes uncertain. Democracy held out the possibility for the satisfaction of worker demands by peaceful means, albeit more slowly and less fully. Socialist parties everywhere fought for universal suffrage, civil liberties, and the other institutions of democracy in order to foster class consciousness and to lend force to worker demands. Not incidentally, these campaigns attracted the workers' support. They did not want to remain second-class citizens. In the United States, workers already enjoyed the rights of citizens. It is also agreed that socialist parties were hindered in their efforts to win support by the single-member district, plurality electoral system and the presidential selection process. These institutions have discouraged the formation of third parties throughout American history.

This circumstance, however, is less significant than another long-standing feature of American politics: the dominance of the Democratic and Republican parties.[64] Before industrialization had proceeded very far and before the industrial working class had grown large, the two established parties had built popular bases. In Europe, the socialist parties were the agents of popular political organization. In the United States, socialists faced the task of displacing a party that already had mass support. Furthermore, both the established parties, and particularly the Democrats after 1912, were quite ready to appropriate socialist proposals if they found popular favor. Not only were socialists unable to prosper as an independent party, they never were able to capture control of either the Democratic or Republican Party. In addition to these political factors, economic and cultural factors also figure in the explanation of the inability of the trade unions to attract more members and of the failure of a socialist party to break the political domination of the established parties.

In the United States, the economy developed differently than in most other industrializing nations. The proportion of the labor force employed in manufacturing never reached the pre–World War I highs attained by Britain and Germany. Britain reached its historical maximum of 51.6 percent in 1911; Germany had 40.9 of its workforce in manufacturing in 1910; Belgium 45.5; France 33.1; and the United States 31.6.[65] The United States did not experience the disruption associated with the industrial revolution in Britain, and to a lesser extent in Germany, in which much of the rural population was driven off the land and into the labor market for industry. Consequently, substantial numbers (31 percent) remained in agricultural employment in the United States just before World War I. The American labor force also included a large sector of white-collar and service workers, which even in 1910 constituted 31 percent of the whole.[66] In sum, the industrial workforce (Marx's *proletariat*) bulked less large in the United States than in other countries. There were fewer people proportionally for unions to organize and to whom a socialist party might make class-based appeals.

In addition, immigration supplied much of the industrial labor force. In 1910 as much as 25 percent of the whole labor force—but a third in manufacturing and half in mining—was foreign-born.[67] On arrival in the States, the immigrants sought community not in the workplace but among those who spoke their language, shared their religion, celebrated their holidays, and ate their food. These ethnic-based ties provided support for successful adaptation to life in America.[68] And it was on this basis that political organization occurred among the immigrants.[69] Ethnicity, then, proved to be stronger than class as a basis for community and as a criterion of interest. Furthermore, many immigrants came to America to acquire a stake before returning home. In the period 1908 to 1910, for every one hundred arrivals in the United States, there were thirty-two departures.[70] Perhaps as much as a third of the working class in 1910 consisted of recent arrivals who did not intend to stay. These workers would presumably give priority to higher wages and shorter hours over basic changes in the economy and government.[71]

Further eroding any sense of class consciousness were the animosities that so often characterized relations among workers. Labor divided into native and "old immigrants" (largely northern and western European and Protestant) on the one hand and "new immigrants" (largely southern and eastern European and Catholic) on the other.[72] This division corresponded more or less with the difference between skilled and unskilled workers. The American Federation of Labor (AFL) organized skilled workers and sought to restrict immigration. White labor, organized and unorganized, was particularly hostile to blacks and to the Chinese, who were regarded as rate-breakers. Only somewhat less virulent were the animosities that divided Protestants and Catholics. To be sure, in some instances these divisions were overcome and common cause was made against management. Transitory exceptions aside, however, division between skilled and unskilled labor and divisions along religious, ethnic, and racial lines burdened any efforts toward an inclusive labor organization and a class-based political party.[73]

These explanations are plausible to be sure, but they are not conclusive for several reasons. First, some identify factors that are common to several countries. Although Britain and France did not institute universal suffrage for males as early as the United States did, they did have more or less democratic regimes with mass electorates in the latter part of the nineteenth century. Furthermore, the single-member, plurality electoral system has not been peculiar to the United States. Britain and Canada continue to use such a system, and many European countries did until World War I. As for economic and cultural factors, it is worth noting that the United States was not alone in preserving a large agricultural sector in the course of industrialization. France in fact employed a greater percentage (41 percent) of its labor force in agriculture in the early twentieth century than did the United States. And, while no other nation could match the United States in the number and diversity of its immigrant population, Protestant England and Wales absorbed substantial numbers of Irish Catholics into the workforce in the nineteenth century. These common factors pose a problem for those theories that invoke them. These same factors did not bar the emergence of a socialist party with mass working-class support in other countries. This is not to deny a causal role to these factors. It may be that their effect, along with other things, has been cumulative in the American case and that these factors were an obstacle, wherever they were present, to the organization of the working class into unions and in support of a political party.

Second, many of these explanations fail to be historically specific. The United States has not always been exceptional with respect to the organization of the working class or to the presence of a socialist party. In the pre–World War I period, union membership in the United States was 2.7 million in 1914, about one-fourth of the industrial labor force. This was less than the 30 to 40 percent in Britain, but greater than the 15 percent in France and about equal to the 25 to 30 percent in Germany. The leading group of unions, the AFL, was committed to contending with management on the issues of wages and hours and working conditions and to controlling access to employment in the crafts. In this, the AFL, as well as other unions, could be quite militant. Strikes and violence marked the course of labor-management relations throughout the nineteenth and well into the twentieth century. Politically, the AFL was opposed to socialism and to the formation of a labor party. Even in the AFL, however, socialism had a good deal of support. In 1902 the Socialist Party platform was backed by 46 percent of the votes cast at the AFL convention. A socialist candidate for the union's presidency in 1912 won a third of the votes.

In politics, the first Socialist representative was elected to Congress in 1910. Eugene Debs, the Socialist presidential candidate, won 6 percent of the popular vote in 1912. By 1914 the party could count some twelve hundred

Socialist municipal officeholders and thirty-three legislators in fourteen states.[74] By comparison, the French socialist party (SFIO) reached a prewar high of 103 seats in the national assembly on the strength of 16.8 percent of the total vote. The Labour Party in Britain won 7 percent of the votes in 1910. None of these socialist parties came close to matching the electoral strength or the organizational reach of the SPD, the German socialist party. In the last election before the war (1912), the SPD won 34.8 percent of the votes cast. The party was the political arm of a labor movement that included strong unions, fraternal organizations, newspapers, insurance societies, schools, and other groups. In sum, the United States, Britain, and France were similar—none had a significant socialist party. Germany had the best claim to exceptional status before World War I.

Following that war, socialist parties flourished in Europe, but in the United States they were relegated to the fringes, where they have languished ever since. The conditions identified above contributed to this result, but the World War I period also dealt wounding blows to the Socialist Party of America. Unlike the socialist parties in Europe, which supported their governments in prosecuting the war, the American party came out in opposition. This confirmed for many the charges of "un-American" and "anti-American" that had been made against the party. The Russian Revolution in 1917 and the association of immigrants with socialism also inflamed a nativism that produced the Red Scare and the political repression of socialists.[75] Policies adopted by the Wilson administration also undercut popular support for the Socialist Party. In particular, an income tax law and the Clayton Act, which promised to protect unions against antitrust suits, were measures long sought by the unions. The war, then, must appear in any response to the question: Why is there no socialism in the United States?[76]

Third, no explanation for socialism's failure in the United States can neglect the attitudes, beliefs, and feelings of Americans. This is so because human beings act in light of their attitudes, beliefs, and feelings. Political, social, and economic circumstances have an effect on these things of course, but the connection is not tight. To be sure, most of those who have responded to Sombart's question have imputed various attitudes, beliefs, and feelings to Americans. As we have seen, Louis Hartz ascribed a set of liberal principles to Americans, and Werner Sombart's specification of American attitudes and beliefs is not much different.

Indeed, most commentators have cited widespread beliefs in individualism and antistatism (least government) as significant, if not insurmountable, barriers to the success of socialism. These commentators may well be correct in imputing those beliefs to Americans. Nevertheless, such attribution is based on anecdote and inference. It was only with the introduction of public opinion polling in the 1930s that more reliable evidence for the states of mind of the otherwise inarticulate became available. Furthermore, attitudes and beliefs said to be the consequence of the frontier or of economic abundance or the absence of a feudal past or some other exceptional quality can hardly be ascribed to immigrants who did have a feudal past, had no experience of the frontier, and knew little of economic abundance or any other aspect of American life.[77] It is with respect to attitudes, feelings, and beliefs that the explanation for the absence of a socialist party with mass support needs the most work.

It is true that the United States has never had a socialist party with substantial popular support. In this respect, it has been exceptional when compared with European or with other English-speaking countries since World War I. Although no complete explanation for this has yet been propounded, it is clear that a combination of political, economic, social, and cultural conditions—no one of which has been decisive—erected formidable obstacles that socialists were unable to surmount. The significance of the failure of socialism in the United States is great. We know that socialist parties in Europe have adopted policies to expand opportunity for all and to reduce social and economic inequality. An American socialist party would, one assumes, have done the same. Many of the conditions, however, that worked against the success of socialism in the United States have produced a government that taxes its citizens less and spends less on public domestic goods than most developed countries. As a consequence, the United States has higher infant mortality rates, relatively more people living in poverty, and relatively more people with inadequate health care than other industrialized nations.

CHAPTER 6

THE AMERICAN MISSION

We now move from the realm of the descriptive to the realm of the moral. The theories examined below claim a special status and a mission for Americans. The claims to a special status and a mission have secured general agreement among Americans. More contentious has been the nature of the special status and of the mission and the means whereby the mission is to be accomplished. I call these theories *moral* because they contend that Americans are superior in holiness or virtue and that Americans are obligated to pursue a mission.

MORAL THEORIES: THE PURITANS' COVENANT THEOLOGY

The most enduring and influential theory of American exceptionalism can be found in the covenant theology of the Puritans. In setting out the fundamentals of this theology, we shall turn to John Cotton (1585–1652) and Samuel Willard (1640–1707) among others. Cotton was a first-generation minister at Boston's First Church and leading exponent of Congregational orthodoxy. Willard was the second-generation minister of Old South Church in Boston for some twenty-five years and head of Harvard College from 1701 to 1707. His *A Compleat Body of Divinity* stood for nearly a century as the only systematic elaboration of Puritan theology. According to Willard, Adam in the state of innocence was party to a covenant with God. "As a Reasonable Creature, man was capable of Transacting with God in the way of a Covenant; he was able to understand, and subscribe to the Articles, to give his free Consent, and set his Seal to them.[1] God need not have entered into a covenant with humankind. Men and women are his creatures, and he might have done with them as it pleased him.[2] God, however, chose not to rule arbitrarily over those whom he had created in his own image. Instead, he offered to Adam (representing all humankind) a covenant whereby both parties would be bound. The Puritan understanding of the term *covenant* will sound familiar: "Where two Parties do stand mutually obliged one to another in a voluntary Agreement, there is a Covenant."[3]

The first covenant provided that if Adam were to conduct himself as he should, he and his posterity would be rewarded with eternal life. The rules of right conduct were "given to *Adam* at the first, and written upon the Tables of his Heart."[4] These rules required that "he was to do the Will of God, and nothing else."[5] Because this covenant demanded a certain kind of conduct, it was called a *covenant of works*. Adam did not adhere to its terms; he failed to observe the moral law. Consequently, Adam and all of human-kind suffered the penalty: a life mortal and unhappy. Furthermore, the very faculty, namely, reason, that distinguishes man from the rest of creation and that enables him to discern the moral law has become "woefully *impaired*. Man knock't his head in his fall, and craz'd his understanding, as to divine Truths."[6]

Since the Fall, God has made no similar offer to humankind. Men and women have offended against God's justice and must atone for their transgression. What's more, men and women relying on their own reason and will would be unable to observe a covenant of works. Rather than let humans wander aimlessly in misery and torment, God, in an exercise of will, proposed a new covenant—the *covenant of grace*.[7] Beginning with Abraham, as related in Genesis 17, men and women may avail themselves of new terms. What God now requires is not right conduct but faith. Humans are free to accept or reject God's terms. There is, however, powerful induce-ment to accept those terms provided by the *covenant of redemption*. This cov-enant between God and Christ preceded the covenant of grace and provided the basis for it.[8] As John Cotton explained, "It is not justice for God to pro-nounce a man just upon any other righteousness, besides the righteousness of his son, for *if God should mark what we have done*, no flesh living should be justified in his sight, Psalms 143:2. But through the righteousness of Christ, which is perfect, the Lord justifies everyone that believeth in him."[9] Thus, the covenant of redemption provides a promise that God will uphold his side of the agreement if a man or woman accepts the terms on offer in the covenant of grace. Whether a man or woman accepts the terms depends on God. For "without the work of the spirit there is no faith begotten by any promise. . . . It is the spirit of God that must do it."[10] So, some men and women, under the influence of the Holy Spirit, come to believe and thereby become parties to the covenant of grace. Those who experience the presence of the Holy Spirit are the *elect*—invisible saints and members of the invisible church; they are known only to God. Nevertheless, the Puritans referred to members of their church as *visible saints*, even while the ministry acknowledged that there was only a rough coincidence between those whom God has redeemed and those accepted into membership in the Congregational church (as Puritans called their church).[11]

In the Puritan view, God has concluded covenants not only with individuals but with nations as well. And just as the covenant of grace transforms the life of the individual who has received the Holy Spirit, so too does the national covenant affect the political and social life of a chosen people. The individual redeemed lives in this world but not of it—subject to providence, God's general superintendence of the world by means of the laws of nature (for example, gravity), but with the promise of eternal life. All peoples, including a chosen people, must live according to the laws of nature. Indeed, almost all have lived by the laws of nature alone. The fortunes of such peoples, that is, whether or not they have prospered as nations, have depended on God's will. The fortunes of a chosen people, however, depend on adherence to their covenant with God.[12]

The national covenant does not promise salvation. In this respect it differs from the covenant of grace extended to Abraham and his successors. The covenant of grace was based on predestination—the idea that God chose at the beginning who was to be saved and who damned for all eternity. Only individuals have immortal souls and, therefore, only individuals have been chosen to be saved. Even though chosen as among the saved (the *elect*), an individual may experience misfortune in the form of disease, crop failure, or the death of a child, for example. Some among the damned, on the other hand, may enjoy earthly happiness. Both will receive their just deserts in good time. The saved, party to the covenant of grace, live by faith—the promise of God's redemption. But, as John Rogers, minister at Ipswich, Massachusetts, put it in a 1706 Election Day sermon, "God does not deal thus with Nations, because . . . Publick Bodies & Communities of men as such can only be rewarded & punished in this World. . . . This being the only Season for National Rewards and Punishments, it seemth Reasonable and necessary in some degree, for a present vindication of the Honour and Majesty of the Divine Laws, that a People should be prosperous, or afflicted, according as their general Obedience or Disobedience thereto appears."[13] Nations are mortal. They have no existence beyond this earth. A nation, therefore, cannot conclude an agreement about its salvation but only about its earthly existence.

In the national covenant, God promises to reward the obedience of his chosen people by conferring earthly blessings: their harvests will be bountiful, their children healthy, their concord complete, and their relations with others peaceful. The Puritans counted their blessings and found reassurance that they were indeed a chosen people. "If any people in the world have been lifted up to heaven as to Advantages and Priviledges, we are the people. Name what you will under this Head, and we have had it," said minister, then magistrate, William Stoughton in 1668.[14] He cautioned, however, that all New England is under "a *solemn divine Probation*."[15] God confers earthly benefits on a people only as they observe the terms of the covenant. And the covenant is "only upheld when a people stick close to the law and to the testimony, walking by the holy rules of Scriptures, in conformity to the revealed will of God in his word."[16] Failure to keep the covenant invites God's wrath.

The opportunity to enter into a national covenant is afforded only to a people chosen by God for their faithfulness. Even before that first four hundred Puritan faithful had left for New England's shores, John Cotton, the renowned Puritan minister, assured them that they were a chosen people to whom God had promised a land. Cotton relied for his authority on this point on II Samuel 7:10: "Moreover I will appoint a place for my people Israel, and I will plant them, that they may dwell in a place of their own, and move no more."[17] In sermon after sermon, New England's ministers taught their parishioners to think of themselves as a chosen people. William Stoughton, after carefully distinguishing between the "purely spiritual Covenant" and the "external political covenant," asserted, "*The Lord hath said of New-England, Surely they are my People, Children that will not lie, so hath he been our Saviour.*"[18] Urian Oakes, minister at Cambridge, was of the same mind: "As the words of my Text respect the *Body of a Nation*, even Israel, that was sometimes the peculiar people of God: So give me leave . . . to perswade the *New England Israel* to get and improve this Spiritual wisdom. . . . As you are a people of many Mercies and Priviledges, so I may parallel you with Israel, a people graciously conducted and carried by the mighty hand of God to a place of Rest, and Peace, and Safety, and Liberty."[19] And Cotton Mather, minister of North Church in Boston, declared, "You may see an *Israel* in *America*, by looking upon this Plantation; may Peace be upon this Israel of God!"[20] In their view, New England Puritans had succeeded to the mantle first worn by Old Testament Jews as the chosen people, and New England was the new Canaan—the land promised to the Jews by God. Like the Jews, God had chosen them for the performance of a mission. As John Winthrop (1588–1649), leader of the emigrants and first governor of the Massachusetts Bay Colony, reminded his fellows in a lay sermon aboard the *Arbella*, "We agreed to seek out a place of cohabitation and consortship under a due form of government, both civil and ecclesiastical"; and "We are entered into covenant with him [God] for this work."[21]

The work to be accomplished was twofold. First, New Englanders were to build a society that could serve as a model for the completion of the Reformation. The Puritans were dissatisfied with the reforms carried out in England before their emigration and, later, under the Puritan Commonwealth of Oliver Cromwell. Cotton Mather was repeating a common theme of a half-century of sermons from Congregational pulpits when he said in 1690, "Let all mankind know that we came into the *Wilderness*, because we would quietly worship God, without that *Episcopacy*, that *Common-Prayer*, and those unwarrantable *Ceremonies*, which the *Land of our Fathers Sepulchres*, has been defiled with."[22] And when he observed, "Tis possible, that our Lord Jesus Christ carried some thousands of *Reformers* into the Retirements of an American Dessart . . . that . . . He might there, To them first, and then By them, give a Specimen of many Good things, which He would have His Churches elsewhere aspire and arise unto."[23] Two motifs were recurrent in Puritan sermons to refer to this part of their mission. John Winthrop supplied one of them when he cautioned his fellows, "We shall be as a City upon a Hill."[24] For him, the Massachusetts Bay Colony was to be an exemplar of holiness and of civil and ecclesiastical government for reformist Christianity. The other motif may well have made its first appearance as the title of one of Samuel Danforth's sermons in 1670: *A Brief Recognition of New-Englands Errand Into the Wilderness*.[25] This errand was the reformation of Christendom. It was a task to be undertaken by New Englanders on behalf of God himself.

The second work was grander still: creation of the conditions for the Second Coming of Christ and the end of history—the millennium. The millennium is the thousand-year period referred to in Revelation 20 during which the "saints" (the saved) would rule with Christ over the world in peace and prosperity. The millennium would mark the end of history and, thus, the end of the war, discord, and sorrow that had characterized it. This millennialism in Puritan thought represented a sharp departure from the traditional interpretation of the prophecies in the Books of Daniel and Revelation and elsewhere in scripture. Augustine, the fifth-century Christian convert and Father of the Roman Catholic church, many centuries before had posited in *The City of God* the existence of two cities: the City of

God and the City of Man. The City of God comprises the good angels and the saved, living and dead. It lives by faith. Sacred history is the account of those individuals who, under the treatment of grace, overcome their lusts and come to love God. The earthly city is made up of the ungodly—those who love themselves. It lives to enjoy earthly goods. Using the same earthly goods but to different ends, these two communities of men and women live side-by-side in the world and in time. There is, however, a great gulf between them. Augustine described that part of the heavenly city in the world and in time as a *sojourner*. Between the two cities there is struggle for the allegiance of men and women. In this struggle the City of Man has recourse to those things—fame, power, money, and sex—that permit it to win the loyalty of most and to dominate the City of God in the world. And so it will be until the final judgment. Augustine understood the Revelation prophecy of a kingdom of Christ on earth as allegorical. The great struggle between God and the devil occurs in the hearts and minds of individual men and women. The saved among them can be said to rule with Christ as they triumph, with his help, over their lusts. There could be, he thought, no convergence of sacred and secular history, no incorporation of the City of Man by the City of God. To think that there could be such a convergence and incorporation would require that many abandon the earthly city and that the City of God acquire power over the City of Man. Such a prospect seemed absurd to the fifth-century Augustine.[26]

Many Puritans found that prospect much more likely. Had not the Reformation dealt a grievous wound to the Beast (the devil and his forces)?[27] To be sure, the Roman church had not yet been vanquished, but reformed churches continued to win converts across Europe. And as the priests, the ritual, and canon law were removed and men and women given unimpeded access to the Word, more converts could be expected. For Increase Mather, minister at Boston and president of Harvard College from 1685 to 1701, "that there will a time come when the kingdom of Christ shall be established all the earth over, the thing is certain and sure."[28] There was no settled view about when the great day would dawn, but many believed that the vanguard of Christ's kingdom could be found in New England. Edward Johnson, merchant and government official, observed in 1650, "When England began to decline in religion . . . Christ creates a New England to muster up the first of his forces in."[29] Cotton Mather and Jonathan Edwards held the same view. Mather in his history of New England gave as his intention the "description of *some feeble attempts* . . . to anticipate the State of the *New-Jerusalem*."[30] Edwards, minister at Northampton and, briefly, president of what would become

Princeton, found in that revival of religious feeling in the early 1740s known as the Great Awakening, "the dawning, or at least, a prelude" to the institution of Christ's kingdom. "And there are many things," he said, "that make it probable that this work will begin in America."[31] For Ebenezer Baldwin, minister of First Church in Danbury, Connecticut, the work had begun. In November 1775, in response to the opening volleys of the Revolution, these words were heard from his pulpit: "I would suppose these Colonies to be the foundation of a great and mighty Empire; the largest the world ever saw, . . . which shall be the principal Seat of that glorious Kingdom, which Christ shall erect upon Earth in the latter Days. And that these Calamities are remotely preparing the Way for this glorious Event."[32] Thus, for the heirs of the Puritan clergy, sacred and secular history had converged in what was at the time the historical backwater of colonial America.

This convergence gave sacred significance to the events of American history for the nation had as its mission the realization of sacred ends: the reform of Christianity and the preparation of the conditions for the Second Coming and the end of history. If that mission were to be accomplished, then the national interests of America must be defended. The nation was acting, after all, as an agent of God. Those who opposed American interests were demonized as agents of Satan. Now, Christians have long interpreted history—sacred history—in dramatic terms. Sacred history is the account of a bitter struggle between God and Satan, good and evil, played out in the souls of individuals that culminates in the final judgment. According to the Puritans, there was a parallel struggle between God and Satan on the international plane. This struggle could be seen in the wars fought against the Indians in 1637 and in 1675–76.[33] It could be seen too in the wars fought against the "papist" French and their Indian allies on four occasions from 1689 to 1763.[34] The outbreak of King Philip's War in 1675 provoked John Richardson, minister at Newbury, to observe, "The church of God upon Earth is Militant, in a Civil as well as in a Spiritual sense."[35] For Samuel Nowell, "there is such agreement between the Spiritual and temporal Warfare, that everything belonging to a Souldier, is made use of to resemble some Grace or Duty of a Christian."[36] Nowell, who combined the roles of minister and militia leader, also warned, "The highest piece for Service that ever souldiers were employed in is yet behind [i.e., to come], and is commonly believed not to be very far off: the highest service that ever was done for the Lord Jesus Christ is yet behind, the destruction of *Gog and Magog* [i.e., Satan], so the enemies of the Church are called in Scripture; whether it be Pope or Turk, or whoever else is meant, that shall oppose the advancement of the Kingdome of

Christ."[37] The national mission was to be accomplished not only by propagation of the Gospel but by force of arms. To the themes, then, of chosen people and national mission, the Puritans added another—military prowess. The forces of good must be powerful in the secular as well as the spiritual sense if they are to shape events in the world.[38]

In the preceding paragraphs, I have described a body of thought developed by Puritan leaders over the first century or so of settlement in New England. How widely shared these ideas were among the immigrants up and down the Atlantic seaboard or among New Englanders in particular are questions that have no definite answer. Most people were mute in the sense that they left no written record. We do know that a belief in American exceptionalism was not confined to New England Puritans. John Rolfe of Virginia, who would secure his place in history by marrying Pocahontas, regarded the English migration to the shores of the Chesapeake as that of "a peculiar people, marked and chosen by the finger of God, to possess it, for undoubtedly he is with us."[39] We also know that some religious leaders did not subscribe to such ideas. William Bradford, early governor of Plymouth Plantation, and Robert Cushman, one of Plymouth's founders, denied that New Englanders were a chosen people and that the millennium might be brought closer by their efforts.[40] Roger Williams, better known for his insistence on separation of church and state, made clear his dissent from the prevailing views in a famous exchange with John Cotton.[41] And, decades later, Charles Chauncy, minister of First Church, Boston, for much of the eighteenth century, asked whether "any good end [may] be answered in endeavoring, upon evidence absolutely precarious, to instill into the minds of the people a notion of the millennium state . . . and of America, as that part of the world which is pointed out in the Revelations of God."[42] Not all Puritans, let alone all Americans, of the seventeenth and eighteenth centuries thought alike.

The Puritans advanced a theory of American exceptionalism that identified Americans as a people singled out by God for their holiness (a chosen people) and entrusted with a mission whose goal was the redemption of humankind. These ideas did not die with the colonial Puritans. From the Revolution down to the present day, Americans have turned to the ideas of a chosen people and a national mission in seeking to understand their experience as a people and to justify the course on which they have settled.[43] The persistence of these ideas can be seen in a 1996 survey of Americans that asked respondents to judge the relative importance of various themes of American history in education. Eighty-seven percent said it is important to teach children that America "has had a destiny to set an example for other nations"; 84 percent that "our nation was founded upon Biblical principles"; and 72 percent that "America has a special place in God's plan for history."[44] While these ideas have persisted, they have done so in modified and diverse forms. For the most part, latter-day expression of them has been shorn of any foundation in covenant theology—at least as they have been expressed in the political sphere. In the place of covenant theology, proponents of these ideas have relied on an unadorned appeal to faith or on an appeal to history. The latter requires some explaining.

MORAL THEORIES: A SECULAR VERSION

Alongside the Puritan theory of American exceptionalism, there grew another theory that is secular in nature. I have made reference to this theory earlier—in the chapter on religion and the Constitution. On this theory it was not God who had charged Americans with a mission but history. History should not be understood as having agency—consciousness and intention. Rather, historical circumstances had provided an opportunity to institute the world's first large-scale republican government (all earlier republics had confined citizenship to a small fraction of their populations). James Madison at the Constitutional Convention told his fellow delegates that they "were now digesting a plan which in its operation wd. decide forever the fate of Republican Govt."[45] And his colleague in the writing of *The Federalist*, Alexander Hamilton, observed, "It seems to have been reserved to the people of this country, by their conduct and example, to decide the important question, whether societies of men are really capable or not of establishing good government from reflection and choice, or whether they are forever destined to depend for their political constitutions on accident and force."[46] Those who expounded this secular theory at the time of the Founding invoked Montesquieu and William Blackstone, but even more frequently they appealed to experience, rather than the Bible, to define the mission.[47] For Madison and Hamilton, Americans ought to advance the cause of republican government. By *republican government*, they meant a government in which people enjoyed both political and civil liberty, a government controlled by the people and respectful of individual rights.

Just as historical circumstances at America's birth had provided an opportunity to institute the first republican government, so later circumstances better enabled America to accomplish its mission. Population growth and economic development, and the military strength these things confer, have permitted the United States to exert its power abroad. In 2004

Roger Cohen, columnist for the *Washington Post*, wrote that while European countries are "very nice places full of thoroughly decent people," only the United States can "stop Al Qaeda, prevent terrorists from gaining access to nuclear weapons, oust the Taliban, assuage Central European concerns over Russia, police the Korean Peninsula, watch over Taiwan, disarm Muammar el-Qaddafi of Libya, or, in general, assume the cost of defending free societies." For Cohen, "no greater force for good exists than the United States."[48] In making this claim, Cohen follows many others who have seen in the rise of America to world power an opportunity, even an obligation, to promote the good abroad. Adm. Alfred T. Mahan at the close of the nineteenth century wrote in his widely influential books that the obligation "to maintain right by force if need be" rested on powerful nations because "much is required of those to whom much is given."[49] A half-century later, Henry Luce, the publisher of *Time*, *Life*, and *Fortune*, pronounced the twentieth century the American century. The United States, he said, was the "principal guarantor of the freedom of the seas," "the dynamic leader of world trade," "the training center of the skillful servants of mankind," "the powerhouse of the ideals of Freedom and Justice," and "the Good Samaritan, really believing again it is more blessed to give than to receive."[50]

The secular theory of American exceptionalism differs from that of the Puritans in a number of respects. As indicated above, the nature of the mission changes. Instead of the reform of Christianity and the preparation of conditions for the millennium, the mission is the advance of liberty. This mission is to be accomplished by Americans, not because they have been chosen by God but because historical circumstances have provided them with an opportunity to do so. In addition, on the secular theory, the great struggle in the world is between liberty and tyranny; the Puritans emphasized the struggle between God and the devil. The secular theory also makes the nation—the whole community—rather than the church the agent to carry out the mission. The Puritans, of course, spoke of America and of the colonies, although more typically of New England, as the land of the chosen people. For them, however, the community (America, the colonies, New England) was the community of the faithful, that is, the people of the Congregational Church. Finally, the secular theory accords to reason the place occupied in the Puritan view by faith. It is only by faith that people can come to know God and to rule with Christ. But by unaided reason people can learn of their right to liberty. They may not enjoy liberty because they live under a tyrant. Nevertheless, they know that they ought to have political and civil liberty. This knowledge, of course, is not confined to Americans.

Thomas Jefferson in his first inaugural referred to the "throes and convulsions of the ancient world, during the agonizing spasms of infuriated man, seeking through blood and slaughter his long-lost liberty."[51] People everywhere want to enjoy liberty. It is the mission of the United States to help them realize this aspiration—or so many, perhaps most, Americans have thought.

AN AMENDED RELIGIOUS THEORY

Both the Puritan and secular theories have their contemporary adherents. Neither theory, however, is well designed to secure widespread acceptance. The secular theory fails in this respect because it gives no place to God or to the United States as a redemptive agent. For the religious-minded, these are fatal flaws. The Puritan theory too can have only limited appeal because its ideas about the national mission and the composition of the chosen people are sectarian. No Catholic, for example, is likely to find attractive a theory that regards the Catholic Church as an agent of the devil.

Later generations of Americans developed the ideas of national mission and of Americans as a special people in ways that broadened their appeal. Over the course of the nineteenth and early twentieth centuries, many churchmen joined the fortunes of Christianity with those of political reform.[52] Lyman Beecher, father of Henry Ward Beecher and Harriet Beecher Stowe, Congregational minister, and first president of Lane Theological Seminary in Cincinnati, wrote in 1835 that the millennium "cannot come to pass under the existing civil organization of the nations," namely, "arbitrary despotism and the predominance of feudal institutions and usages." Despots and feudal institutions must be overthrown. "Revolutions and distress of nations will precede the introduction of the peaceful reign of Jesus Christ on the earth." Beecher asked, "Where shall the central energy be found, and from what nation shall the renovating power go forth?" The answer was the United States for "what nation is blessed with such experimental knowledge of free institutions . . . as our own?"[53]

Later in the century, Washington Gladden, minister of the First Congregational Church in Columbus, Ohio, member of the Columbus city council for one term, and leader in a movement to apply Christian principles to social problems, asserted, "All these glowing promises made by the old prophets, of the triumphs yet to be won for the kingdom of God in the world, are made to the nation and not to the church." Gladden was no less persuaded that "God has commissioned this nation, within the last few years, in some unwonted and impressive ways, to show the non-Christian nations what Christianity means."[54] The line of development marked out by Beecher and Gladden produced a religious theory far less sectarian and more secular than the Puritan theory.

Although no single theory, religious or secular, commands a consensus, it is possible to identify a cluster of ideas that are common to all moral theories of American exceptionalism. First, Americans are a special people, superior in holiness or civic virtue. Second, Americans as a nation have a mission as charged by God or permitted by historical circumstances. And, third, this mission is the advance of liberty—understood as preparatory to the millennium or as a good in its own right.

DISPUTE OVER CARRYING OUT THE MISSION

On either understanding of liberty, slavery mocked the pretensions of Americans as a chosen people. Had not Madison acknowledged at the Convention that black slavery was "the most oppressive dominion ever exercised by man over man"?[55] And had not his fellow Virginian, Thomas Jefferson, called slavery "the most unremitting despotism on the one part and degrading submission on the other"? Slavery, he wrote, made him "tremble for my country when I reflect that God is just."[56] Only a hypocrite could claim liberty as the national mission and turn a blind eye to slavery. Most Americans, however, were far less troubled by this inconsistency between the ideal and practice of liberty in the United States than by the thought that only by revolution could slavery be abolished. The Constitution, after all, had placed slavery beyond national control. For this reason William Lloyd Garrison, the ardent abolitionist, called the Constitution an "agreement with hell." During the first half of the nineteenth century, antislavery sentiment grew in the North and the South felt more and more under attack. Congressional attempts to resolve the North-South dispute over the extension of slavery were unable to bridge the gulf between the contending views of the American prospect. The South regarded Lincoln's victory at the polls in 1860 as threatening to slavery itself. Within weeks of his inauguration, Southern cannonballs slammed into Fort Sumter, and the nation was plunged into the bloodiest war of its history.

A chosen people, a national mission, the advance of liberty as that mission—Americans have not much dissented from any of these ideas. The great struggle has been over how the national mission ought to be pursued in concrete circumstances. Some, like Lincoln, looked inward and saw the great disparity between America's asserted devotion to liberty and its practice. At Gettysburg, he emphasized the "unfinished work" yet to be done and "the great task remaining" before Americans as they carried out the mission set by the founders. Lincoln declared that the founders had created "a new nation, conceived in liberty, and dedicated to the proposition that all men are created equal." In making this declaration, he appealed to what he regarded as the spirit of the founding as expressed in the Declaration of Independence rather than to the letter of the Constitution.[57] He asked that "we here highly resolve that . . . this nation, under God, shall have a new birth of freedom—and that government of the people, by the people, for the people, shall not perish from the earth."[58] The victory of Union arms and the passage of the postwar amendments went some distance toward realization of those aspirations.

In the early twentieth century, the Reverend Matthew Gladden decried the wage slavery created in the course of industrialization. The depredations of unrestrained capitalism brought him to "admit that our industry in many of its phases is brutalized by greed; that we harbored the growth of a plutocracy, whose presence is a shame and a curse to us, and have bred . . . a proletariat whose helpless misery is the dismay of our philanthropy."[59] He called for the adoption of better working conditions and recognition of a right to organize.[60] Gladden and others in the Social Gospel movement regarded such measures as the application of Christian principles to social problems. President Franklin Delano Roosevelt sounded a similar theme throughout his administrations. In a speech in 1936, for example, he proclaimed, "This generation of Americans has a rendezvous with destiny." And that destiny is to advance the cause of liberty by erecting defenses against economic misfortune. "'Necessitous men are not free men,'" he explained. "Liberty requires opportunity to make a living— . . . a living decent according to the standard of the time, a living which gives men not only enough to live by, but something to live for."[61] Social Security, minimum wage laws, and collective bargaining rights came out of this understanding of liberty.

In 1963 Martin Luther King, also called on Americans to honor their commitments. The Emancipation Proclamation, he said, had come as a "joyous daybreak to end the long night of captivity," but one hundred years later, "the Negro is still not free." He is "crippled by the manacles of segregation" and the "chains of discrimination." He urged that America "rise up and live out the true meaning of its creed: 'We hold these truths to be self-evident: that all men are created equal.'"[62] Congress responded by adopting the Civil Rights Act of 1964 and the Voting Rights Act of 1965 as well as other civil rights legislation.

For Lincoln, Gladden, Roosevelt, and King, the United States was meant to pursue its mission by serving as an exemplar, a model that other nations might follow. In taking this view, they followed the Puritans of seventeenth-century New England who sought to build a "City upon a Hill." And like those Puritans of old, Lincoln, Gladden, Roosevelt, and King were no less insistent that America must live up to its own standards, if it were to be an exemplar. Perhaps Albert Gallatin, secretary of the treasury under Jefferson, put this position most succinctly in the midst of the war with Mexico in the mid-1840s. He admonished his fellow Americans in this way: "Your mission was to be a model for all other governments and for all other less-favored nations, to adhere to the most elevated principles of political morality, to apply all your faculties to the gradual improvement of your own institutions and social state, and by your example to exert a moral influence most beneficial to mankind at large." Gallatin's convictions were ignored by an administration that appealed to what he called "the thirst of unjust aggrandizement by brutal force."[63] Both Lincoln and Ulysses S. Grant, by the way, shared his view of the war with Mexico.[64]

In addition to the idea of America as an exemplar of liberty, some Americans have claimed that the United States, by force of arms if necessary, ought to safeguard the liberty of others as it might be threatened by an oppressor and even to extend liberty to others as they might suffer under an oppressor. The U.S. government has always invoked this idea whenever it has employed force beyond its borders. Throughout the nineteenth century, the title that this idea took was *manifest destiny*. The apparent originator of the phrase put it this way: "[It is] our manifest destiny to overspread and to possess the whole of the continent which Providence has given us for the development of the great experiment of liberty and federated self-government entrusted to us."[65] Presumably what made this destiny manifest was the fact that the United States had the power and the will to realize it. Under the mantle of manifest destiny, the United States faced down Mexico over the annexation of Texas, secured settlement of the Oregon controversy with Britain, and in a war with Mexico acquired California and the New Mexico territory. The last-named acquisitions disappointed the more ambitious expansionists who had campaigned for "all-Mexico." Indeed, some thought that "until every acre of the North American continent is occupied by the citizens of the United States, the foundations of the future empire will not have been laid."[66]

Following decades of preoccupation with domestic matters—the Civil War and its consequences—Americans looked beyond North America's shores. And manifest destiny underwent a revival—this time with an explicit racial cast. Josiah Strong, a Congregational minister, wrote in 1891,

"This race [Anglo-Saxons] of unequaled energy, with all the majesty of numbers and the might of wealth behind it—the representative, let us hope, of the largest liberty, the purest Christianity, the highest civilization—having developed peculiarly aggressive traits calculated to impress its institutions upon mankind, will spread itself over the earth." He saw in this a divine appointment. "For, if this generation is faithful to its trust, America is to become God's right arm in his battle with the world's ignorance and oppression and sin."[67] Albert J. Beveridge, senator from Indiana and close friend of President Theodore Roosevelt, just a few years later announced, "God has not been preparing the English-speaking and Teutonic peoples for a thousand years for nothing. . . . He has made us adepts in government that we may administer government among savage and senile peoples. . . . And of all our race He has marked the American people as His chosen Nation finally to lead in the regeneration of the world."[68] These words were spoken in justification of the occupation of territory seized during the Spanish-American War. "Porto Rico is ours and ours for ever; the Philippines are ours and ours for ever; and Cuba ought to have been ours." Indeed, *the sovereignty of the Stars and Stripes can be nothing but a blessing to any people and to any land.*"[69] The Republicans thought these views sufficiently popular that they adopted the speech from which the last two quotations were taken as a national campaign document in 1900.

The career of manifest destiny ended in the years leading up to World War I. The idea of a national mission did not. President Woodrow Wilson expressly disavowed any territorial ambitions in announcing American entrance in the war. He has been followed in this by all the wartime presidents who succeeded him. The United States, Wilson said, "is fighting for no advantage or selfish object of her own, but for the liberation of peoples everywhere from the aggressions of autocratic force."[70] In order that aggression be forever banished, he proposed at war's end the institution of the League of Nations. (The Federal Council of Churches wired the White House that the proposed League was the "political expression of the Kingdom of God on earth."[71]) The war had presented Americans, he thought, with an "opportunity for which they have sought to prepare themselves . . . ever since the days when they set up a new nation in the high and honorable hope that it might . . . show mankind the way to liberty."[72] The League, Wilson believed, was that way. "The stage is set, the destiny disclosed. . . . It was of this that we dreamed at our birth. America shall in truth show the way."[73] One could with equal facility quote Presidents Franklin Roosevelt, John Kennedy, and Ronald Reagan among others attesting to an American mission to advance the cause of liberty. Let it suffice, however, to find this theme in more recent expression.

After the terrorist attacks on September 11, 2001, President George W. Bush in a series of speeches set out the administration's position. He declared to Congress before the month's end that "in our grief and anger we have found our mission. . . . The advance of human freedom . . . now depends on us."[74] In later speeches, he asserted that "the advance of freedom . . . is the calling of our country" and America's "heritage."[75] This mission, he claimed, is of divine origin. To the UN General Assembly, he announced, "The outcome of the conflict [with Afghanistan] is certain: There is a current in history and it runs toward freedom. . . . We're confident, too, that history has an Author who fills time and eternity with His purpose."[76] The United States also pursues divine purposes in Iraq according to the president. "I sent," he said, "American troops to Iraq to make its people free, not to make them American."[77] He had earlier informed the U.S. Chamber of Commerce that "Liberty is both the plan of Heaven for humanity, and the best hope for progress here on Earth."[78] In making these speeches, President Bush sought to elicit support for his policies by invoking themes made familiar by repetition ever since the Puritans. There is no suggestion of manipulation here. Presidents and ordinary Americans have drunk from the same well of justification.

Before proceeding any further, several observations are in order. First, all of this begs the questions of whether or not American intervention abroad, although undertaken in the name of liberty, has in fact been intended to protect or extend liberty or has had the effect of protecting or extending liberty. These are questions beyond the scope of this essay. Second, the two principal views about how the United States ought to advance liberty in the world are not mutually exclusive. One could, without contradiction, subscribe to both views. Thus, it might be maintained, the United States ought to advance liberty by serving as an exemplar of liberty and to extend liberty to others by force of arms if necessary. Third, these two views do not coincide with the positions called *isolationism* and *internationalism*. Liberty—in the sense of national independence—does figure in the dispute between isolationists and internationalists. The central issue in that dispute, however, is national security. The isolationist maintains that national security is best protected by noninvolvement in world affairs—no alliances, neutrality between belligerents, and defense at the nation's borders. The internationalist, on the other hand, asserts that national security is best protected by involvement—alliance with like-minded nations, mutual defense, and defense at a distance. Intercontinental ballistic missiles and international terrorism have consigned isolationism to irrelevance, but in an earlier day its advocates had a powerful voice in American politics. Fourth, the two principal views about how the United States ought to advance liberty in the world do not coincide with *pacifism* and *militarism*. The pacifist insists that force must not be met with force. Even the proponent of the view that the United States ought to advance liberty *only* by serving as an exemplar and never by using force abroad could maintain as well that the United States might need to defend itself by force. There is more coincidence between militarism and the view that the United States ought to extend liberty to others by force if necessary. The militarist wants a strong military, and he who would extend liberty by force requires one. The militarist, however, does not specify the ends to be served by a strong military beyond national security, while the end of liberty is central to the other position.

If the two principal views about how the United States ought to advance liberty in the world are not contradictory and do not coincide with other positions known to have divided Americans, how have these views divided Americans? They have been invoked in disputes about the course that America ought to take in concrete circumstances and when the United States has gone to war. The government has always invoked the idea of defending or extending liberty abroad in justification of going to war but never has this idea been relied on exclusively or even primarily. Wilson in World War I and Roosevelt in World War II, for example, gave higher priority to national security. The younger President Bush too in expounding his reasons for going to war in Iraq seemed to give priority to national security: "I sent American troops to Iraq to defend our security." He then asserted, "I sent American troops to Iraq to make its people free."[79] On another occasion, he said, "We must stand up for our security, and for the permanent rights and hopes of mankind."[80]

The American critics of U.S. intervention abroad have often claimed that, in the particular circumstances existing at the time, liberty could not be advanced by force of arms, the costs of extending liberty in this way were too high, and the advance of liberty was not the government's real motivation. Critics of American intervention in Vietnam made all these claims. Many of these same critics, Martin Luther King, for example, also pointed to the United States as a country where liberty really was at stake and where its cause could be advanced and ought to be advanced so that America could be an exemplar.

Furthermore, while the two views about how the United States ought to advance liberty in the world are *in principle* not contradictory, they may well be contradictory *in practice*. A society, it has been said, cannot have both guns and butter. This is a shorthand way of saying that no society's resources, not even those of the United States, are unlimited. The advance of liberty both at home and abroad requires the expenditure of resources. (War is particularly profligate in the consumption of resources.) Therefore, the advance of liberty at home and the advance of liberty abroad are in competition.

CONCLUSION

Many differences distinguish the United States from other countries. It has had the most productive economy in the world for well over a century and, until recently, the highest standard of living (gross domestic product per capita). The United States has the longest-running democracy and the oldest written constitution. And Americans are more religious, more patriotic, and participate more in voluntary associations than the citizens of other industrialized nations. None of these differences, however, makes the United States exceptional—if by *exceptional*, we mean qualitatively different. With respect to the foregoing qualities, the United States is measured on the same scale as other countries.

The United States is distinguished as well by a history without feudalism and the deference and dependence that characterized it. The legacy of slavery, however, has been as enduring and influential in American life as the legacy of feudalism for Europeans and in some of the same ways. Certainly slavery and its fruits have burdened the struggle for equality in America fully as much as feudalism has burdened that struggle in Europe. The United States is distinguished also by a history without a significant socialist party. This made the United States exceptional among Western industrialized countries for much of the twentieth century. The consequences of socialism's failure in America are still being felt in the form of high rates of poverty, the most unequal distribution of income and wealth among industrialized nations, and great inequalities in health care and education. Nevertheless, the United States is no longer the outlier with respect to socialism—at least as socialism was understood early in the twentieth century. The European socialist parties have given up their revolutionary rhetoric altogether; they have largely abandoned the nationalization of industry as a policy for the transformation of capitalism; and, in general, they have adopted a less utopian, more pragmatic outlook. In sum, European socialist parties have now drawn closer to the Democratic Party.

Some of the differences mentioned above, as well as others, have been a source of considerable pride to many Americans. Americans are not, of course, the only people who have taken pleasure in the achievements of their countrymen and in the distinctive qualities of their country. Exceptionalism is not a belief confined to Americans.[81] Neither Americans nor others ought to be faulted for such feelings. No harm is worked when an American feels proud of the lunar landing, the sacrifice of U.S. servicemen for the liberation of Europe from the Nazis, the discoveries of Jonas Salk and Albert Sabin for the prevention of polio, or the creation of jazz. Harm may well be worked, however, when the distinctive qualities of one's country are thought to confer superiority. This harm may be nothing more reprehensible than arrogance. But much greater harm is possible. The magnitude of the potential harm depends on that to which a people feels entitled by virtue of its superiority. The likelihood of harm depends on the possession of power. So, when feelings of superiority, a large conception of entitlement, and national power come together, the danger that harm, great harm, may be done is enormous.

Few peoples, including Americans, seem to have avoided the move from "we are exceptional" to "we are superior." The universality of those feelings and that move suggests that the identity—the sense of selfhood—of many, perhaps most, persons is bound up with feelings about the nation. The *we* in "we are exceptional" and "we are superior" are we Americans or we Japanese or we French. Thus, an American who asks, Who am I? seeks an answer, to significant degree, in the response to the question, What is an American?

The answer given by the moral theories described above is that Americans are exceptional and that they have a mission. Are any of these theories true? Is it the case, as the religious theories contend, that God has made Americans a chosen people and charged them with a world-historical mission? The difficulties that stand in the way of answering this question are insurmountable. Those who purport to know God's will as the consequence of mystical experience or biblical interpretation rely on faith. But faith is not evidence amenable to public scrutiny.

The secular theory presents a problem in interpretation. If we understand that theory, when it speaks of a national mission, to say no more than that historical circumstances have created an opportunity for Americans to advance the cause of liberty, then in this respect the theory is true. Thus, at the time of the Founding, Americans were a people who, for the most part, spoke the same language, shared similar religious convictions, and were of the same ethnic background (save, of course, for their African slaves). It is relevant too that property was widely distributed among them and that no powerful neighbors resided on their borders. The absence of such favorable circumstances has often impeded the institution of stable government, let alone government protective of liberty, in other parts of the world. These were among the circumstances that made America unique at the time and that created the opportunity to advance the cause of liberty.

If we understand the secular theory to say that historical circumstances created an *obligation* to institute government protective of liberty, then we must continue our inquiries. Certainly there is nothing in the account above that might be said to create obligation. One of the ways, however, in which obligations are acquired is by consent.[82] You, let us say, agree voluntarily and knowingly with another to do or not to do something. You have thereby acquired an obligation to perform as you agreed. This recognition provides the needed clue. Another circumstance that existed at the time of the Founding did create obligation. Americans were a people who had declared themselves devoted to political and civil liberty. They had made such declarations for generations as members of their church congregations, as participants in town meetings, as members of Committees of Correspondence, and in many other associations. They had already given consent to governments designed to protect liberty. These statements require qualification. Only some Americans had made such declarations, and certainly the consent given by many to their colonial and confederation governments was tacit, that is, inferred from their actions—principally their obedience and their participation in political life. Some Americans were more bound than others by their commitments. The politically active were more bound than the man-in-the-street, because they had more voluntarily and more knowingly (more willfully) committed themselves to one another. We can see the commitment at its strongest in the signers of the Declaration of Independence who "pledge[d] to each other our lives, our fortunes, and our sacred honor." As a consequence (bearing in mind the above qualification), Americans did have an obligation—to one another. In this sense, it is true that historical circumstances had created an obligation to institute in America government that protected liberty. This understanding implies nothing, of course, about any obligation that Americans might have to promote liberty abroad by example or by intervention. And, although succeeding generations are not bound by their predecessors, Americans have continued to declare their commitment to liberty down to the present day. Thus, the myth of a national mission has expressed American aspirations, and at the same time it has obscured the constraints on liberty for many Americans.

CHAPTER 7

THE MARKET

Two remarkable works appeared in 1776: America's Declaration of Independence and Adam Smith's *Wealth of Nations*.[1] These works marked the coming of age of the modern era. The Declaration set out truths that had become, Jefferson said, "self-evident": "All men are created equal"; "they are endowed by their Creator with certain inalienable rights"; and governments derive "their just powers from the consent of the governed." Smith was no less forthright in his advocacy of what he called "the obvious and simple system of natural liberty" and which we know as *capitalism* or the *market*. For him, if economic preferences and restraints were removed, then "every man, as long as he does not violate the laws of justice" could be left "perfectly free to pursue his own interest his own way."[2] Taken together, the Declaration and the *Wealth of Nations* sought to lift from the shoulders of the individual the yoke of crown, church, guild, and manor. These feudal institutions ought to be replaced by democratic government and the market. It is the latter of these—the market—that will occupy our attention in this chapter. What is the market? How did it come to be? How does it work? What are its consequences? What recommends it?

THE MARKET DEFINED

The market is a social system that coordinates the production and distribution of goods and services by means of transactions (buying and selling) into which the parties enter to voluntarily exchange property.[3] This definition requires some elaboration. The market is not a place, even though many market transactions occur face-to-face in a particular location—at the neighborhood grocery store, for example. Other market transactions, including many retail purchases, are carried out electronically or by telephone. The financial market does most of its business in this way, that is, at a distance. The market is better understood as a web in which the activities of many are coordinated in such a way that many human wants are satisfied.[4]

The *parties* to market transactions may be individuals or groups of individuals organized as the state, a corporation, an agricultural co-op, a church, or any other kind of association. As this list of possible participants suggests, an economy need not be populated mainly by enterprises privately owned to qualify as a market system.[5] As long as prices and the allocation of resources are left largely to the market, a market system exists. We shall be concerned in this chapter, however, with the so-called *free enterprise* or *capitalist* system, that is, a market system in which privately owned enterprises are the principal producers of goods and services. The transactions into which these parties enter must not be compelled; there must be no legal or physical compulsion to buy or sell. If, for example, the state conscripts you into the armed forces, the market is no longer doing the coordinating. You as a draftee did not sell your labor in the market. *Production* refers not only to manufacturing but also to any "bringing forth" and is intended to include such goods and services as canned pineapples, automobiles, research labs, musical performances, physical therapy, and the installation of hot water heaters. *Distribution* refers to the shares accorded to the claimants (that's all of us) to society's product—the goods and services produced. For most of us, these shares are distributed in the form of wages or salary. Profits (interest and dividends) and rent are the other forms that distributions may take. Finally, the state may attempt to exclude some things from the market— heroin, cockfighting, and the products of child labor, for example—but the market is open to anything that can be bought and sold. And anything can be bought and sold that is scarce in the sense that demand exceeds supply, and the seller can withhold it if the buyer will not meet the seller's price. The specification above of the meaning of the several terms in the definition of the market gives no attention to "buying and selling." These activities lie at the heart of the market system. Their significance is so great, however, that I postpone any consideration of them until they can be dealt with at greater length later in the chapter.

The market is a response to the problem of human survival and flourishing in a world that has often yielded its bounty only reluctantly.[6] The market is one of the three principal ways that humans have contrived to respond to this problem. (Custom and command are the others; they are described below.) Scarcity, then, requires society to provide some organization by which its members can be fed, clothed, and housed and in which its members can develop the intellectual, aesthetic, and moral capacities characteristic of human beings. In the performance of the latter function, families and churches, schools and professional associations, clubs and artistic groups, and the state figure prominently. But these groups too are participants in economic life and are significantly affected by it. Society must also organize in response to the human tendency to multiply needs endlessly. It is not enough that one have food on the table, a roof over one's head, and clothes on one's back. Contemporary Americans, for example, also demand cable connection to the Internet, single-family housing in the suburbs, an SUV in the garage, higher education, and vacations in exotic places. It is the American dream.

ALTERNATIVES TO THE MARKET

For much of history, custom and command have provided the necessary organization of human activity for the production and distribution of goods and services.[7] The market system made its first appearance only in the last few centuries. There have long been marketplaces of course. Ancient texts make frequent mention of the use of money, of trade, and of buying and selling. These activities, however, engaged relatively few people and were themselves subjected to the restraints of custom and command. The marketplaces of medieval England and France, biblical Israel, ancient Greece, and Puritan Massachusetts scarcely touched the lives of their inhabitants. It was not the marketplace that fed, clothed, and housed most medieval Englishmen and Frenchmen, Israelites, ancient Greeks, or Bay Colony Puritans.

Instead, most people obtained the necessaries of life by following the well-worn paths marked out by custom. In the largely agrarian societies of the pre-industrial past, sons followed their fathers into the fields to learn how to plant, irrigate, and harvest. Others learned how to care for livestock or how to fish as their fathers and their fathers before them had. Younger males also bore responsibility for the community's defense (and expansion). Still others became political, military, or religious leaders. As societies became sufficiently wealthy, a more elaborate division of labor occurred. Some became miners, potters, or metalworkers, for example. Custom almost everywhere consigned women to the household, where the fire had to be tended; food prepared; clothes made, cleaned, and repaired; and children cared for. Mothers taught daughters how to dry, grind, and preserve foodstuffs and to spin and weave. Production was very inefficient, and, therefore, almost all human effort had to be devoted to the production of necessaries.

More particularly, agriculture produced little more than was required by the peasant to maintain himself and his family. Typically, a landlord (some political, military, or religious leader) would appropriate most, if not all, of that excess. Thus, not only did custom assign people to the jobs that needed doing, it also distributed the product of society's labors. Disproportionate shares went to political, military, and religious leaders, and women were slighted in favor of men.

Superimposed on the customary life of premodern societies, a system of command also organized society. Political, military, and religious leaders emerge even in primitive societies; they have been a characteristic feature of human societies throughout history. Their rule usually supported custom. This is not surprising as custom was the source of their authority. In consequence, long-standing ways of production and distribution were perpetuated. When rulers were able to acquire sufficient power and legitimacy to rule over large numbers of people, they could bring about change. By commanding taxes and conscripting labor, rulers could undertake projects well beyond the capacity of any household. In antiquity, exactions made from the peasantry and the conscription of labor—slave labor—permitted the Athenians to build temples, the pharaohs their pyramids, and the Romans aqueducts and roads. In these ancient societies, slaves made up a large fraction of the labor force. Perhaps as much as a third of the population of Periclean Athens and of Republican Rome was slave.[8] On the backs of slaves and others in some form of involuntary servitude the cities of the ancient world were erected. Out of the cities came the art, architecture, and philosophy that make up so much of the legacy of that period. At the time, the dramas of Sophocles, the statues of Phidias, and the teachings of Aristotle delighted their audiences, but those audiences were urban and not rural. The city's production of art and literature did nothing to relieve the tedium and harshness of rural life. And certainly the city produced next to nothing to increase the production of the necessaries of life.[9]

The fall of Rome in 410 AD brought great institutional change. The government of Rome had knit together the peoples of the Empire with a common language, law, and currency. The proconsuls, supported by the swords and spears of the legions, kept the peace internally and provided protection against marauding bands at the borders until the fall of Rome brought political chaos and vulnerability to attack. So insecure did life become that people turned for safety and sustenance to local organization. (In ensuing centuries the spread of Christianity established the sole bond among the peoples of the West.) This local organization—the manorial estate—was rural. The cities of the vanquished Roman Empire went into sharp decline. They depended on trade and movement of goods from the country. The health of their inhabitants required clean water and sewage systems. Provision of these things could no longer be sustained in the chaos of the times.

The manor long organized much of medieval life. Custom and command defined relations among its members and their relation to the land. The manor included a large tract of land ranging in size from a few hundred to thousands of acres. A lord who might be a knight or church official controlled the land. He (it was always a he) served as administrator, judge, and military leader. To him all other members owed obedience and labor. He provided them with a measure of physical security, food from his storehouses in hard times, and the use (for a fee) of his mills, ovens, and draft animals. The land and its inhabitants were not devoted to production for sale. They supported, first, a military order and, second, a church. This was the core of feudalism.

The land was not for sale. Two widespread practices kept estates intact and warriors at their head: entail and primogeniture. Entail confined transmission of an estate to a single family, and primogeniture restricted inheritance to the eldest son. The lord, then, was tied to the land. Serfs planted and harvested the food and fiber, hewed the wood, and drew the water. They occupied the lowest rung in the feudal hierarchy and made up the great bulk of the population. A serf could not leave his plot to take up another within the same manor or move to another manor without permission of his lord and only then on payment of a fee. He too was tied to the land. He might owe from three to five days' labor a week to the lord. The remainder of the week could be devoted to his own plot. From its yield he needed to feed his family and make in-kind payments to the lord. The serf's labor was not for sale.

The revival of the cities after many centuries of decline provided a home for another characteristic institution of the time—the guild. The guilds controlled what there was of manufacturing in the Middle Ages and produced much of what was for sale. They organized the trades and professions whose specialized goods and services could not be had at the manor: armorers, hatmakers, wheelwrights, and so on. Each guild was composed of the masters of a particular trade or profession and established to regulate not only the pursuit of that trade or profession but also much else in the lives of its members: their dress and conduct, for example. Under the authority of the masters, journeymen and apprentices learned on the job. The guild regulated the wages that could be paid journeymen, the number and length of apprenticeships, the conditions of work, the process of production, and the quality and price of goods and services. The guild, then, suppressed competition and any acquisitive urges that might arise among its members. The end for the guilds was not profits but preservation of a way of life.

Custom and command continued everywhere down to the eighteenth century as the principal systems for the production and distribution of goods and services. Markets existed, but they touched the lives of relatively few. There was little movement from job to job or place to place. The household was the primary economic unit—it was within its bounds that many of a family's needs were met, if they were met at all. Agriculture was the principal occupation. This is not to deny the occurrence of change or the variety of customs and laws manifest in the Western societies of the pre-industrial past. It is to emphasize the continuity in the underlying structure of society.

OBSERVATIONS ON CUSTOM AND COMMAND

Before we leave this description of the preindustrial past in which the systems of custom and command predominated, several observations can be made. First, both the custom and command systems were well-known to the Bible as were the vigorous marketplaces of Israel and beyond. The Bible does not neglect to speak about many aspects of them all. Two matters are of particular interest here because they bear on the conditions for a market system, namely, slavery and the charging of interest. The King James Version, unlike some others, refers variously to *bondmen, servants, maids, handmaids,* and *menservants* among other locutions.[10] By any other name, they were still slaves.[11] The Bible places the origins of slavery in Noah's curse on Canaan for an act of Canaan's father. Ham had seen Noah naked in his tent. All the progeny of Ham were therefore to be enslaved.[12] There is controversy over whether or not the Bible condones slavery. It nowhere specifically condemns the practice. The Old Testament lays down many regulations concerning the buying, selling, and treatment of slaves.[13] The New Testament too betrays an acceptance of slavery. Whether that is a resigned acceptance or not is unclear. Slaves are repeatedly admonished to obey their masters, not simply out of fear but out of love for their masters and love of God.[14] Furthermore, Christ does not seize on the opportunity presented by the centurion to condemn slavery. The centurion had come to Christ to ask that he heal his sick slave. Jesus healed the slave, and he praised the centurion for his faith.[15] Now, putting aside any moral consideration, slavery is incompatible with the market. Slavery is not a voluntary exchange. And, unless labor is legally free to go where the returns are greatest, the market is not allocating to its most efficient use.

The Bible's prohibition on the charging of interest also imposed a formidable barrier to market transactions. In a handful of instances, the Old Testament condemns the lending of money or goods at interest.[16] The typical borrower, we are to understand, is poor. Who else would borrow except the unfortunate? Deuteronomy distinguishes brothers from foreigners. While a fellow Jew may not be charged interest, a foreigner may be.[17] The New Testament is silent on the whole subject. Over many centuries, the Old Testament provisions were understood by the Catholic Church to prohibit the charging of interest. This understanding would prevail until the sixteenth century and the Reformation. Civil law generally followed religious teaching. The significance of the prohibition on interest is great. Without interest, there can be no capital market. Without interest, little capital will be put at risk to expand or innovate.

Beyond these matters, the Bible, and more particularly the New Testament, encourages an attitude toward life that is remote from that the market fosters. The market is very much of this world. Even the faithful, of course, while they live out an earthly existence require food, clothing, and shelter. The market makes these things and much else available. From the biblical point of view, it is no sin to possess more than the necessaries. And, for its part, the market is indifferent to the beliefs of its participants. The only quality necessary for participation is possession of something to exchange. In principle, then, there is no conflict between participation in the market and living by faith. The Bible, however, clearly expects that in practice fallen men and women will have great difficulty in keeping their priorities straight.[18] Their first concern should be salvation. If they want to be rich (to get ahead, to keep up with the Joneses, to realize the American dream), they may forget the condition of their souls. One who carefully weighs the costs and benefits of proposed actions, who seeks the best price, who closely calculates profit and loss, and who seeks to maximize utility—all qualities that the market rewards—has little time for contemplation of the life eternal. "They that will be rich fall into temptation and a snare, and into many foolish and hurtful lusts."[19] Most will succumb to the siren call of money and, consequently, "it is easier for a camel to go through the eye of a needle, than for a rich man to enter into the kingdom of God."[20]

Second, my emphasis in this description of the premodern economy has been on the cooperation that enabled people to produce at least subsistence for most (interrupted by the occasional famine) and enough more for a relatively few to cultivate the arts, devise codes of law, explore the mysteries of life, and enjoy whatever luxury was available. One should not infer that this cooperation was always willing or that all were satisfied with their allotted portion of the social product. It may never have occurred to most that there might be another way to allocate jobs and to divide the product of their labors. Nevertheless, desperation and perceived injustice were common enough to spark recurrent slave and peasant uprisings in antiquity and in the Middle Ages. And, among the favored, the ambitious sought to unseat the current holders of political, military, and religious power. Custom and command, then, were not always successful in securing cooperation.

Third, despite the long pedigrees of custom and command, both have significant flaws. Custom stands in the way of change—change in the tools, materials, and techniques that might (and many did) increase productivity. Custom also assigns people, generation after generation, to the same jobs whether they have a talent for them or interest in them or not. And custom allots portions of the social product to its producers without much regard to the effort expended, the risks run, or the skill required by those who work at a particular occupation.

Command has problems of its own. Unlike custom, command does not necessarily resist change. Indeed, as we have seen, rulers have brought about change that increased productivity and general well-being. But, however necessary command may be in realizing some worthwhile ends, many people do not like to be told what to do. Therefore, rulers must expend precious resources to secure obedience—resources that might be used to feed, clothe, and house people. Furthermore, under the dictatorships of the ancient and medieval periods (and of modern times as well), rulers commanded that people work to realize purposes they probably did not share. The production and distribution of goods and services by command reflects, after all, the rulers' priorities about how the resources of society ought to be allocated and how the social product ought to be distributed. The advent of democratic government has increased the coincidence between the rulers' priorities and those of the ruled. It has not eliminated, although it has mitigated, the problem of obedience.

Fourth, as Karl Marx, the nineteenth-century social thinker, points out, custom and command distinguished among jobs in this way:

head—hand
city—country
male—female
rulers—ruled

These distinctions, Marx maintains, persist under a market system as well, but they appeared so obviously in ancient and medieval times that I introduce the idea here. It is these distinctions that Marx calls the *division of labor*.[21] He does not deny that division of labor has another meaning. Adam Smith, for example, adopts the more conventional meaning in his famous description of the making of pins: one person draws out the steel, another cuts it, another attaches the head, and so on.[22] Marx also does not deny the significance that Smith claims for division of labor as Smith understands it, namely, it vastly increases productivity. Nevertheless, for Marx, writing in 1845–46, we miss seeing the forest for the trees if we think that the division of labor involves nothing more than the assignment of people to different tasks.

Those who worked with their heads gave orders to those who worked with their hands. Those who worked in the city gave orders to those who worked in the country and so on. Thus, those on the left side of the columns above were superiors and those on the right inferiors. There was, of course, overlap among the groups on each side of the divide. More is at issue than who gets to give the orders. Those on the left were accorded higher status and received greater material rewards. Furthermore, the assignment of this person rather than that person to a particular job was often made irrespective of the talent or interest of that person in the job. Finally, in the course of a person's life, there was neither variety in the jobs done nor time to pursue avocations.

Smith, the market's great advocate, agrees with much of this analysis of the social bases for division of labor *in a market system*. He also agrees with Marx on the effects of division of labor at least with respect to the "far greater part of those who live by labour, that is, of the great body of the people." To quote Smith:

> The understandings of the greater part of men are necessarily formed by their ordinary employments. The man whose whole life is spent in performing a few simple operations . . . has no occasion to exert his understanding. . . . The torpor of his mind renders him, not only incapable of relishing or bearing a part in any rational conversation, but of conceiving any generous, noble, or tender sentiment. . . . Of the great and extensive interests of his country he is altogether incapable of judging; and . . . he is incapable of defending his country in war.[23]

Both Smith and Marx regard these effects as harmful. As a remedy, Smith proposes that government encourage a multiplicity of religious sects and provide elementary education for all. Marx believes that a much more radical change will be necessary—nothing less than the institution of a new social order. At the time, however, communist society was nothing more than a sketchy blueprint in Marx's mind. The new social order of the eighteenth and nineteenth centuries was the market system. It is to its emergence that the following section is devoted.

THE RISE OF THE MARKET

How did the market come to displace custom and command as the predominant system for the production and distribution of goods and services? To answer this question, it will be helpful to identify the conditions for the existence of the market.[24] First, people must be free to dispose of themselves as they see fit. More particularly, short of working force or fraud on others, people must be free of legal restraints on using their time and energy in their own way. Neither slave nor serf enjoyed this kind of personal freedom. To put this another way, they were not free to sell their labor. Second, people must be able to sell, use, and deny to others the use of desired things. The United States and other Western societies have accorded the several facets of this capacity the status of property rights. Such desired things must include land, tools, buildings, bank accounts, stocks and bonds that are often used to produce income as well as articles of (typically) personal consumption like a house, car, and clothing. Under feudalism, land was not for sale, and property could not be lent at interest. Third, the only legal way, aside from gifts, to acquire desired goods and services is by buying them, that is, by offering something acceptable to the seller in exchange. In antiquity and in the Middle Ages, the nobility and clergy by custom and law appropriated what they wanted from the lower orders. Fourth, money must become the medium of exchange. Money eliminates the need for a buyer to find a seller willing to accept what he has on offer. Sellers are quite willing to accept money, which can then be exchanged for what the seller wants. Furthermore, money (more precisely, the desire to acquire it) motivates people to forsake much production for household use and, instead, to produce what buyers want. These are necessary conditions for the existence of the market. Without change, however, in the attitude of many toward the making of money and, more generally, toward earthly life, the market would never have transformed society.

Calvinism contributed to change in the attitude of Europeans toward earthly affairs.[25] This was not because the Calvinist teaching was more secular or less committed to the salvation of souls than Roman Catholicism. If anything, Calvin (1509–1564) was less willing to accommodate the ways of this world. He rejected the medieval idea of the two standards, which prescribed one way of conduct for those who had taken up the monastic life and another for everyone else. All, according to Calvin, are equally bound to the same counsels of perfection if they are to follow Christ's way.[26] Nevertheless, Calvinism figures in the explanation for the emergence of the market system in two ways.

First, Calvin taught that humankind is subject to two callings from God. All are called to salvation. This calling is universal and makes no distinction among persons—all are equally sinners and equally in need of God's forgiveness in order to join his eternal kingdom. In this world, human beings are not equal but arrayed in different ranks and orders. They are called to different vocations: husband, father, wife, farmer, merchant, soldier, magistrate, and so on. The discharge of the duties of one's vocations is to serve God by serving one's fellows.[27] There is God's work to be done in this world, his love to be made manifest—not only by propagation of the Word but by faithful performance of the duties of one's vocations.[28] Many found encouragement in this teaching to work hard and to be thrifty and prudent. Calvin denied that by such self-denial one could earn salvation. It is by faith alone that salvation could be gained, and faith is a gift of God's grace.[29] Nevertheless, good works are a manifestation of faith and thus might confirm to oneself and others that one was among the elect.

Second, Calvin revised the long-standing prohibition on usury, the lending of property at interest. Like other Christian theologians, he distinguished between those rules in Scripture that are eternal and those that are time-bound. Many of the social and economic rules of the Old Testament he held to be time-bound, overturned by Christ's teaching and example. The prohibition on usury is among those obsolete rules. God, according to Calvin, did not forbid usury altogether. In order that Jews and foreigners be on an equal footing, he permitted the Jews to charge interest of foreigners. Calvin claimed the same right for Christians so that they might be on an equal footing with Jews. He did leave in place the principles of charity and equity as limits on the charging of interest.[30] Why ought not Christians be under the same prohibition as Jews were with respect to one another? Because, Calvin answered, Christ's calling is universal. No distinction is to be made between brother and foreigner. Calvin thereby preserves the idea of Christian universality, but, it would seem, at the expense of Christian brotherhood—everyone is to be treated as a foreigner.[31]

Historical explanation is complex, and any satisfactory explanation of the rise of the market system must recognize the relevance of many forces. It is worth noting that many of these forces were at work before the Reformation and Calvin in particular. In addition, then, to Calvinism, the following deserve mention: The growth of the cities encouraged the production of foodstuffs and fibers for sale rather than home consumption. Innovations in agriculture like three-field rotation of crops, the use of fertilizers, and better equipment (horseshoes, horse harness, and the scythe) realized efficiencies that permitted landlords to release (dispossess) some of their tenants.[32] In England, the development of the wool trade led to the enclosure of once common fields and the displacement of millions who had lived and worked on them. A similar event played out in northern Germany. In this way a more mobile labor force available for hire was created. The exposure of the Crusaders to the riches of the East and the increased availability of exotic goods fueled acquisitive desires. The voyages of exploration and colonization opened up new markets and brought increased wealth. The invention of firearms destroyed the dominance of the armored knight on the battlefield. Increased literacy—encouraged by Protestantism—and the invention of the printing press destroyed the dominance of the clergy over knowledge. Both these developments encouraged people outside the nobility to aspire to a better life on this earth. This list is not comprehensive; it provides some notion of the range of forces that produced the market. But, before we leave this matter, one other circumstance must be identified.

The development of centralized government promoted the transformation to a market system. In their struggles with the feudal nobility for power and authority, the monarchies forged alliances with the growing merchant class. The merchants exacted interest on their loans to monarchs and recognition of their rights to freedom and property. Furthermore, as the monarchies acquired more power and authority, they were able to better protect property rights. They also established uniform currencies and standards of measure. They funded scientific and technological research and voyages of discovery. They constructed the infrastructure of roads, canals, and bridges over which trade could occur. They eliminated local restrictions on trade. All this the monarchies did—not to create a self-regulating market but to increase national wealth. They believed that this end could best be realized by state intervention in the economy, a policy known as *mercantilism*.[33] So, while local restrictions were lifted, national regulations were imposed. Instead of competition, the state subsidized favored industries. Instead of free trade, the state imposed tariffs.[34] Nevertheless, as a consequence of state action, and the other forces identified above, the market emerged.

The market first became well entrenched in Britain during the eighteenth century. Over the first half of the nineteenth century, North America and the rest of Europe followed in Britain's footsteps. The transformation was not sudden; the market system was centuries in the making as indicated by the causal factors identified above. Furthermore, the penetration of the market into society varied from country to country. Jean-Baptiste Colbert (1619–1683), finance minister to Louis XIV, inquired of a merchant, How may we help you? The merchant responded, *"Nous laissez-faire,"* that is, leave us alone.[35] The self-regulating market thereby acquired a slogan. Ever since, advocates of less governmental restraint have held up *laissez-faire* as the ideal. Colbert rejected such a policy for his country. Market participants, both consumers and producers, government officials, and most citizens everywhere, have done the same—although for different reasons. Even in the heyday of the relatively unrestrained market in the United States—the latter part of the nineteenth century—state governments imposed significant controls on the market,[36] and the national government regulated the market by means of the tariff. It also promoted economic development by subsidizing such industries as the railroads, shipbuilding, and agriculture. The influence of custom on economic life during this period can be seen in the racial and gender discrimination practiced in hiring, promotion, and wages. Nowhere, then, did the market displace entirely the reign of custom and command in the coordination of social life. But, it must be added, government and society conceded significant control to the vast organizations known as corporations that began to emerge in the latter part of the nineteenth century.

The rise of the market system saw the creation of complex networks among the participants. These networks include people who provide transport services, supply materials and advice (financial and legal) to producers, or erect buildings for the storage of goods or for retail sales, to name a few. Those who assemble the land, capital, and labor to do such things and to make goods and services available to buyers are called *entrepreneurs*. Their decisions can have significant consequences for many. Among these decisions are the following: the geographic location of the enterprise; the character of the product; hiring and promotion practices; production effort (how many units to produce); level of investment in research and development, plant, labor, advertising, and political activity; price-cost relations (profit); and returns to stockholders. Despite the significant consequences these decisions have for others, those who make them are largely unaccountable to anyone but themselves. The chief executive officers and their boards sit at the top of hierarchical organizations. The organizations they run are command systems. Neither their stockholders nor their employees, let alone the general citizenry, have any real say in the making of many of these decisions.

In competitive markets, the corporations must take into account, of course, the preferences of customers in making decisions about the character of the product, production effort, and price.

As the market expanded and technological innovation occurred, entrepreneurs transformed their enterprises into corporations.[37] These organizations realize economies of scale and confer some control over the volatility of the market.[38] In the United States, they acquired the rights of persons under the 14th Amendment.[39] Many corporations have grown larger than some nation-states. In a 2002 study, corporations were found to constitute fifty-two of the world's one hundred largest economic entities. That study ranked countries by gross domestic product (GDP) and corporations by sales. Wal-Mart ranked nineteenth—just behind Belgium and ahead of Sweden. General Motors, Exxon-Mobil, Ford, and General Electric followed close behind.[40] The individual employee or consumer is always overmatched in any transaction with these giants. And the general citizenry is often overmatched by them in the making of public policy.

The political power that such size confers is great. It has enabled corporations to secure protection from government in the form of tariffs; tax exemptions—those accorded to mining companies that mine on federal lands, for example; subsidies—those given to the oil, gas, and lumber industries, for example; funds for research and development—support for the pharmaceutical companies; loans, loan guarantees, and insurance—the Overseas Private Investment Cooperation and the Export-Import Bank, both government agencies, support American businesses in the international market. The value of these several forms of aid totals billions of dollars annually.[41] Political power has also permitted the corporations to secure from government laws that discourage trade union recruitment and depress trade union power (Taft-Hartley, right-to-work laws) and to block the passage of environmental legislation (the application of CAFE standards to SUVs and trucks) or modify its implementation (relaxation of requirements to install air pollution devices on coal-fired power plants).

In sum, the economic system that came to predominate in the twentieth century was not the self-regulating market of economic theory. Throughout the West government remained, and remains today, a significant participant in economic life. Only the corporations eclipse its role in ordering the economy. The United States and other Western countries have what are known as *mixed economies*—a mix of market and command systems. Although custom goes largely unacknowledged in this characterization, it too continues to have an effect on how people go about producing and distributing goods and services. In rejecting the self-regulating market, what have the Western democracies given up?

THE THEORY OF THE SELF-REGULATING MARKET

Adam Smith first gave expression to the theory of the self-regulating market. Its latter-day advocates under the banner of laissez-faire have sought to reduce the governmental presence in economic life so that the market's promise might be more fully realized. In describing this theory, I shall elaborate the meaning of *buying* and *selling* in the definition of the market given at the outset. On this theory, human beings act out of self-interest. As consumers, they search for the highest quality in what they want at the lowest price. As producers, they seek the highest price for what they have on offer whether it is a day's labor or some product, an automobile, say. Because all are similarly motivated, interests conflict and people compete for buyers and for jobs. In what must be the most famous passage in all economics literature, Smith observed, "It is not from the benevolence of the butcher, the brewer, or the baker, that we expect our dinner, but from their regard to their own interest."[42]

The butcher, the brewer, and the baker, of course, hand over their wares only for a price. What is to prevent them from charging exorbitant prices? The butcher, the brewer, and the baker around the corner. If a seller charges more for his wares of the same quality than his competitors or if he pays less than others to his workers, he will soon find that he has no buyers or workers. To quote Smith again, "By directing [his] . . . industry in such a manner as its produce may be of greatest value, he intends only his own gain, and he is in this, as in many other cases, led by an invisible hand to promote an end which was no part of his intention."[43] That end is the allocation of people to jobs and the distribution of the social product to its many claimants. It is self-interest restrained by competition that induces people to take up the jobs that society needs to be done. It is self-interest restrained by competition that induces people to produce what others want and are able to pay for.

Prices are set as a result of many transactions.[44] These transactions reflect the decisions that people make about what they value and the talents and assets that they have available to exchange. The result of these transactions is to bring supply and demand into balance. In this sense, the resources of society are efficiently allocated. Those with the greater talents and assets are obviously much advantaged in these transactions.

The process of establishing prices is dynamic. Technological innovation can bring new products to the market or reduce the costs of production.

People's preferences and assets also change. In both these cases, the market responds by adjusting prices and, thereby, reallocating land (and other natural resources), labor, and capital (including buildings, tools, and transport facilities) to new uses. For example, technological innovation worked reduction in the price of computers. People saw possibilities for the use of computers in their businesses and homes. This spurred demand for computers and, consequently, the allocation of more land, labor, and capital to the production of computers. The market is self-regulating in this way.

If the price mechanism is to work as just described, then perfect competitiveness must characterize the market. This requires that several conditions must be met. First, no one producer or a few producers must be able to significantly affect prices or demand. Second, labor and capital must be completely mobile. Third, there must be no significant barriers to entrance into the market. And, fourth, consumers must be informed and rational, and their preferences must be fairly stable. None of these conditions is very well satisfied in the real world. Where they are sufficiently satisfied, often by government intervention, most of the market's promise can be realized. Before we examine the benefits claimed for the market, let us first take notice of the forces that prevent the full realization of the self-regulating market.

The proponents of laissez-faire single out government as the chief culprit. In their view, government intervention occurs in response to misplaced demands for justice made by people acting as citizens. Collective bargaining, the minimum wage, and the redistributive policies of the welfare state are often cited as instances of this kind. These policies certainly do constrain the market. Fully as significant, however, are the actions of people acting as producers and consumers, that is, as market participants. Producers want protection from foreign competition and environmentalists, subsidies for favored goods, and support for research and development. They have often been able to secure these wants from government. On the consumer side, much government regulation has sought to reduce information asymmetries: producers know a great deal about their products; consumers often know very little. Government brings the real market closer to the theoretical market by creating the opportunity for consumers to be better informed. Consumers want fuller disclosure of the components of goods for sale. They want protection against adulterated foodstuffs and drugs, flammable fabrics, and automobile "lemons." They also want assurances that the physicians and attorneys they consult meet certain standards. Government has provided these assurances and those protections. It has done so as much in response to producers as consumers. Producers thereby acquire a kind of certificate of wholesomeness, safety, or competence. All of this is explicable within market theory itself. That theory teaches that human beings are self-interested, and the actions described above are the actions of self-interested men and women.

Within the market system lies another force acting against self-regulation: the division of labor. The division of labor increases productivity. Large enterprises can institute a more elaborate division of labor (and thereby lower costs) than a small business. Large enterprises drive small businesses out of business. The tendency in this process, then, is toward monopoly—the domination of an industry by one firm. Monopolistic power eliminates competition as a restraint on self-interest. Price is no longer determined by market competition but by the heads of enterprises. And the barriers to access to the market in monopolistic industries are high if not insurmountable. The development of the market in the United States saw the emergence of near-monopolies in many industries by the end of the nineteenth century.[45] It was not monopoly, however, that came to characterize the structure of American business but oligopoly—the domination of an industry by several firms. Economic historians have advanced various reasons for this development.[46] Among those reasons is the adoption of antitrust legislation.[47] Here too government intervention by promoting competition brings the real market closer to the theoretical market. To be sure, "closer" is not very close. Oligopolistic competition is far from Adam Smith's free-for-all.

Nor, in the real world, is labor nearly as mobile as market theory assumes.[48] Both labor and the buyers of labor want to reduce the uncertainties of unbridled competition. They enter into contracts with one another in order to do so. Neither employer nor employee under contract can respond immediately to price changes in the market. This reduces the importance of price in the hiring of labor. The effect is to delay the balancing of supply and demand in the labor market. The employee gains job security—at least for a while. The employer gains the assurance that he will have workers in the morning, that he can recoup investment in on-the-job training, and that he can expect greater commitment and effort from his employees. The continued influence of these forces—self-interest, the division of labor, and the desire to avoid the fluctuations of the market—will always prevent the full realization of the self-regulating market. Even though the real-world market falls short of the theoretical market in many respects, large claims are made for the market's superiority over custom and command. That superiority would be even more pronounced, according to some, were government intervention confined to protection against force and fraud.[49] Is it true that the market more efficiently uses available resources, better fosters growth, and confers more freedom than other ways of organizing the production and distribution of goods and services?

EFFICIENCY: TECHNOLOGICAL

Efficiency is an important test of any economic system. Resources are limited, and there are many to feed, cloth, and house. Across Africa, hunger and disease are the constant companions of most owing to a scarcity of food, medicine, potable water, and so on. Even in the United States with the most productive economy in the world, wants go unsatisfied. In part, this is a consequence of unequal distribution of the social product. Many Americans must forego meals and medical care because they cannot afford them. For even the wealthiest Americans, scarcity is a problem. Some suffer from Parkinson's, Alzheimer's, or other maladies for which there is no cure. Had the society devoted more resources to medical research perhaps a cure might have been found. Efficiency permits the greatest satisfaction of wants from the available resources.

There are two kinds of efficiency: technological and allocative. Technological efficiency permits more product to be obtained from a fixed amount of resources—more iron produced than before from the same amount of ore, more wheat from the same acreage, for example. In part, technological efficiency is realized by the introduction of new machinery or processes. The development of hybrid grains, fertilizers, and pesticides and the introduction of engine-driven planters and harvesters have brought huge increases in agricultural efficiency. The market clearly enjoys a great advantage over custom in this regard. Custom resists change to the long-established, familiar way of doing things.

It is not so clear that the market enjoys any such advantage over command systems. In the American case, the national government has long played a large role in research and development. Military considerations, although not only military considerations, have spurred much government involvement. The U.S. government provided money and expertise early in the nineteenth century to the development of interchangeable parts.[50] Later in that century, the Navy offered contracts to the steel companies to produce higher quality steel with which to armor its ships. The consequence was modernization of the steel industry.[51] During World War II, government agencies participated in the development and production of penicillin, the first antibiotic.[52] Government agencies also harnessed nuclear energy for both military and civilian uses. In the more recent past, the transistor, the computer, and the Internet were all developments financed in part by the government.[53] The national government through such agencies as the National Science Foundation and the National Institutes of Health finances today (and has for decades) much of the basic research in this country and a good deal of research that has commercial application like the extraction of ethanol from orange peels and the development of pharmaceuticals.[54]

Technological efficiency is also realized by the division of labor. One of the basic resources (factors of production) used in production is human labor (the others are land and capital). Despite the automation of many industrial processes, we are far from the day when production can be turned over entirely to machines. The division of labor remains as important as ever to the realization of technological efficiency. Therefore, it must not be abolished as Marx sometimes seems to suggest would happen under communism.[55] If the division of labor remains indispensable to technological efficiency, must its undesirable aspects as pointed out by Smith and Marx be accepted? Does the market perpetuate, or even exacerbate as Marx believed, the qualities of division of labor characteristic of antiquity and the Middle Ages? I shall take up the second of these questions first.

Recall Marx's charges against the division of labor: it creates superiors and inferiors; gives disproportionate rewards to those who work in the city, or are male, or are rulers; assigns jobs on the basis of irrelevant criteria and with little concern for the interests or talents of a person in the job. Finally, so this indictment runs, division of labor is corrosive of those qualities—intellectual, moral, and aesthetic—distinctive of human beings. Are these charges true? In some particulars, yes; in others, no. In one particular, Marx's indictment requires qualification. In general, it remains true that those who work with their heads give orders to those who work with their hands. Furthermore, the former usually receive greater material rewards and higher status than manual workers. And manual work is often more routine, less intellectually challenging, and performed under more difficult or dangerous conditions than intellectual work. Nevertheless, exceptions come readily to mind. Some skilled manual workers like electricians, plumbers, and autoworkers can command greater incomes than some white-collar workers, teachers, and artists, for example, who appear on the "head" side of Marx's taxonomy.

While the division of labor in a market system creates superiors and inferiors, the relationships no longer fall along quite the same lines as Marx suggested. No longer is the country subordinate to the city and the city parasitic on the country, only taking and giving nothing in return. It was the market that brought this about. The city continues, of course, to be dependent on the country for the provision of foodstuffs and all the other produce of the primary industries. The city now must pay for them. Furthermore, the city supplies manufactured goods and many services to the country. Electricity, the automobile, and the Sears and Roebuck catalog—all products of the city—transformed rural life in the first half of the twentieth century, and it has been further transformed by television and the Internet in more recent decades. Marx's complaint about the "idiocy of rural life" has been misplaced for decades in the developed world.[56]

The market too changed the relationship between wealth and power. In antiquity and in the Middle Ages, wealth followed power. The rulers—political, military, and religious—were the powerful. They received wealth and status. In market societies, on the other hand, power follows wealth. The market promotes the formation of huge enterprises, the corporations, whose individual assets rival those of many contemporary nations. Those who command these assets, the chief executive officers, are legally among the ruled. In fact, however, they have great influence over rulers in the making of public policy, and the policies that they make for their corporations significantly affect the lives of their employees and the communities in which the corporation is located. And, of course, because corporate officers are personally wealthy, should they seek public office, their wealth confers a great advantage. Marx recognizes that the wealthy have power. They might even be said (Marx says so) to be among the rulers—as they are in important respects. Marx, however, fails to take notice of the change in the relationship between wealth and power brought about by the market.

The division of labor in a market system often allocates jobs on the basis of irrelevant criteria. No ethical principles inform the market except those that market participants bring to their transactions. Thus, as the American experience testifies, if employers hold racial and gender prejudices, then the market will exclude blacks and women from all but the least-skilled and lowest-paying jobs whatever their talents and interests may be.[57] More generally, the market is indifferent to the principle of equality of opportunity. The fact that some participants in the labor market have had little education and poor health care while others have been able to discover their interests and develop their talents is of no concern to the market. Marx, and Smith before him, saw this clearly.[58]

The division of labor in a market system gives disproportionate rewards to those who are male or are rulers. I include the corporate rulers among the class of rulers as Marx did. What ought to be the measure of reward?

The market provides a measure, and on that measure women are paid less than men for doing comparable work.[59] This gap has persisted ever since women entered the workforce in large numbers; today it runs about 20 percent. On that measure, too, corporate executives are paid substantially more than the average worker. This differential has grown steadily over the last four decades. In Colorado, the fifty top-paid corporate executives had a median compensation of $5.34 million in 2005. This was 131 times the average annual pay ($41,000) of all employed Coloradans. There was, by the way, one woman among the top fifty.[60] The CEOs (chief executive officers) at the nation's largest corporations receive 400 to 500 times the pay earned by the average worker.[61]

What other measures of reward might be used? Relevant considerations are effort expended, risks run, skills required, and responsibility borne. Does the CEO of a large American corporation expend much more effort than a high school biology teacher, a trash collector, or a lumberjack? Does the CEO run greater physical risks than a foundry worker, a coal miner, or a tuna fisherman? Does the CEO run greater personal financial risks than the small businessman opening up a new store or a farmer planting in the spring? On all these counts, the answer is either "no" or "not much more." The skills required of a CEO are less common than those of the average worker, but are those skills rarer than those of a gifted teacher, physician, or research biochemist? CEOs bear considerable responsibility, but is that responsibility much greater than that borne by an air-traffic controller, a federal judge, a state governor, or an army general—let alone the president of the United States to whom we give a measly $400,000 and the use of a nice house at a good address and a large airplane. It ought to be remembered too that pay is not the CEOs' only compensation. They are accorded high status, and they are able to exercise considerable power—rewards denied to most other workers. Even if we concede that CEOs deserve to be paid more than others on one or more of these measures, do they really deserve so much more? If the answer is "no," as I conclude it must be, then CEOs are disproportionately paid. I am not alone in this conviction. Adam Smith observes, "All for ourselves, and nothing for other people, seems, in every age of the world, to have been the vile maxim of the masters of mankind."[62]

Finally, Marx and Smith contend that the division of labor in a market system is corrosive of those qualities distinctive of human beings. Instead of fostering talents and gratifying interests, it makes people into machines—in two ways. The division of labor requires workers to perform the same small number of operations over and over again. Some jobs like gutting fish in a cannery or monitoring the conveyor belt in a bottling plant are far more repetitive than some others. Farming, serving as a policeman, or repairing automobiles offer more variety. Nevertheless, for all the labor-saving advances of the last two hundred years, repetition remains characteristic of many jobs. Marx and Smith believe that people need to learn new things, to experience variety and challenge, and to converse with their fellows, if they are to flourish as human beings. Many people do regard the job largely as an activity to make money—undertaken because one must in order to live one's real life the rest of the time. The job is not an activity in which one's interests are gratified and one's talents developed.[63]

The second way in which humans are made into machines is by a prolonged workweek. In the United States in 1850, the average workweek across all industries, agricultural and nonagricultural, was about seventy hours. For nonagricultural workers, the workweek was about sixty-six hours or eleven hours a day, six days a week.[64] A century earlier in England, the workweek for some was even longer.[65] A workweek of such long duration left little time for anything else. As noise, dirt, danger, and temperature extremes were among the other working conditions, people—men, women, and children—were simply used up to die an early death. It was the effects of long hours on women and children that first drew the attention of reform-minded legislators early in the twentieth century.

Must we accept the undesirable aspects of division of labor lest we lose the benefits it provides in technological efficiency? Clearly we do not need to accept those undesirable aspects. The workday for many can and has been reduced to eight hours. Racial and gender discrimination has been reduced in the work place by legislation. The hierarchical relations between labor and management have been altered in some industries by the institution of joint councils that discuss production problems and, in some countries, decide on a solution.[66] The disproportionate rewards allotted to corporate leaders have been reduced slightly by the progressive income tax and could be further reduced. It would not seem that efficiency has been much affected by the imposition of such nonmarket controls.[67] All the countries in which such controls have been adopted continue to grow economically. Would those economies have grown faster in the absence of such controls? Perhaps, but the gains would have been modest and at the expense of significant improvement in the lives of workers.

EFFICIENCY: ALLOCATIVE

Allocative efficiency is the allocation of society's resources to the production of goods and services in the quantities and of the quality wanted and at the prices consumers are willing to pay. Whose preferences are to prevail? Or, to put the question a little bit differently, whose values are to provide the criterion for allocative efficiency? If a government wants more tanks, and either through command or purchase secures their production, then from the government's point of view, society's resources have been more efficiently allocated. The government's values might or might not be shared by the society at-large. If individual consumers want more cell phones and by their purchases secure their production, then from the point of view of consumers, society's resources have been more efficiently allocated. You or I might not agree with the prevailing allocation as determined by our fellow consumers. In short, there is no absolute criterion. Any criterion of allocative efficiency is relative to some person or group. The allocation of society's resources to increased production of this good or that service has as a necessary consequence giving up the enjoyment of more of some other good or service, whoever decides. More cell phones, fewer bicycles or symphonic performances or pizzas. Every choice has a cost. Resources are limited.

In the theoretical market, prices permit the consumer (an individual, a church group, a corporation, or the government, for example) to determine the relative values of what is acquired and what is foregone. Thirty dollars for a sweater has a cost of lunch for two at a neighborhood café or half an hour's massage and so on. If prices are to perform this function, they must reflect all costs. In a real market system, like that of the United States, prices reflect costs only more or less. This is so in part because producers are often able to shift some costs from consumers to third parties (the economists' *externalities*). Producers pursue such a strategy because it enables them to set lower prices and thereby to attract more buyers. Thus the price of an automobile does not reflect the costs of air pollution borne by the general public. The price of electricity generated by coal-fired plants in the West does not reflect the costs of acid rain that must be borne by people in the East. The price of motorcycles does not reflect the costs of noise pollution that must be borne by the general public. Prices do not reflect the costs of health care as more and more employers abandon health care plans for their employees, past and present. These employers continue to maintain their machines—it is a cost of production. The gap between real costs and the costs reflected in prices reduces the allocative efficiency of real markets. But there are other more significant inefficiencies in market allocation.

The market allocates to many too little to eat, inadequate medical care, and uncomfortable, if not dangerous, housing. For the poor, market allocation is not efficient.[68] The market is not efficient for all the claimants to the social product because it responds only to effective demand—to cash. Another significant consequence of the market, then, is poverty for many. Indeed, the less constrained by welfare policy, the more people the market impoverishes. The United States, which has the most miserly welfare policies among Western developed nations, also has the highest percentage of poor.[69] To be sure, the poor of the developed nations are not the poor of the Third World. Adam Smith exaggerated only a bit (as of 1776) when he observed that, owing to increased productivity, the standard of living of "the very meanest person in a civilized country . . . exceeds that of many an African king, the absolute master of the lives and liberties of ten thousand naked savages."[70]

Times have changed. African kings today live like Donald Trump. Many of their subjects continue to live lives of the most desperate want. By the standard of the Third World, the poor in the economies of the developed world are relatively well-off. Nevertheless, poverty in the United States retains its bite. Meals skipped, chronic diseases untreated, and housing, cold in the winter and hot in the summer, are the lot of America's poor.[71] Furthermore, by the standards of the developed world, America's poor (and those of the other developed countries) are relatively deprived.[72] The magnitude of relative deprivation is revealed in table 7.1, which shows the distribution of income.

There has always been great inequality. It is increasing, and the beneficiaries are clustered at the very top. In 1998 "the 13,000 richest families in America had almost as much income as the 20 million poorest households; those 13,000 families had incomes 300 times that of average families."[73] Wealth (assets minus debts) is even more concentrated than income (see table 7.2).

The concentration of wealth today rivals that of the period before the Great Depression when the top 1 percent of households held 44.2 percent of all household wealth in 1924.[74] When the market rather than government distributes goods like education and health care—as it does in the United States to a significant degree—then those who have little income and wealth are unable to secure as much of them or as high in quality as they may need. Equal opportunity does not exist under such circumstances.

The market fails to allocate jobs to all who want or need them. For example, from 1960 to 2001 in the United States, millions who wanted and sought employment were out of work every year. In 2001 some 6.7 million constituting 4.8 percent of the American civilian labor force were unemployed.[75] Almost 33 percent of the unemployed were out of work for five weeks or

TABLE 7.1
HOUSEHOLD SHARES OF AGGREGATE INCOME BY FIFTHS
IN THE UNITED STATES: SELECT YEARS 1967–2001

Year	Share of Aggregate Income					
	Lowest Fifth	Second Fifth	Third Fifth	Fourth Fifth	Highest Fifth	Top 5 Percent
2001	3.5	8.7	14.6	23.0	50.1	22.4
1992	3.8	9.4	15.8	24.2	46.9	18.6
1980	4.3	10.3	16.9	24.9	43.7	15.8
1967	4.0	10.8	17.3	24.2	43.8	17.5

Source: U.S. Census Bureau, Housing and Household Economics Statistics Division, *Historical Income Tables—Income Equality* at www.census.gov/hhes/www/income/histinc/ie3.html.

more and 28 percent for fifteen weeks or more.[76] Another 4.6 million wanted a job in 2001 but for various reasons were not counted as part of the labor force.[77] In their attempt to find work, many had become so discouraged that they had stopped looking. Since almost all Americans must work to acquire an income (beyond the small minimums accorded some by welfare programs and excluding heirs to family fortunes), the loss of a job initiates a steady decline in standard of living. Unemployment also has a harmful effect on the mental health of the jobless.[78] The late Pope John Paul II

TABLE 7.2
DISTRIBUTION OF TOTAL HOUSEHOLD WEALTH IN
THE UNITED STATES BY HOUSEHOLDS, 2001

Percent of Households	Percent of Wealth Owned	Cumulative Percent
Top 1%	32.7	
Next 4%	25.0	57.7
Next 5%	12.1	69.8
Next 40%	27.4	97.2
Bottom 50%	2.8	100.0

Source: Arthur B. Kennickell, "A Rolling Tide: Changes in the Distribution of Wealth in the U.S., 1989–2001," 9, at www. federalreserve.gov/pubsfeds/2003/200324/20032 4/pap.pdf.

stated in a 1999 address, "Work is an essential element for everyone. It contributes to his personal growth because it is an integral part of his everyday life. . . . Work also ensures every individual a place in society, through the justifiable feeling of being useful to the human community and through the growth of fraternal relations; further more, it enables him to participate responsibly in the life of his country and to contribute to the work of creation."[79] In saying this, the pope was repeating a theme set out more fully in his encyclical *Laborem exercens*.[80] The response of Western governments to the problem has been unemployment benefits. This is a patch, and an ill-fitting one at that. In the United States, benefits typically run out after twenty-six weeks and provide only a third of one's former weekly wages. Furthermore, benefits do nothing to address the loss of identity and dignity. Government could become the employer of last resort as it did in the United States during the Great Depression.[81] The Works Progress Administration and the Civilian Conservation Corps put millions to work building roads and libraries, producing theatrical performances, and writing histories. There is certainly much that needs doing that the market neglects.

The market fails to allocate resources to what are known as *public goods*. These are goods that most people, in some cases virtually everyone in the society, want but whose enjoyment cannot be confined (or confined at acceptable cost) to those willing to pay for them. National defense, police protection, bridges and highways, and the education of the young are among those goods. This list could be much elaborated: highways free of roadside litter, flood control, and a host of public health measures like small pox vaccination and sewage disposal to name a few. Now, people do hire private security guards, but in the absence of a public force, the private guards would be overwhelmed. The use of at least some bridges and highways can be confined to those who pay a toll, but if all bridges and highways were tollways, commerce would be much slowed. And, yes, it is in employers' interest to have an educated workforce. It is not in the interest of any one employer to help pay for the general education of a nation's youth. Even the largest employer will hire only a tiny fraction of the workforce. The problem that arises in connection with public goods is the *free rider*. Some (the free riders) recognize that they can enjoy the benefits of, say, the lighting of streets at night without paying for it themselves as long as there are enough others willing to foot the bill. Cooperation cannot always be left to voluntary transaction. It must sometimes be secured by compulsion. Government, of course, does not rely on voluntary subscription to light the streets. It levies taxes to secure the necessary funds.

GROWTH

Some claim that the market fosters economic growth, and, more particularly, the market unconstrained by nonmarket controls like minimum wage laws, collective bargaining, and welfare policies best fosters growth. In evaluating this claim, we can ignore the question: Is growth desirable? This question, of course, arises only in the developed countries where minimum standards of living have long been exceeded. It is clear that in the process of increasing productivity tremendous wastes are created and natural resources exhausted. Global warming is only the most alarming and pervasive of the consequences. Growth exacts a direct toll on its producers as well. Increasing productivity often requires working longer days and more years, which leaves less time to cultivate other talents or to give to family and friends. These considerations aside, continued growth blunts the force of the distribution question by providing modest increase in the living standards of the poor.

It is not hard to understand why the claimed relationship between the market and growth has been made. As we have seen, the market became predominant in the countries of North America and Western Europe early in the nineteenth century. And, since 1820, all these countries have experienced "substantial and sustained growth. Before 1820 no country, not even the UK, achieved growth rates equal to the minimum achieved since that date."[82] Has this been a coincidence of two events (the market and "substantial and sustained growth") or has the market promoted growth? Economic historians are not sure. Smith emphasized parsimony, extension of the market, and division of labor as the causes of increased productivity. Marx pointed to capital accumulation and technological innovations. Others argue for the role of increased literacy and secularization. None of these factors, however, is distinctive of the market. Save for extension of the market, all have occurred as well under command systems in the modern age.

The distinctive characteristic of the market system is a kind of allocative efficiency. Does this allocative efficiency better foster growth than command systems? We shall not attempt to answer this question here. The West has rejected command as the predominant way to organize the economy for a variety of reasons—not simply because it may retard growth.

The question concerning the market and growth that is asked is this: Do nonmarket controls on the market retard growth? Examination of table 7.3 is instructive. The nations whose growth performance is reported span the range of mixed economies from the Scandinavian countries with their well-developed welfare and industrial (government planning) policies to the United States, where the market is far less restrained. Included too are non-Western nations like Japan and Singapore in which government exerts considerable influence on investment decisions.[83] The USSR also appears. The table reports figures from several sources with some overlap in the periods covered as noted.

The table shows that all the Western countries have experienced growth over the whole of the post–World War II period. Japan, Singapore, and the USSR also had robust rates of growth during the periods reported. Furthermore, one or another, and sometimes two or more, of the countries with more developed welfare and industrial policies exceeded the United States in rate of growth in every period covered. This only suggests that government controls do not retard growth. If a number of factors contribute to growth, then the presence of several of them could promote growth notwithstanding government controls on the market. The table does cast doubt on the contention that the unencumbered market has anything like a decisive influence on growth. Thus, the relatively unencumbered market of the United States in the 1980s grew at a rate of 2.7 percent, while Norway and Canada with their more encumbered markets grew at a faster pace.

FREEDOM

Among the other benefits claimed for a market system is that it confers freedom. By definition, the transactions into which market participants enter are voluntary. Thus, in the market one is free to buy this product or that or to buy nothing. One is also free to take this job or that one. Earlier in this chapter, in speaking about the conditions for a market system, I put these things in somewhat different words. There, I spoke of what we customarily speak of as rights: the rights to use my time and energy as I see fit and to sell, use, and deny to others the use of desired things. If a market system exists, then these freedoms must exist. In a pure command system, in contrast, one's choice among goods and services would be curtailed altogether.[84] You must take this apartment or do without. You can buy this type of coffee or none at all. The government planners would determine the range of choice. Similarly, government planners would simply assign one a job. Under such a system, one would have no consumer choice and no occupational choice. These are freedoms that most of us value highly and enjoy as market participants.

The market requires that sellers be free to advertise their goods and services and that buyers be able to acquire information about the goods and services for sale. Therefore, the market implies some measure of freedom of speech and press. The market also requires that sellers and buyers be

TABLE 7.3

AVERAGE ANNUAL RATES OF GROWTH OF REAL GDP

	UN Statistical Yearbook				Gould		Madd	IMF	
	1950–60	1960–67	1970–75	1975–81	1950–60	1960–65	1950–73	1979–88	1989–98
United States	2.9	5.1	2.8	3.1	3.2	4.5	3.7	2.7	2.3
Denmark	3.2	4.5	2.2	2.1	3.3	4.9	4.0	2.1	2.0
Norway	3.6	5.2	4.7	4.2	–	–	4.0	3.0	3.3
Sweden	3.6	4.7	2.9	1.2	3.3	5.1	3.8	2.2	1.2
France	3.5	5.1	4.2	2.8	4.4	5.1	5.1	2.2	1.9
Germany	7.9	4.3	2.4	3.5	7.6	4.8	6.0	1.8	2.7*
Netherlands	4.6	4.8	3.5	2.5	4.9	4.8	4.8	1.6	2.9
UK	2.7	3.2	2.4	1.2	2.6	3.3	3.0	2.5	1.7
Canada	3.9	5.6	5.2	3.1	3.9	5.5	5.2	3.2	1.8
Japan	8.8	9.6	9.8	5.0	9.5	9.6	9.7	3.8	2.4
Singapore	–	–	9.8	9.0	–	–	–	7.3	8.0
USSR	–	–	–	–	7.5	4.9	–	–	–

* Data through 1991 apply to West Germany only.

Source: United Nations, *Statistical Yearbook* (New York: United Nations, 1968 and 1982); J. D. Gould, *Economic Growth in History: Survey and Analysis* (London: Methuen, 1972), 22–23; Angus Maddison, *Phases of Capitalist Development* (Oxford: Oxford University Press, 1982), Table 3.2, 45; and International Monetary Fund, *World Economic Outlook, October 1997* (Washington, DC: International Monetary Fund, 1997).

free to move about in their search for a sale or a buy. Therefore, the market implies some measure of freedom of movement. These too are not negligible freedoms. They would seem to mark out the scope of freedom in a market system.

Several things are worth noticing about market freedom. First, some of the freedom enjoyed in a market system can be enjoyed in predominantly command systems. Just as there have been no pure market systems, so there have been no pure command systems. Some command systems, Tito's Yugoslavia, for example, have used markets to recruit labor for socially owned enterprises.[85] Others, like Communist China (particularly since 1978), have used markets to distribute a wide range of products to satisfy consumer demands.[86] One or another command system has also recognized and protected rights of property, particularly, in goods and services intended for household consumption.[87] In Poland after 1956 and Yugoslavia after 1948, farms were largely in private hands.[88] I do not mean to minimize the differences between market and command systems in these regards. I do mean to point out that the freedom claimed for the market is not quite so distinctive as some of its advocates think.

Second, although market transactions are voluntary, the alternatives among which some people must choose can be quite limited. In general, the greater one's talents and the larger one's assets, the wider the range of choice. Moreover, large assets can compensate for little talent. Obviously, there are substantial differences among persons in both talents and assets. Not everyone starts out in the same place as a market participant. The professional basketball player is never confronted with the necessity to choose among several unsafe, uncomfortable tenement flats. The heir to a fortune is never confronted with the necessity to choose between going hungry and taking a dangerous, dirty job. Many others, however, are confronted by such choices. For them, the compulsion exerted by the need to work might well seem more significant than the freedom conferred by the market. Command systems, of course, cannot relieve what is a general human condition. Most of us must work. Command systems, however, may, and often have, compounded the problem by compelling a particular employment. Market freedom is to be preferred over the command alternative or, for that matter, over customary arrangements. Nevertheless, market freedom is far from being the same for everyone. It is distributed very unequally.

Third, we enjoy market freedom as one among many market participants—each of us pursuing "his own interest in his own way." There are other freedoms at least as important that we enjoy as fellow citizens in a political community of a particular sort. These are the well-known freedoms set out in the Constitution and the Bill of Rights that enable us to pursue the common interest: the rights of speech, press, and assembly; the right to vote; and the right to run for public office. Nothing in the definition of the market system implies democracy. Indeed, in modern times, many nations with a predominantly market system are not democratic: Taiwan, Singapore, Indonesia, Egypt, and Pakistan, for example. Nevertheless, modern representative democracy did grow up alongside the market.

The market, it might be contended, also confers freedom and promotes democracy by dispersing power. Instead of concentrating power to decide production and distribution questions in the hands of a small band of government bureaucrats as command systems do, the market disperses power to everyone in the society. This power is synonymous with market freedom, and its possession encourages people to demand control over political leaders. There is some truth in this. As a society of consumers, we have an effect on what is produced, in what quantities, and of what quality. This is what is known as *consumer sovereignty*. That sovereignty, however, is very unequally possessed. One's share is roughly proportionate to one's fortune. Furthermore, that sovereignty does not extend to the process of production. It is heads of enterprises who determine the location of the enterprise, hiring and promotion practices, waste disposal, and profit margins among other things.

On the distribution side, the case for popular control in a market system is difficult to make. This is so because the market for labor determines income (the form in which shares of the social product are distributed). The market may demand that one or another employer hire labor, but that employer can usually choose among many applicants. That is real power, and it is joined with all the other powers that employers possess: the determination of working conditions, hours, promotion practices, and so on. Employers are a relatively small part of the whole society. There is concentration of power, not dispersion, in the employer-employee relationship. And nowhere is that concentration more evident than in the corporations. Furthermore, a small businessman may be a tyrant in his relations with his employees, but he tyrannizes over only a few. The power of the corporations is such that they affect the lives of us all, in part by exerting influence over the making of public policy. So constant, well funded, and astute is the political participation of the corporations that democratic control is imperiled, not promoted.

CONCLUSION

The market system is highly flawed. It fails to allocate resources to public goods like highways, elementary education, and police. It imposes costs on people not party to a particular market transaction. Water, air, and noise pollution are among them. It leaves many in poverty with too little to eat, inadequate medical care, and dilapidated housing. It fails to employ, even in the best of times, millions who want and need to work. It concentrates power in corporations. This reduces the very competition that restrains the self-interest on which the market is founded. And, those same corporations can often thwart the will of democratic majorities. Even the freedom claimed for the market turns out to be less than advertised: the rich and the talented have a wide range of choices; the poor and the disabled have little. This indictment is damning.

Is there a superior alternative? Not among the other major systems. Custom tends to preserve the status quo whatever its inequities and inefficiencies. Had the custom of early twentieth-century America prevailed, a whole race would continue to be consigned to the most tedious and low-paying jobs. A recital of custom's defects might be much prolonged. I assume that such a recital is unnecessary. Custom is unacceptable as a system for the production and distribution of goods and services. What about command?

A command system would require the creation of a huge bureaucracy, which, even in a democracy, would be scarcely more amenable to popular control than the corporate hierarchies. The thought of a governmental bureaucracy deciding, say, how many refrigerators to produce and who is to assemble automobile engines is alarming. More alarming still is the realization that government would be the sole decision maker and that its decisions would be backed by compulsion. Furthermore, in the absence of the information provided by the market about consumer preferences, it is difficult to see how the shortages and surpluses that so plagued the Soviet Union could be avoided. In light of its inefficiencies and its reliance on compulsion, the command system is unappealing.

It would seem that we are stuck with the market—not the market of economic theory but the market in conjunction with a government that plays an important role in the economy. It is this alternative that has emerged in all the developed nations of the West and is known as the mixed economy. This hybrid comes in many variations. In some countries, the government is more prominent than in others. One measure of this difference is government expenditures expressed as a percentage of GDP. For Sweden, the percentage is about 60; for the United States about 30. The appropriate role for government remains controversial.[89] Let us briefly review the ways in which government can support the market and compensate for its failings.

Government is necessary to provide the very conditions under which the market exists. Chief among these is respect for persons and property. Voluntary observance of this principle cannot be depended upon. Some people must be compelled to abstain from assault, theft, and the like. Compulsion is also necessary to collect the taxes that enable government to provide all those goods and services that the market fails to produce or to produce in sufficient quantity because it is not in the self-interest of market participants to do so: public health measures, for example. In addition, government can bring the real world market closer to the theoretical ideal. By reducing information asymmetries between sellers and buyers, government promotes a better-informed consumer. By proceeding against monopoly and such practices as price-fixing, government promotes competition. This much of an agenda for government in the mixed economy is relatively uncontroversial.

The third candidate for inclusion on that agenda is more controversial. The corporations resist mightily government efforts to regulate those transactions that have undesired consequences for third parties. This resistance is readily explicable. The corporations are looking out for their own interests. This resistance, however, defies market principles. The government by requiring the fitting of catalytic converters to automobiles, for example, makes prices more fully express real costs and thereby increases the market's allocative efficiency. Beyond these things, just what should be left to the market, particularly with regard to the distribution of the social product, is more controversial still.

In reflecting on the place to be accorded the market in society, recognize that the market relies on self-interest restrained by competition to realize the public good. This is not the market's purpose. It has no purpose. The public good realized by the market is the unintended consequence of the actions of market participants who intend only their own good. In that sense, the market's public good is arrived at irrationally. It is not discovered in a discussion among citizens in which alternatives are considered, arguments made, and evidence presented. What is the market's public good? It is the gross domestic product—the value of all the goods and services produced by the society in a year. The gross domestic product, however, tells us nothing about how those goods and services were produced. By child labor? By desperate men and women ready to take whatever jobs the market has to offer? By processes that create toxic wastes? Nor does the gross domestic product tell us anything about how those goods and services are distributed.

Are they widely distributed or do a relatively few enjoy inordinately large shares? The market is indifferent to such considerations.

The market has no conscience. For some, this is a great recommendation for the market. It is morally neutral—a space where people with different beliefs can cooperate with one another for the satisfaction of their respective wants. But is an institution that ignores the different starting places of the participants truly neutral, or is it simply morally obtuse? People do, after all, come to the market with very different assets and talents to exchange and leave it with very different wants unsatisfied. Few will join me in bemoaning the absence of a Picasso from my office wall, but should a society that declares allegiance to the principle of equal opportunity be similarly dismissive about a child denied medical care because her parents cannot foot the bill?

NOTES

CHAPTER 1: RELIGION AND THE CONSTITUTION

1. William Few, "Autobiography of Colonel William Few of Georgia," *Magazine of American History* 7 (November 1881): 343–58.

2. John Locke, *An Essay Concerning Human Understanding*, ed. Alexander Campbell Fraser, 2 vols. (New York: Dover, 1959), 1: 438.

3. This matter is the subject of a new book by David L. Holmes, *The Faiths of the Founding Fathers* (New York: Oxford University Press, 2006).

4. Peter Marshall and David Manuel, *The Light and the Glory* (Old Tappan, NJ: Revell, 1977); and *From Sea to Shining Sea: Discovering God's Plan for America in the First Half-Century of Independence, 1787–1837* (Old Tappan, NJ: Revell, 1986); and Tim LaHaye, *Faith of Our Founding Fathers* (Brentwood, TN: Wolgemuth and Hyatt, 1987), 1, 22.

5. Michael Novak, *On Two Wings: Humble Faith and Common Sense at the American Founding* (San Francisco: Encounter Books, 2002), 7–9.

6. Marshall and Manuel, *Light and the Glory* and *From Sea to Shining Sea*.

7. James H. Hutson, *Religion and the Founding of the American Republic* (Washington, DC: Library of Congress, 1998), 78; Justice William Rehnquist in dissent in *Wallace v. Jaffree*, 472 U.S. 38 (1985); Attorney General Edwin Meese III, "The Supreme Court of the United States: Bulwark of a Limited Constitution," a speech delivered to the American Bar Association in Washington, July 9, 1985, and reprinted in *South Texas Law Review* 27 (1986): 455–66; Anson Phelps Stokes, *Church and State in the United States*, 3 vols. (New York: Harper, 1964), 1: 541; and LaHaye, *Faith of Our Founding Fathers*, 195.

8. Michael J. Malbin, *Religion and Politics: The Intentions of the Authors of the First Amendment* (Washington, DC: American Enterprise Institute for Public Policy Research, 1978), 15; and Novak, *On Two Wings*, 114.

9. Max Farrand, ed., *The Records of the Federal Convention of 1787*, rev. ed., 4 vols. (New Haven, CT: Yale University Press, 1966), 1: 450–52.

10. Peter Marshall and David Manuel, *From Sea to Shining Sea for Children: Discovering*

God's Plan for America in the First Half-Century of Independence, 1787–1837, with Anna Wilson Fishel (Grand Rapids, MI: Revell, 1993), 18–19. They get it wrong in the adult edition, too, in their assertions that Franklin's motion was not seconded (it was—by Roger Sherman) and that the motion occurred three months after deliberations had begun (it was one month into the Convention). For similar claims see also Rev. William C. Heyer, *American Trust in Providence* (Boston: R. G. Badger, 1925), 36–37; Dan Smoot, *The Hope of the World* (Dallas, TX: Tom Newman, 1958), 21–22; Marshall E. Foster and Mary E. Swanson, *The American Covenant: The Untold Story* (Thousand Oaks, CA: Mayflower Institute, 1982), 11–12 and 97; and LaHaye, *Faith of Our Founding Fathers,* 57–58 and 122–24.

11. See James Madison's notes in Farrand, *Records,* 1: 450–52. On the integrity of those notes, see James H. Hutson, "The Creation of the Constitution: The Integrity of the Documentary Record," in *Interpreting the Constitution: The Debate over Original Intent,* ed. Jack N. Rakove (Boston: Northeastern University Press, 1990), 156–58 and 162–68. Only Robert Yates among the other note takers at the Convention mentions the incident at all. Compare the entries of Yates, William Paterson, and Rufus King in Farrand, *Records,* 1: 453–59; John Lansing and Pierce Butler in James H. Hutson, *Supplement to Max Farrand's "The Records of the Federal Convention of 1787"* (New Haven, CT: Yale University Press, 1987), 125–26; and George Washington's diary in Hutson, *Supplement,* 126. All those just mentioned agree that the delegates met in convention on the two days subsequent to Franklin's motion.

12. Farrand, *Records,* 1: 452.

13. Ibid., 3: 227.

14. For a summary of Anti-Federalist objections, see Jackson T. Main, *The Antifederalists: Critics of the Constitution, 1781–1788* (Chapel Hill: University of North Carolina Press, 1961), 119–67.

15. I owe this characterization to Edwin S. Gaustad, *Faith of Our Fathers: Religion and the New Nation* (San Francisco: Harper & Row, 1987), 113.

16. Timothy Dwight, *A Discourse in Two Parts,* 2nd ed. (Boston: Flagg and Gould, 1813), 24.

17. Chauncey Lee, *The Government of God* (Hartford, CT: Hudson and Goodwin, 1813), 43.

18. George Mason, *The Papers of George Mason,* ed. Robert A. Rutland, 3 vols. (Chapel Hill: University of North Carolina Press, 1970), 1: 274–91; James Madison, *The Papers of James Madison,* ed. William T. Hutchinson et al. (Chicago: University of Chicago Press, 1962–1991), 8: 295–306; James Wilson, *The Works of James Wilson,* ed. Robert G. McCloskey, 2 vols. (Cambridge, MA: Harvard University Press, 1962), 1: 241–42; and Alexander Hamilton, *The Papers of Alexander Hamilton,* ed. Harold C. Syrett, 27 vols. (New York: Columbia University Press, 1961–1987), 1: 86–88.

19. Hamilton, *Papers,* 1: 87–88.

20. John Dickinson, *The Political Writings of John Dickinson, 1764–1774,* ed. Paul L. Ford (New York: Da Capo Press, 1970).

21. Wilson, *Works*, 1: 133.

22. Benjamin Franklin, *The Autobiography of Benjamin Franklin*, ed. Leonard W. Labaree et al. (New Haven, CT: Yale University Press, 1964), 114–15; and *The Writings of Benjamin Franklin*, ed. Albert Henry Smyth, 10 vols. (New York: Macmillan, 1905–1907), 10: 85.

23. Wilson, *Works*, 1: 144.

24. On this point, see Peter R. Henriques, *Realistic Visionary: A Portrait of George Washington* (Charlottesville: University of Virginia Press, 2006).

25. Madison expressed that skepticism in *The Federalist* 10—see Alexander Hamilton, James Madison, and John Jay, *The Federalist Papers*, ed. Clinton Rossiter (New York: New American Library, 1961), 81—and in a letter to Jefferson October 24, 1787, in Madison, *Papers*, 10: 213. His later view can be found in a letter to F. Beasley, November 20, 1825, in *The Writings of James Madison*, ed. Gaillard Hunt, 9 vols. (New York: G. P. Putnam's Sons, 1910), 9: 230.

26. George Washington, *Writings: George Washington*, ed. John Rhodehamel (New York: Library of America, 1997), 971.

27. Hamilton et al., *Federalist Papers*, 346.

28. Farrand, *Records*, 3: 141.

29. Ibid., 3: 302–303.

30. See Wilson, *Works*, 1: 143–44; and Jared Sparks, *The Life of Gouverneur Morris, with Selections from His Correspondence and Miscellaneous Papers* (Boston: Gray and Bowen, 1832), 3: 483.

31. Farrand, *Records*, 3: 380.

32. They were joined by John Jay, who was not a delegate to the Convention and who wrote just five essays of the total of eighty-five.

33. Harry S. Stout, "Rhetoric and Reality in the Early Republic: The Case of the Federalist Clergy," in *Religion and American Politics: From the Colonial Period to the 1980s*, ed. Mark A. Noll (New York: Oxford University Press, 1990), 62–76.

34. Peter Gay, *The Enlightenment: An Interpretation*, 2 vols. (New York: Knopf, 1966–1969), describes the development of the idea of progress in eighteenth-century Europe in vol. 2, ch. 2.

35. George Washington, *The Papers of George Washington, Confederation Series*, eds. W. W. Abbot and Dorothy Twohig (Charlottesville: University Press of Virginia, 1987–2002), 4: 215–16.

36. Hamilton et al., *Federalist Papers*, 33.

37. Ibid., 104.

38. Farrand, *Records*, 1: 422–23.

39. Ibid., 515.

40. Ibid., 529.

41. Ibid., 452.

42. George Washington, *The Papers of George Washington, Presidential Series*, ed. Dorothy Twohig (Charlottesville: University Press of Virginia, 1987–2007), 2: 175.

43. Rodney Stark and Roger Finke, "American Religion in 1776: A Statistical Portrait," *Sociological Analysis* 49 (1988): 39–51; see also Patricia U. Bonomi and Peter R. Eisenstadt, "Church Adherence in the Eighteenth-Century British

American Colonies," *William and Mary Quarterly*, 3rd series, 39 (April 1982): 245–86; and Jon Butler, "Church Membership: Less Than God-Fearing," in *Mapping America's Past: A Historical Atlas*, eds. Mark C. Carnes and John A. Garraty (New York: Henry Holt, 1996), 50–51.

44. Donald S. Lutz, "The Relative Influence of European Writers on Late Eighteenth-Century American Political Thought," *American Political Science Review* 78 (March 1984): 189–97.

45. The Anglican Church did, of course, have such government in England. The oversight exercised by the Bishop of London in whose see the colonial church was located was remote and infrequent. The Congregational Church was organized at the local level. There was no national organization, and state meetings were infrequent.

46. Madison, *Papers*, 1: 106.

47. I rely in the rest of this section on Thomas J. Curry, *The First Freedoms: Church and State in America to the Passage of the First Amendment* (New York: Oxford University Press, 1986), chs. 5–7.

48. Gaustad, *Faith of Our Fathers*, Appendix B, 163.

49. Maryland repealed its constitutional provision permitting general assessment in 1810.

50. Massachusetts maintained its establishment until 1833, and New Hampshire until 1819.

51. Gaustad, *Faith of Our Fathers*, Appendix B, 163.

52. Ibid., 168 and 172.

53. Neither Rhode Island nor Connecticut adopted new constitutions, so they are not mentioned here.

54. Madison, *Papers*, 8: 298–304; or Gaustad, *Faith of Our Fathers*, Appendix A, 141–49.

55. Stokes, *Church and State in the United States*, 1: 393–94. In pages 366 to 397 he recounts the story of the Virginia struggle with excerpts from many of the relevant documents.

56. As quoted by Curry, *First Freedoms*, 212.

57. Ibid.

58. Ibid.

59. Ibid.

60. The Federalist case as made by Alexander Hamilton can be found in *The Federalist* 84 and by James Madison at the Virginia state ratifying convention in Jonathan Elliot, ed., *The Debates in the Several State Conventions on the Adoption of the Federal Constitution*, 2nd ed., 5 vols. (Philadelphia: J. B. Lippincott, 1901–1907), 3: 330; and in a letter to Jefferson in Madison, *Papers*, 11: 297–300.

61. Merrill Jensen, John Kaminski, and Gaspare Saladino, eds., *The Documentary History of the Ratification of the Constitution*, 18 vols. (Madison: University of Wisconsin Press, 1976–), 2: 288, 309–11, 386, 392, 399, 459, 597, 710–11; 3: 374; 6: 1453; 8: 250; 9: 772, 802, 821; 10: 1213; 13, 466, 525, 535; and Herbert J. Storing, ed., *The Complete Anti-Federalist*, 6 vols. (Chicago: University of Chicago Press, 1981), 2.27.55, 3.3.29, 4.22.4, 6.10.6.

62. Jensen et al., *Documentary History*, 2: 592, 710–11; and Storing, *Complete Anti-Federalist*, 3.3.29, 3.13.5, 5.4.7.

63. Jensen, *Documentary History*, 2: 710–11; 13: 466; and Storing, *Complete Anti-Federalist*, 2.7.55, 2.8.86.

64. Charles C. Tansill, ed., *Documents Illustrative of the Formation of the Union of the American States* (Washington, DC: Government Printing Office, 1927), 1026.

65. There is no record of the proceedings of the New Hampshire ratifying convention.

66. The proceedings are reprinted in full in Stokes, *Church and State*, 1: 541–43.

67. Gaustad, *Faith of Our Fathers*, Appendix A, 156.

68. James Madison, *The Papers of James Madison, Presidential Series*, ed. Robert A. Rutland (Charlottesville: University Press of Virginia, 1984–2000), 3: 176.

CHAPTER 2: ORIGINAL INTENT

1. William H. Rehnquist, "The Notion of a Living Constitution," *Texas Law Review* 54 (May 1976): 693–706; and Robert H. Bork, "Original Intent and the Constitution," *Humanities* 7 (1986): 22, 26–27.

2. Charles Warren, *The Making of the Constitution* (Boston: Little, Brown, 1937), 810–12, provides dates of attendance for each of the delegates.

3. Farrand, *Records*, 3: 373.

4. See Hutson, "Creation of the Constitution," 166–68; and Leonard Levy, *Original Intent and the Framers' Constitution* (New York: Macmillan, 1988), 286–88.

5. Farrand, *Records*, 3: 362.

6. Ibid., 133–35.

7. Ibid., 2: 221.

8. Ibid., 632.

9. Ibid., 3: 297

10. Ibid., 2: 645–46.

11. Ibid., 3: 357.

12. Ibid., William Pierce of Georgia, 3: 100–101; Pierce Butler of South Carolina, 3: 102–103; George Washington of Virginia, 3: 103–104, 242; James Wilson of Pennsylvania, 3: 160–62; Hugh Williamson of North Carolina, 3: 238–39; Robert Morris of Pennsylvania, 3: 242–43; and James McHenry of Maryland, 2: 649.

13. William Jackson, secretary to the Convention, kept the *Journal*, in which he recorded the motions made and assigned a number to each division of the delegates. The *Journal* is reproduced in Farrand, *Records*. Jackson misreported Vote 313. Instead of four "ayes" to five "noes," it should have been seven states "aye" to two "no" with Massachusetts absent. Connecticut changed its vote on 313 to make the division 8 to 1.

14. Farrand, *Records*, 2: 318–19.

15. There is not much there apart from, for example, random comments by James Wilson in Jensen et al., *Documentary History*, 2: 583; and by Oliver Ellsworth in Elliot, *Debates*, 2: 195.

16. Hamilton et al., *Federalist Papers*, 417–18.

17. Madison, *Papers*, vol. 15.

18. Hamilton, *Papers*, vol. 15.

19. Levy, *Original Intent*, ch. 1.

20. On the removal power, see *Debates and Proceedings of the Congress of the United States (Annals of Congress)*, comp. Joseph Gales (Washington, DC: Gales and Seaton, 1834), 1: 42 and 603; on the bank, ibid., 2012.

21. Washington, *Papers, Confederation Series*, 5: 422.

22. The figures cited below can be found in U.S. Bureau of the Census, *Historical Statistics of the United States: Colonial Times to 1957* (Washington, DC: Government Printing Office, 1960), and in the current issue of the annual *Statistical Abstract*.

23. Susan B. Carter, Roger L. Ransom, and Richard Sutch, "Family Matters: The Life-Cycle Transition and the Antebellum American Fertility Decline," in *History Matters: Essays on Economic Growth, Technology, and Demographic Change*, eds. Timothy W. Guinnane, William A. Sundstrom, and Warren Whatley (Stanford, CA: Stanford University Press, 2004), 271–327; William A. Sundstrom and Paul A. David, "Old-Age Security Motives, Labor Markets, and Farm-Family Fertility in Antebellum America," *Explorations in Economic History* 25 (1988): 164–97; Richard Hofstadter, *America at 1750: A Social Portrait* (New York: Knopf, 1971), ch. 1; J. Potter, "The Growth of Population in America, 1700–1860," in *Population in History: Essays in Historical Demography*, ed. D. V. Glass and D. E. C. Eversley (Chicago: Aldine, 1965), 644, 649, and 662–63; James H. Cassedy, *Demography in Early America: Beginnings of the Statistical Mind, 1600–1800* (Cambridge, MA: Harvard University Press, 1969), 173; and John Demos, "Families in Colonial Bristol, Rhode Island: An Exercise in Historical Demography," *William and Mary Quarterly*, 3rd Series, 25 (1968): 44–46.

24. This is the contention of Bernard Bailyn, *The Ideological Origins of the American Revolution* (Cambridge, MA: Harvard University Press, 1967).

25. L. H. Butterfield, Marc Friedlaender, and Mary-Jo Kline, eds., *The Book of Abigail and John: Selected Letters of the Adams Family, 1762–1784* (Cambridge, MA: Harvard University Press, 1975), 121.

26. Farrand, *Records*, 1: 135.

27. Ibid., 2: 364.

28. Ibid., 373.

29. Ibid., 415–16.

30. Hamilton et al., *Federalist Papers*, 441.

31. Edwin J. Perkins, *The Economy of Colonial America*, 2nd ed. (New York: Columbia University Press, 1988), 57–60.

32. Farrand, *Records*, 3: 584.

33. Ibid., 3: 103. See also the comment of Franklin, 3: 131; Washington, 3: 131; Pierce, 2: 100–101; Wilson, 3: 138; Hamilton, 3: 332–33; Davie, 3: 341; and Spaight, 3: 346.

34. Hamilton et al., *Federalist Papers*, 230.

35. Ibid.

36. This characterization is not mine. From whom I acquired it I cannot recall despite my efforts to track it down.

37. Farrand, *Records*, 3: 477.

38. Ibid., 1: 242.

39. Ibid., 1: 447–48, 486; and 2: 10.

40. Ibid., 1: 491.

41. Ibid., 2: 26.

42. Ibid., 1: 492.

43. Ibid., 255.

44. Ibid., 561.

45. Ibid., 562.

46. See the comments in Farrand, *Records*, of Hamilton, 1: 466; Madison, 1: 486, 601 and 2: 9–10; Charles Pinckney, 1: 510; King, 1: 566; and G. Morris, 1: 604.

47. Ibid., Paterson, 1: 561; King, 1: 586; and Morris, 1: 603–604.

48. Ibid., 1: 587.

49. Ibid., 593.

50. Ibid., Pinckney, 2: 30; and Williamson, 2: 32.

51. Ibid., 2: 56–57.

52. Elliot, *Debates*, 4: 286.

53. See Farrand, *Records*, 1: 593 and 2: 364–65.

54. See the comments in Farrand, *Records*, of Gouverneur Morris, 1: 533; John Rutledge, 1: 534; Rufus King, 1: 541; Pierce Butler, 1: 542; and James Wilson's dissent, 1: 584.

55. See Hamilton et al., *Federalist Papers*, particularly numbers 10 and 51.

56. This thesis was developed by Jackson T. Main in *The Antifederalists* (pp. 271–81), but it was first suggested by Orin Libby in "Geographical Distribution of the Vote of the Thirteen States on the Federal Constitution," *Bulletin of the University of Wisconsin* 1 (1897): 14. For graphic representation of the division, see Lester J. Cappon, ed., *Atlas of Early American History: The Revolutionary Era, 1760– 1790* (Princeton, NJ: Princeton University Press, 1976), 63; and Van Beck Hall, *Politics without Parties: Massachusetts, 1780–1791* (Pittsburgh, PA: University of Pittsburgh Press, 1972), particularly 286–87 for Massachusetts.

57. For identification of their assets and sources of income, see Forrest McDonald, *We the People: The Economic Origins of the Constitution* (Chicago: University of Chicago Press, 1958), 44, 69–70, and 72.

58. See the state-by-state surveys of Robert A. Becker, *Revolution, Reform, and the Politics of American Taxation, 1763–1783* (Baton Rouge, LA: Louisiana State University Press, 1980), 113–218; and David P. Szatmary, *Shays' Rebellion: The Making of an Agrarian Insurrection* (Amherst: University of Massachusetts Press, 1980), ch. 7, particularly 124–26.

59. Willi Paul Adams, *The First American Constitutions: Republican Ideology and the Making of the State Constitutions in the Revolutionary Era*, trans. Rita and Robert Kimber, expanded ed. (Lanham, MD: Rowman & Littlefield, 2001), 315–27, summarizes property qualifications for the vote and for office in the several states. Cf. Alexander Keyssar, *The Right to Vote: The Contested History of Democracy in the United States* (New York: Basic Books, 2000), 328–29.

60. Chilton Williamson, *American Suffrage: From Property to Democracy, 1760–1860* (Princeton, NJ: Princeton University Press, 1960), 22–23, identifies those difficulties.

61. See Adams, *First American Constitutions*, 197–205; and Williamson, *American Suffrage*, 25–39.

62. Jefferson famously commented on the malapportioned districts in Virginia in response to Query XIII in his *Notes on the State of Virginia*. See Thomas Jefferson, *Writings: Thomas Jefferson*, ed. Merrill D. Peterson (New York: Library of America, 1984), 244.

63. Keyssar, *Right to Vote*, ch. 1; and Becker, *Revolution*, 113–218 passim.

64. John S. Bassett, "The Regulators of North Carolina, 1765–1771," *Annual Report of the American Historical Association* (1894): 141–212.

65. Woody Holton, "'From the Labours of Others': The War Bonds Controversy and the Origins of the Constitution in New England," *William and Mary Quarterly*, 3rd Series, 61 (April 2004): 271–316 and particularly the tables on 308–14.

66. Edwin J. Perkins, *American Public Finance and Financial Services, 1700–1815* (Columbus: Ohio State University Press, 1994).

67. Forrest McDonald and Ellen Shapiro McDonald, *Requiem: Variations on Eighteenth-Century Themes* (Lawrence: University Press of Kansas, 1988), 69.

68. Jackson T. Main, *The Social Structure of Revolutionary America* (Princeton, NJ: Princeton University Press, 1965), 106.

69. To be sure, they were genuinely alarmed. Shays's Rebellion provoked Washington to express his concern about the "combustibles in every state" who might burst into flames, and he feared that "a step or two more must plunge us into inextricable ruin" (see Washington, *Papers, Confederation Series*, 4: 482 and 360). James Wilson, the most consistent majoritarian among the delegates, said later, "The flames of internal insurrection were ready to burst out in every quarter . . . and from one end to the other of the continent, we walked on ashes, concealing fire beneath our feet" (see Jensen et al., *Documentary History*, 2: 577). See also William Blount in a letter of December 7, 1786, in *Letters to Members of the Continental Congress*, ed. Edmund Burnett, 8 vols. (Washington, DC: Carnegie Institute of Washington, 1921–1936), 8: 516; Pierce Butler in a letter of March 3, 1788, as quoted by Szatmary, *Shays' Rebellion*, 127; and George Mason in his *Papers*, 2: 768.

70. Hamilton, *Papers*, 3: 609.

71. Farrand, *Records*, 1: 26–27; see also 1: 51.

72. Ibid., 1: 48.

73. Ibid., 49

74. Ibid., 32.

75. Ibid., 583.

76. Ibid., Roger Sherman, 1: 48 and 359; Pierce Butler, 1: 50; Charles Pinckney's motion, 1: 132 as seconded by John Rutledge and the latter's comment at 1: 359; Charles Cotesworth Pinckney's view, 1: 137; and that of John Francis Mercer, 2: 205.

77. The debate and votes on popular election of the lower house occurred on May 31, June 6, and June 21—see ibid., 1: 48–50, 132–38, and 358–60. The debate and vote on the property qualification for voting occurred on August 7—see ibid., 2: 201–206.

78. Ibid., 1: 135.

79. See Garry Wills, *Explaining America: The Federalist* (Garden City, NY: Doubleday, 1981), 268–70; and Gordon S. Wood, "Interests and Disinterestedness in the Making of the Constitution," in *Beyond Confederation: Origins of the Constitution and American National Identity*, eds. Richard Beeman, Stephen Botein, and Edward C. Carter II (Chapel Hill: University of North Carolina Press, 1987), 69–109.

80. For example, Wilson in Farrand, *Records*, 2: 469, and Jensen et al., *Documentary History*, 2: 483–84; and Rufus King in Farrand, *Records*, 1: 266, 301 and 2: 92. The Convention meeting as a Committee of the Whole adopted the principle of popular ratification early on (June 12) by a vote of 6 to 3 with two states divided. Ellsworth later sought to secure ratification by the state legislatures—a motion defeated 7 states to 3. The Convention then reaffirmed its commitment to popular ratification 9 to 1. The Convention revisited the matter one more time on August 31 when by a vote of 10 to 1 it decided to submit the Constitution to popularly chosen state ratifying conventions. See Farrand, *Records*, 1: 122–23, 214, and 232; 2: 88–93 and 475–79.

81. Farrand, *Records*, 3: 374.

82. Robert A. Dahl undertakes that task in his usual thoughtful way in *How Democratic Is the American Constitution?* (New Haven, CT: Yale University Press, 2001).

CHAPTER 3: SEPARATION OF POWERS

1. William B. Gwyn, *The Meaning of Separation of Powers: An Analysis of the Doctrine from Its Origin to the Adoption of the United States Constitution* (New Orleans, LA: Tulane University, 1965); M. J. C. Vile, *Constitutionalism and the Separation of Powers* (Oxford: Clarendon Press, 1967); and Bradford Wilson and Peter W. Schramm, eds., *Separation of Powers and Good Government* (Lanham, MD: Rowman & Littlefield, 1994), give broad treatment to these matters.

2. *The Federalist* 49 in Hamilton et al., *Federalist Papers*, 314.

3. Charles A. Beard, *An Economic Interpretation of the Constitution* (New York: Macmillan, 1913); James MacGregor Burns, *The Deadlock of Democracy: Four-Party Politics in America* (Englewood Cliffs, NJ: Prentice-Hall, 1963): Robert A. Dahl, *A Preface to Democratic Theory* (Chicago: University of Chicago Press, 1956); E. E. Schattschneider, *Party Government* (New York: Farrar and Rinehart, 1942); and J. Allen Smith, *The Spirit of American Government* (Cambridge, MA: Harvard University Press, 1965).

4. George W. Carey, "Separation of Powers and the Madisonian Model: A Reply to Critics," *American Political Science Review* 72 (1978): 151–64; David F. Epstein, *The Political Theory of the Federalist* (Chicago: University of Chicago Press, 1984); and Wills, *Explaining America*.

5. Hamilton et al., *Federalist Papers*, 303.

6. Ibid., 352.

7. Ibid., 301.

8. Ibid., 327.

9. Ibid., 342.

10. Ibid., 226–27.
11. Ibid., 321.
12. Ibid., 483.
13. Ibid., 302.
14. Ibid., 313.
15. Ibid., 310–13.
16. Ibid., 322.
17. Ibid., 327.
18. Ibid., 309.
19. Ibid., 316.
20. Ibid., 316.
21. Ibid.
22. Ibid., 78 and 51.
23. Ibid., 289.
24. Ibid., 78.
25. Ibid., 296.
26. Ibid., 380.
27. Ibid., *The Federalist* 10 and 324.
28. Ibid., 324.
29. Madison, *Papers*, 5: 83 and 8: 300.
30. Hamilton et al., *Federalist Papers*, 78.
31. Ibid., 324–25.
32. Ibid., 81.
33. Ibid.
34. Ibid., 226 and 380–82.
35. Madison, *Papers*, 9: 354.
36. Farrand, *Records*, 1: 134.
37. Madison, *Papers*, 10: 212.
38. Hamilton et al., *Federalist Papers*, 268.
39. Ibid., 82.
40. Ibid., 386.
41. Farrand, *Records*, 1: 422.
42. Hamilton et al., *Federalist Papers*, 384.
43. Ibid., 77–79.
44. Farrand, *Records*, 1: 422; Hamilton et al., *Federalist Papers*, 79.
45. Farrand, *Records*, 1: 422.
46. Madison, *Papers*, 9: 349. See also Hamilton et al., *Federalist Papers*, 84; and Madison, *Papers*, 9: 318, 397.
47. Hamilton et al., *Federalist Papers*, 84; and Madison, *Papers*, 9: 384.
48. Farrand, *Records*, 1: 422–23.
49. Hamilton et al., *Federalist Papers*, 80–81.
50. Ibid., 82–83.
51. This is the view of George W. Carey, *The Federalist: Design for a Constitutional Republic* (Urbana: University of Illinois Press, 1989), 133; Cushing Strout, "Introduction," in J. Allen Smith, *Spirit of American Government*, xlvii–xlviii; and

Wills, *Explaining America,* 258. Harvey C. Mansfield Jr., *America's Constitutional Soul* (Baltimore: John Hopkins University Press, 1991), 122; and Drew R. McCoy, *The Last of the Fathers: James Madison and the Republican Legacy* (Cambridge: Cambridge University Press, 1989), 43 and 137, may well share this view.

52. Hamilton et al., *Federalist Papers,* 385.
53. Ibid., 322.
54. Ibid., 379.
55. Ibid., 384.
56. Farrand, *Records,* 1: 421.
57. Ibid., 562.
58. Madison, *Papers,* 11: 287–88.
59. Farrand, *Records,* 2: 93.
60. Ibid., 73.
61. Ibid., 1: 99–100.
62. Ibid., 1: 104, 2: 73–74 and 298.
63. Ibid., 2: 589.
64. Ibid., 1: 108.
65. Ibid., 2: 110.
66. Ibid., 587.
67. Madison, *Papers,* 11: 298.
68. Ibid., 12: 204.
69. Hamilton et al., *Federalist Papers,* 322–24.
70. Ibid., 346.
71. Madison, *Papers,* 9: 355–56; Farrand, *Records,* 1: 133; Hamilton et al., *Federalist Papers,* 81, 268, 315, 342, and 360; and Madison, *Papers,* 10: 213.
72. Hamilton et al., *Federalist Papers,* 83–84.
73. Ibid., 343–44.
74. Ibid., 350–51.
75. Ibid., 82–83.
76. Farrand, *Records,* 1: 486.
77. Ibid., 135–36.
78. Ibid., 485–87.
79. Ibid., 78–79.
80. Ibid., 486–87.
81. Hamilton et al., *Federalist Papers,* 378.
82. Ibid., 241.
83. Madison, *Papers,* 9: 357.
84. Hamilton et al., *Federalist Papers,* 100.
85. Madison, *Papers,* 9: 357.
86. Hamilton et al., *Federalist Papers,* 324.
87. Ibid., *The Federalist* 10, 78.
88. As contended by Epstein, *Political Theory,* 5.
89. Madison, *Papers,* 10: 209–214.
90. Hamilton et al., *Federalist Papers,* 226.
91. Madison, *Papers,* 9: 348–57.

92. Hamilton et al., *Federalist Papers*, *The Federalist* 41–43.

93. Ibid., 333.

94. Ibid., 283–86.

95. Ibid., 255–56.

CHAPTER 4: TYRANNY OF THE MAJORITY

1. Hamilton et al., *Federalist Papers*, 241.

2. Few disagreed about the desirability or the grounds for one or another of these provisions. As we saw in the last chapter, Madison favored them all except for equality of representation in the Senate, and he favored them as defenses against tyranny of the majority—what he called a factional majority.

3. Lindsay Rogers, "Barrier Against Steamrollers," and Walter Lippmann, "Minorities Should Not Be Coerced," in *Bishop and Hendel's Basic Issues of American Democracy*, ed. Samuel Hendel, 7th ed. (New York: Appleton-Century-Crofts, 1973), 490–94.

4. James Madison, *The Federalist* 10 and 51, in Hamilton et al., *Federalist Papers*, 78 and 323–24; Alexis de Tocqueville, *Democracy in America*, trans. George Lawrence (New York: Harper & Row, 1969), 246–61; and John Stuart Mill, *On Liberty*, in *Utilitarianism, On Liberty, Considerations on Representative Government, Remarks on Bentham's Philosophy*, ed. Geraint Williams (London: Dent, 1993), 71–73.

5. John Stuart Mill, "De Tocqueville on Democracy in America [II]," in *Collected Works of John Stuart Mill*, ed. J. M. Robson, 33 vols. (Toronto: University of Toronto Press, 1963–1991) 18: 178. See also Tocqueville, *Democracy in America*, 255.

6. Mill, *On Liberty*, 99–100.

7. Ibid., 99.

8. Farrand, *Records*, 1: 133–34.

9. Warren E. Miller and Donald E. Stokes, "Constituency Influence in Congress," *American Political Science Review* 57 (March 1963): 43–56; Robert S. Erikson, "Constituency Opinion and Congressional Behavior," *American Journal of Political Science* 22 (August 1978): 511–35; Alan Monroe, "Consistency Between Public Preference and National Policy Decisions," *American Politics Quarterly* 7 (January 1979): 3–19; and Benjamin I. Page and Robert Y. Shapiro, "Effects of Public Opinion on Policy," *American Political Science Review* 77 (March 1983): 175–90.

10. For national policy on Cuba, see the *Gallup Poll Monthly*, May 1999, 49–50, and May 2000, 33; on gun control, see *Gallup Poll Monthly*, January 2000, 59–60, and November 2000, 30–32; and on state educational policies, see *Gallup Poll Monthly*, June 1998, 17–18, and August 1999, 35–37.

11. The classic study is Angus Campbell et al., *The American Voter* (New York: Wiley, 1960), chs. 8–10. Richard G. Niemi and Herbert F. Weisberg, eds., *Controversies in Voting Behavior*, 3rd ed. (Washington, DC: CQ Press, 1993), ch. 6, review the literature concerning the sophistication of the American electorate.

12. Russell Hardin, "Public Choice Versus Democracy," in *Majorities and Minorities*, eds. John W. Chapman and Alan Wertheimer (New York: New York University Press, 1990), 184–203.

13. Steven J. Rosenstone and John Mark Hansen, *Mobilization, Participation, and Democracy in America* (New York: Macmillan, 1993), treat these points in detail.

14. Much might be done to promote satisfaction of these conditions and, thereby, to increase popular control over government. See Benjamin R. Barber, *Strong Democracy: Participatory Politics for a New Age* (Berkeley: University of California Press, 1984).

15. William H. Flanigan and Nancy H. Zingale, *Political Behavior of the American Electorate*, 9th ed. (Washington, DC: CQ Press, 1998), 133–34; and Sidney Verba and Norman H. Nie, *Participation in America: Political Democracy and Social Equality* (New York: Harper & Row, 1972), part 3. Robert S. Erikson and Gerald C. Wright, "Votes, Candidates, and Issues in Congressional Elections," in *Congress Reconsidered*, eds. Lawrence C. Dodd and Bruce I. Oppenheimer, 5th ed. (Washington, DC: CQ Press, 1993), 91–114, contend that these limits are the ideological tendencies "liberal" and "conservative."

6. The nature and variability of these limits are identified in Flanigan and Zingale, *Political Behavior*, ch. 6.

7. Hamilton et al., *Federalist Papers*, 83.

8. James S. Fishkin makes this point in *Tyranny and Legitimacy: A Critique of Political Theories* (Baltimore, MD: Johns Hopkins University Press, 1979), ch. 3.

9. James H. Jones, *Bad Blood: The Tuskegee Syphilis Experiment* (New York: Free Press, 1981); T. G. Benedek, "The 'Tuskegee Study' of Syphilis: Analysis of Moral Versus Methodological Aspects," *Journal of Chronic Diseases* 31 (1978): 35–50; W. J. Curran and S. M. Hyg, "Law-Medicine Notes: The Tuskegee Syphilis Study," *New England Journal of Medicine* 289 (1973): 730–31.

20. I paraphrase Robert A. Dahl, *Democracy and Its Critics* (New Haven, CT: Yale University Press, 1989), 108–114 and 129–30.

21. Ibid., 220–24.

22. Since three levels of government were involved, they may have incurred any culpability unequally.

23. William Dudley, ed., *Hurricane Katrina* (Detroit: Greenhaven Press, 2006); Jed Horne, *Breach of Faith: Hurricane Katrina and the Near Death of a Great American City* (New York: Random House, 2006); Christopher Cooper and Robert Block, *Disaster: Hurricane Katrina and the Failure of Homeland Security* (New York: Times Books, 2006); and Ivor van Heerden and Mike Bryan, *The Storm: What Went Wrong and Why During Hurricane Katrina: The Inside Story from One Louisiana Scientist* (New York: Viking, 2006), among others contribute to answering the question.

24. Brian Barry, *Political Argument: A Reissue with New Introduction* (Berkeley: University of California Press, 1990), 12–13 and 61–66.

25. The full text is in an appendix to Roger Daniels, *Prisoners without Trial: Japanese Americans in World War II* (New York: Hill and Wang, 1993), 129–30.

26. The *New York Times Index* under the heading "United States-Foreign Population" has nearly four double-columned pages of small print citations for 1942 alone— nearly all devoted to Japanese-American internment. The online archive of the *Los Angeles Times* under the heading "Japanese evacuation" cites dozens of

articles for the war years. See also Greg Robinson, *By Order of the President: FDR and the Internment of Japanese Americans* (Cambridge, MA: Harvard University Press, 2001), 125–26, 190, and 200–201; U.S. Commission on Wartime Relocation and Internment of Civilians, *Personal Justice Denied: A Report* (Washington, DC: Government Printing Office, 1992), 67–72, 77, 80, and 225–27.

27. U.S. Commission, *Personal Justice Denied*, 3.
28. Daniels, *Prisoners*, 132.
29. U.S. Commission, *Personal Justice Denied*, 51–67.
30. Ibid., 67–72. Robinson, *By Order*, chs. 1–2, describes the development of FDR's attitudes toward the Japanese.
31. *Lawrence v. Texas*, 539 U.S. 558 (2002).
32. *Meyer v. Nebraska* 262 U.S. 390 (1923).
33. *Loving v. Virginia* 388 U.S. 1 (1967).
34. *Turner v. Safley* 482 U.S. 78 (1987). See also *Zablocki v. Redhail* 434 U.S. 374 (1978).
35. I borrow here from the majority opinion in *Lawrence v. Texas* written by Justice Sandra Day O'Connor.
36. The first two appear among the four given by Dahl, *Democracy and Its Critics*, ch. 10. The third is adumbrated in the same place.
37. *Dred Scott v. Sandford* 19 Howard 393 (1857); *Plessy v. Ferguson* 163 U.S. 537 (1896); *Minersville v. Gobitis* 310 U.S. 586 (1940); *Korematsu v. United States* 323 U.S. 214 (1944); and *Dennis v. United States* 341 U.S. 494 (1951).
38. On the Red Scare, see Robert K. Murray, *Red Scare: A Study in National Hysteria, 1919–1920* (New York: McGraw-Hill, 1955), chs. 11 and 13; Zechariah Chafee, *Free Speech in the United States* (Cambridge, MA: Harvard University Press, 1941), chs. 2, 5, 9, and 10; and Murray B. Levin, *Political Hysteria in America: The Democratic Capacity for Repression* (New York: Basic Books, 1971), ch. 2. On the McCarthy period, see Peter Irons, *The Courage of Their Convictions* (New York: Free Press, 1988), chs. 4 and 8; Alan Barth, *The Rights of Free Men: An Essential Guide to Civil Liberties* (New York: Knopf, 1984), chs. 1–2; and Walter Goodman, *The Committee: The Extraordinary Career of the House Committee on Un-American Activities* (New York: Farrar, Straus, and Giroux, 1968), chs. 7, 10, and 14.
39. Robert A. Dahl first posed this question in "The City in the Future of Democracy," *American Political Science Review* 61 (1967): 953–70.
40. Lani Guinier, *The Tyranny of the Majority: Fundamental Fairness in Representative Democracy* (New York: Free Press, 1994), takes up these matters with respect to American blacks. See the introduction for her analysis of the problem and chapter 4 for proposed remedies.

CHAPTER 5: WHY NO SOCIALISM?

1. The origin of the term *American exceptionalism* may well be found in Tocqueville, *Democracy in America*, 455–56.
2. Among these foreign commentaries, see James Bryce, *The American Commonwealth* (New York: Macmillan, 1910); Harold J. Laski, *The American Democracy: A Commentary and Interpretation* (New York: Viking Press, 1948); Gunnar Myrdal, *An American Dilemma: The Negro Problem and Modern Democracy* (New York:

Harper, 1944); H. G. Wells, *The Future in America: A Search after Realities* (New York: Harper, 1906); and the collections by John G. Brooks, *As Others See Us: A Study of Progress in the United States* (New York: Macmillan, 1908); Henry Steele Commager, ed., *America in Perspective: The United States through Foreign Eyes* (New York: Random House, 1947); Bernard Lewis, Edmund Leites, and Margaret Case, eds., *As Others See Us: Mutual Perceptions, East and West* (New York: International Society for the Comparative Study of Civilizations, 1986); Donald W. Robinson, ed., *As Others See Us: International Views of American History* (Boston: Houghton Mifflin, 1969); and Robert W. Smuts, *European Impressions of the American Worker* (New York: King's Crown Press, 1953).

3. The Organization for Economic Cooperation and Development (OECD) was formed in 1961. The United States was a founding member. The OECD performs research and analysis for member countries. Initially the membership included twenty Western European and North American states. It has taken in additional members from East Asia and Eastern Europe and now numbers thirty. It includes most, but not all, industrialized nations. Notable omissions are China, India, and Russia.

   The European Union grew out of European treaty organizations established soon after World War II. The Treaty of Maastricht (1993) created the EU, which in early 2008 counted twenty-seven European countries as members.

4. Seymour Martin Lipset, *American Exceptionalism: A Double-Edged Sword* (New York: Norton, 1996), 26.

5. Ibid., 43.

6. On the differences between the European and American parties, see Leon D. Epstein, *Political Parties in Western Democracies* (New Bruinswick, NJ: Transaction Books, 1980) and *Political Parties in the American Mold* (Madison: University of Wisconsin Press, 1986).

7. For their observations on this point see Henry J. Abraham, *The Judicial Process: An Introductory Analysis of the Courts of the United States, England, and France*, 2nd ed. (New York: Oxford University Press, 1968), ch. 7; and Robert G. McCloskey, *The American Supreme Court* (Chicago: University of Chicago Press, 1960), 225.

8. Abraham, *Judicial Process*, 299.

9. Lipset, *American Exceptionalism*, 40.

10. On the weakness of the political parties, see Everett Carll Ladd, *Where Have All the Voters Gone? The Fracturing of America's Political Parties*, 2nd ed. (New York: Norton, 1982).

11. Lipset, *American Exceptionalism*, 40.

12. Ibid., 22, 71–72, and 289.

13. *OECD in Figures: Statistics on the Member Countries* (Paris: Organization for Economic Cooperation and Development, 2004), 36–37.

14. Ibid., 38–39.

15. Richard Rose, "Is American Public Policy Exceptional?" in *Is America Different? A New Look at American Exceptionalism*, ed. Byron E. Shafer (Oxford: Clarendon Press, 1991).

16. U.S. Department of State, *World Military Expenditures and Arms Transfers*, 28th ed. (Washington, DC: Government Printing Office, 2003).

17. *OECD in Figures*, 66–67.

18. Rose, "American Public Policy," 207.

19. Ibid., 192–93 and 205–10.

20. See Angus Maddison, *The World Economy: Historical Statistics* (Paris: Development Centre of the Organization for Economic Cooperation and Development, 2003); Simon Kuznets, *Economic Growth of Nations: Total Output and Production Structure* (Cambridge, MA: Harvard University Press, 1971); and *OECD in Figures*, 12–13.

21. This calculation was made from Maddison, *World Economy*, tables 1b, 2b, and 5b. The principal omission from the calculation is the Soviet Union.

22. UN Department for Economic and Social Information and Policy Analysis, *Trends in International Distribution of Gross World Product* (New York: United Nations, 1993), 224–25, table A.1.

23. U.S. Central Intelligence Agency, *The World Factbook 2007* available online at www.cia.gov/cia/publications/factbook.

24. Ibid., 8–9 and 66–67.

25. Lipset, *American Exceptionalism*, 26.

26. Michael Forster and Mark Pearson, "Income Distribution and Poverty in the OECD Area: Trends and Driving Forces," *OECD Economic Studies*, no. 34 (2002/1), 38.

27. Michael Forster and Marco Mira d'Ercole, *Income Distribution and Poverty in OECD Countries in the Second Half of the 1990s*, OECD Social, Employment and Migration Working Papers, no. 22, March 10, 2005, 72–74.

28. Ronald Inglehart et al., ed., *Human Beliefs and Values: A Cross-Cultural Sourcebook Based on the 1999–2002 Values Surveys* (Mexico: Siglo XXI, 2004), tables E190 and 191. See also J. Rytina, W. Form, and J. Pease, "Income and Stratification Ideology: Beliefs about the American Opportunity Structure," *American Journal of Sociology* 75 (1970): 703–16.

29. G. Fields and Efe A. Ok, "Measuring Movement of Incomes," *Economica* 66 (1999): 455–71, survey the controversies over empirical questions.

30. Seymour Martin Lipset and Reinhard Bendix, *Social Mobility in Industrial Society* (Berkeley: University of California Press, 1967), 289.

31. Robert Erikson and John H. Goldthorpe, *The Constant Flux: A Study of Class Mobility in Industrial Societies* (Oxford: Clarendon Press, 1992), ch. 9. Erikson and Goldthorpe's summary is on page 321. See also Robert Erikson and John H. Goldthorpe, "Are American Rates of Social Mobility Exceptionally High?" *European Sociological Review* 1 (1985): 1–22.

32. Lawrence Mishel, Jared Bernstein, and Heather Boushey, *The State of Working America 2002/2003* (Ithaca, NY: ILR, 2003), 75–78; Miles Corak, ed., *Generational Income Mobility in North America and Europe* (New York: Cambridge University Press, 2004); and Gary Solon, "Cross-Country Differences in Intergenerational Earnings Mobility," *Journal of Economic Perspectives* 16 (2002): 59–66.

33. D. Checchi, A. Ichino, and A. Rustichini, "More Equal and Less Mobile? Education Financing and Intergenerational Mobility in Italy and in the US,"

Journal of Public Economics 74 (1999): 351–93; and Peter Gottschalk and E. Spolaore, "On the Evaluation of Economic Mobility," *Review of Economic Studies* 69 (2002), 191–208.

34. Martin N. Marger, *Social Inequality: Patterns and Processes* (Mountain View, CA: Mayfield, 1999), 155–56 and 158–60; and Jonathan Kozol, *Savage Inequalities: Children in America's Schools* (New York: Crown, 1991).

35. Daniel Golden, *The Price of Admission: How America's Ruling Class Buys Its Way into Elite Colleges—and Who Gets Left Outside the Gates* (New York: Crown, 2006).

36. Lipset, *American Exceptionalism*, 19, 26, and 289.

37. Inglehart, *Human Beliefs*, tables F028, A006, F050, F051, and F054.

38. Andrew M. Greeley is doubtful that Europe has become significantly more secular in the postwar period. See his *Religion in Europe at the End of the Second Millennium: A Sociological Profile* (New Bruinswick, NJ: Transaction Books, 2003).

39. Inglehart, *Human Beliefs*, tables G006 and E012.

40. Tocqueville, *Democracy in America*, 513.

41. Inglehart, *Human Beliefs*, tables A064–A079.

42. Ibid., tables A081–A096.

43. Robert D. Putnam, *Bowling Alone: The Collapse and Revival of American Community* (New York: Simon & Schuster, 2000), 127–33.

44. *OECD in Figures*, 44–45, 34–35, 50–51, and 48–49.

45. *OECD in Figures*, 68–69.

46. Rose, "American Public Policy," 191.

47. Andrew Greeley does not ignore this question in his *Religion Around the World: A Preliminary Report*, National Opinion Research Center, 23/4, June 10, 1993, 55–56.

48. Tocqueville, *Democracy in America*, 9.

49. Karl Marx, *The Eighteenth Brumaire of Louis Bonaparte*, in Karl Marx and Friedrich Engels, *Collected Works*, 50 vols. (New York: International Publishers, 1975–2004), 11: 11.

50. Letter from Engels to Sorge, January 6, 1892, in Marx and Engels, *Collected Works*, 49: 307.

51. The Amsterdam Speech, September 8, 1872, in *The Marx-Engels Reader*, ed. Robert C. Tucker, 2nd ed. (New York: Norton, 1978), 523.

52. Tocqueville, *Democracy in America*, 194.

53. Louis Hartz, *The Liberal Tradition in America: An Interpretation of American Political Thought Since the Revolution* (New York: Harcourt, Brace, 1955), 62.

54. See also Daniel Bell, "'The Hegelian Secret': Civil Society and American Exceptionalism," in Shafer, *Is America Different?* 46–70; Daniel J. Boorstin, *The Genius of American Politics* (Chicago: University of Chicago Press, 1953); and David M. Potter, *People of Plenty: Economic Abundance and the American Character* (Chicago: University of Chicago Press, 1954).

55. Daniel T. Rodgers, *Contested Truths: Keywords in American Politics Since Independence* (New York: Basic Books, 1987); and John Lukacs, "American History: The Terminological Problem," *American Scholar* 61 (1992): 17–32.

56. As Richard Hofstadter observed in "Reflections on Violence in the United States," in *American Violence: A Documentary History*, eds. Richard Hofstadter and Michael Wallace (New York: Knopf, 1970), 11.

57. U.S. Bureau of the Census, *Historical Statistics*, 218: Series H452–454. See also Jessie Parkhurst Guzman, "Lynching," in *Racial Violence in the United States*, ed. Allen D. Grimshaw (Chicago: Aldine, 1969), 56–59.

58. G. David Garson and Gail O'Brien, "Collective Violence in the Reconstruction South," in *Violence in America: Historical and Comparative Perspectives*, eds. Hugh Davis Graham and Ted Robert Gurr (Beverly Hills, CA: Sage, 1979), 243–60. The quotes are from pages 247–48.

59. See chapters 4–7 in Grimshaw, *Racial Violence*; and the works cited by Leslie V. Tischauser, *Black/White Relations in American History: An Annotated Bibliography* (Lanham, MD: Scarecrow Press, 1998), 92–101.

60. For figures on strikes see U.S. Bureau of the Census, *Historical Statistics*, Series D764–778: 99. Philip Taft and Philip Ross, "American Labor Violence: Its Causes, Character, and Outcome," in *Violence in America*, 187–241.

61. Werner Sombart, *Why Is There No Socialism in the United States?* (White Plains, NY: M. E. Sharpe, 1976), 15.

62. Engels's observations can be found in letters to Friedrich Sorge on February 8, 1890, October 24, 1891, January 6, 1892, December 31, 1892, and December 2, 1893; to Florence Kelley-Wischnewetzky on June 3, 1886; and to Hermann Schluter on March 30, 1892, in Marx and Engels, *Collected Works*. See also H. G. Wells, *Future in America*, 72–76; and Morris Hillquit, *Socialism in Theory and Practice* (New York: Macmillan, 1909), 162–65; and *History of Socialism in the United States*, 5th ed. (New York: Funk & Wagnalls, 1910), 139–40 and 349.

63. Ann Archer, "Why Is There No Labor Party? Class and Race in the United States and Australia," in *American Exceptionalism? U.S. Working Class Formation in an International Context*, eds. Rich Halpern and Jonathan Morris (New York: St. Martin's, 1997); Daniel Bell, *Marxian Socialism in the United States* (Princeton, NJ: Princeton University Press, 1967); Jean Heffer and Jeanine Rovet, eds., *Why Is There No Socialism in the United States?* (Paris: Editions de l'École des Hautes Études en Sciences Sociales, 1988); C. T. Husbands, "Introduction," in Sombart, *Why Is There No Socialism*; Jerome Karabel, "The Failure of American Socialism Reconsidered," *The Socialist Register* 18 (1979), 204–27; Seymour Martin Lipset, "Why No Socialism in the United States," in *Sources of Contemporary Radicalism*, eds. Seweryn Bialer and Sophia Sluzar (Boulder, CO: Westview, 1977), 31–149; Seymour Martin Lipset and Gary Marks, *It Didn't Happen Here: Why Socialism Failed in the United States* (New York: Norton, 2000); Gary Marks, *Unions in Politics: Britain, Germany and the United States in the Nineteenth and Early Twentieth Centuries* (Princeton, NJ: Princeton University Press, 1989), ch. 9; and Aristide R. Zolberg, "How Many Exceptionalisms?" in *Working-Class Formation: Nineteenth-Century Patterns in Western Europe and the United States*, eds. Ira Katznelson and Aristide R. Zolberg (Princeton, NJ: Princeton University Press, 1986), 397–455.

64. Lipset and Marks make much of this in *It Didn't Happen Here*, 58–71.

65. For the United States, see U.S. Bureau of the Census, *Historical Statistics*, 74:

Series D72-122; and for Britain, France, and Germany, see B. R. Mitchell, comp., *International Historical Statistics: Europe, 1750–1993*, 4th ed. (New York: Stockton Press, 1998), 145–60; Zolberg, "How Many Exceptionalisms?" 438.

66. U.S. Bureau of the Census, *Historical Statistics*, 74: Series D72-122.

67. E. P. Hutchinson, *Immigrants and Their Children, 1850–1950* (New York: Wiley, 1956), 202: table 38.

68. Gerald Rosenblum, *Immigrant Workers: Their Impact on American Labor Radicalism* (New York: Basic Books, 1973), 145–51.

69. Ira Katznelson, *City Trenches: Urban Politics and the Patterning of Class in the United States* (New York: Pantheon, 1981); Husbands, "Introduction"; and Karabel, "Failure of American Socialism."

70. U.S. Bureau of the Census, *Historical Statistics*, 56: Series C88-100 and 64: Series C156-170. See also Michael Piore, *Birds of Passage: Migrant Labor and Industrial Societies* (New York: Cambridge University Press, 1979), 151–53.

71. Rosenblum, *Immigrant Workers*, 34–51 and 151–58.

72. Isaac A. Hourwich, *Immigration and Labor: The Economic Aspects of European Immigration to the United States* (New York: Putnam's, 1912), ch. 7; Hutchinson, *Immigrants and Their Children*, 101–105: tables 25ab, 124–31: tables 29ab, 161–63: table 33, 202: table 38, and his summary on p. 275; and Gwendolyn Mink, *Old Labor and New Immigrants in American Political Development: Union, Party, and State, 1875–1920* (Ithaca, NY: Cornell University Press, 1986), ch. 2.

73. Edna Bonacich, "Advanced Capitalism and Black/White Relations: A Spilt Labor Market Interpretation," *American Sociological Review* 41 (1976): 34–51; Mike Davis, *Prisoners of the American Dream: Politics and Economy in the History of the U.S. Working Class* (New York: Verso, 1986); and Katznelson, *City Trenches*.

74. James Weinstein, *The Decline of Socialism in America, 1912–1925* (New York: Monthly Review Press, 1967), 93–118.

75. Robert Goldstein, *Political Repression in Modern America, 1870 to the Present* (Cambridge, MA: Shenkman, 1978), 103-64.

76. As Aristide Zolberg argues in "How Many Exceptionalisms?" 450.

77. On the significance of the frontier, see Frederick Jackson Turner, *The Frontier in American History* (New York: Henry Holt, 1920). On the significance of economic abundance, see Potter, *People of Plenty*.

CHAPTER 6: THE AMERICAN MISSION

1. Samuel Willard, *A Compleat Body of Divinity* (New York: Johnson Reprint, 1968), 153.

2. Ibid., 153–54; and Increase Mather, "Awakening Truths Tending to Conversion," in *The Puritans*, eds. Perry Miller and Thomas H. Johnson (New York: American Book Co., 1938), 335–36.

3. Willard, *Compleat Body*, 153.

4. Samuel Willard, "The Character of a Good Ruler," in *Puritans*, 251. This sermon is reproduced in full in Sacvan Bercovitch, ed., *A Library of American Puritan Writings*, 22 vols. (New York: AMS Press, 1982–97), 1: 2. This sermon and other materials cited below in *American Puritan Writings* are paginated separately.

5. Willard, *Compleat Body*, 154.

6. Ibid., 15.

7. Ibid., 246–57.

8. Ibid., 275–79.

9. John Cotton, "A Treatise of the Covenant of Grace," in *The Puritans in America: A Narrative Anthology*, eds. Alan Heimert and Andrew Delbanco (Cambridge, MA: Harvard University Press, 1985), 151.

10. Ibid., 152–53.

11. John Cotton, "The New Covenant," in *Puritans*, 314–18. See also the sources cited by Perry Miller and his discussion in *The New England Mind: The Seventeenth Century* (New York: Macmillan, 1939), 68–81; and "A Platform of Church Discipline," in *American Puritan Writings*, 6: 21–23.

12. I am indebted for this comparison of the two covenants to Miller, *New England Mind*, 479.

13. As quoted in Ibid., 480.

14. William Stoughton, "New-Englands True Interest: Not to Lie," in *Puritans*, 245. This sermon appears in full in *American Puritan Writings*, vol. 1. See also Thomas Shepard Jr., "Eye-Salve," in *Puritans in America*, 253; and Cotton Mather, "A Pillar of Gratitude," as quoted in *The Wall and the Garden: Selected Massachusetts Election Sermons, 1670–1775*, ed. A. W. Plumstead (Minneapolis: University of Minnesota Press, 1968), 144.

15. Ibid., 244, and *American Puritan Writings*, 1: 16.

16. Samuel Willard, "The Only Sure Way," in *Wall and the Garden*, 98. See also Shepard, "Eye-Salve," 252; and Stoughton, "New-Englands True Interest: Not to Lie," in *American Puritan Writings*, 1: 12–14.

17. John Cotton, "God's Promise to His Plantations," in *Puritans in America*, 76.

18. Stoughton, "New-Englands True Interest," in *Puritans*, 243; and in *American Puritan Writings*, 1: 16.

19. Urian Oakes, "New-England Pleaded With," in *American Puritan Writings*, 1: 17.

20. Cotton Mather, "The Serviceable Man," in *Puritan Political Ideas 1558–1794*, ed. Edmund S. Morgan (Indianapolis: Bobbs-Merrill, 1965), 241.

21. John Winthrop, "A Model of Christian Charity," in *Puritans in America*, 89–90.

22. Mather, "Serviceable Man," 243.

23. Cotton Mather, "Magnalia Christi Americana," in *The Puritans*, 166–67. On both of these points, see also Samuel Danforth, "A Brief Recognition of New-Englands Errand into the Wilderness," in *Wall and the Garden*, 65; Shepard, "Eye-Salve," 258; and Peter Bulkeley, "The Gospel-Covenant," in *Puritans in America*, 120.

24. Winthrop, "Model of Christian Charity," 91. Winthrop relied here on Matthew 5: 14.

25. Plumstead, *Wall and the Garden*, 57–77. See Plumstead's comments on origins and citations to other occurrences of the expression, 48n4–5.

26. For the two cities see St. Augustine, *The City of God*, trans. Henry Bettenson (London: Penguin, 1984), book 14, chs. 1–4 and 28; book 15, chs. 1–8; and book 19, chs. 1–8, 11, 17, and 24. For St. Augustine's interpretation of Revelation see ibid., book 20, chs. 7–17.

27. On identification of the papacy with Satan see Thomas M. Brown, "The Image of the Beast: Anti-Papal Rhetoric in Colonial America," in *Conspiracy: The Fear of Subversion in American History*, eds. Richard O. Curry and Thomas M. Brown (New York: Holt, Rinehart and Winston, 1972), 1–20.

28. Increase Mather, "The Mystery of Israel's Salvation," in *Puritans in America*, 243. See also Jonathan Edwards, "A Humble Attempt," in *Apocalyptic Writings*, ed. Stephen J. Stein, vol. 5 of *The Works of Jonathan Edwards*, 22 vols. (New Haven, CT: Yale University Press, 1957–2003), 337.

29. Edward Johnson, "Wonder-Working Providence of Sion's Savior in New England," in *Puritans*, 143–44. The full text is in Edward Johnson, *Johnson's Wonder-Working Providence 1628–1651*, ed. J. Franklin Jameson (New York: Scribner's, 1910).

30. Cotton Mather, *Magnalia Christi Americana: Books I and II*, ed. Kenneth B. Murdock (Cambridge, MA: Harvard University Press, 1977), 123.

31. Jonathan Edwards, "Some Thoughts Concerning the Present Revival of Religion in New England," in *Puritanism and the American Experience*, ed. Michael McGiffert (Reading, MA: Addison-Wesley, 1969), 160. The full text is in Jonathan Edwards, *The Great Awakening*, vol. 4 of *Works*. See also Samuel Sewall, "Phaenomena quaedam Apocalyptica," in *Puritans in America*, 292–93; and Perry Miller's comments on the millennialism of the late seventeenth and early eighteenth centuries in *New England Mind*, 185–90.

32. Ebenezer Baldwin, "The Duty of Rejoicing Under Calamities and Afflictions," as quoted in J. F. Maclear, "The Republic and the Millennium," in *The Religion of the Republic*, ed. Elwyn A. Smith (Philadelphia: Fortress Press, 1971), 185n3. Baldwin was not alone in these sentiments as Nathan O. Hatch demonstrates in his *The Sacred Cause of Liberty: Republican Thought and the Millennium in Revolutionary New England* (New Haven, CT: Yale University Press, 1977), particularly ch. 4: 146–51. See also Winthrop Hudson, ed., *Nationalism and Religion in America* (New York: Harper & Row, 1970), 49 and 52.

33. See Johnson, *Johnson's Wonder-Working Providence*, 165, for the devil's role in provoking the Pequot War of 1637; and William Hubbard, *Narrative of the Troubles with the Indians* (1677) for his reappearance in 1675 as the ultimate cause of King Philip's War as quoted in Richard Slotkin, *Regeneration Through Violence: The Mythology of the American Frontier, 1600–1860* (Middletown, CT: Wesleyan University Press, 1973), 88.

34. See Jonathan Mayhew, "A Sermon Preached," in *Wall and the Garden*, 310.

35. John Richardson, "The Necessity of a Well Experienced Souldiery," as quoted in Harry S. Stout, *The New England Soul: Preaching and Religious Culture in Colonial New England* (New York: Oxford University Press, 1986), 83.

36. Samuel Nowell, "Abraham in Arms," in *So Dreadful a Judgment: Puritan Responses to King Philip's War, 1676–1677*, eds. Richard Slotkin and James S. Folsom (Middletown, CT: Wesleyan University Press, 1978), 285.

37. Ibid., 286.

38. Stout, *New England Soul*, 82–85 and ch. 12.

39. As quoted in Perry Miller, *Errand into the Wilderness* (Cambridge, MA: Harvard University Press, 1956), 119.

40. William Bradford, "Of Plymouth Plantation," in *Puritans in America*, 57; Robert Cushman, "Discourse," in *Chronicles of the Pilgrim Fathers of the Colony of Plymouth from 1602 to 1625*, ed. Alexander Young, 2nd ed. (Baltimore, MD: Genealogical Publishing, 1974), 240–41.

41. Roger Williams and John Cotton, in *Puritans in America*, 196–209.

42. Ibid., 12.

43. See, for example, George Marsden, "Evangelicals, History, and Modernity," in *Evangelicalism and Modern America*, ed. George Marsden (Grand Rapids, MI: Eerdmans, 1984), 95–97; James Franklin Love, *The Mission of Our Nation* (New York: Fleming H. Revell, 1912), 122; and William G. McLoughlin, *Billy Graham: Revivalist in a Secular Age* (New York: Ronald Press, 1960), 142.

44. James Davison Hunter and Carl Bowman, *The State of Disunion: 1996 Survey of American Political Culture*, 2 vols. (Ivy, VA: In Media Res Educational Foundation, 1996), 1: 4–5.

45. Farrand, *Records*, 1: 422–23.

46. Hamilton et al., *Federalist Papers*, 33.

47. See the comments of Elbridge Gerry, in Farrand, *Records*, 1: 515; Gouverneur Morris, 1: 529; Benjamin Franklin, 1: 452; and Washington, *Papers, Confederation Series*, 2: 175.

48. Roger Cohen, "Globalist: U.S. 'Greatest' Rhetoric Alienates Many Abroad," *International Herald Tribune*, September 15, 2004.

49. Alfred T. Mahan, *Lessons of the War with Spain and Other Articles* (Boston: Little, Brown, 1899), 286–87; and *The Interest of America in Sea Power, Present and Future* (Boston: Little, Brown, 1898), 104.

50. Henry R. Luce, *The American Century* (New York: Farrar and Rinehart, 1941), 36 and 39.

51. Jefferson, *Writings*, 493.

52. See Hatch, *Sacred Cause of Liberty*, 171n92.

53. Lyman Beecher, *Plea for the West* (Cincinnati, OH: Truman and Smith, 1835), 9–10.

54. Washington Gladden, "The Nation and the Kingdom," in *The Social Gospel in America, 1870–1920*, ed. Robert T. Handy (New York: Oxford University Press, 1966), 141 and 152.

55. Farrand, *Records*, 1: 135.

56. Jefferson, *Writings*, 288 and 289.

57. As Garry Wills suggests in his *Lincoln at Gettysburg: The Words That Remade America* (New York: Simon & Schuster, 1992).

58. Abraham Lincoln, *Abraham Lincoln: Speeches and Writings*, ed. Don E. Fehrenbacher, 2 vols. (New York: Library of America, 1989), 2: 536.

59. Gladden, "The Nation and the Kingdom," 144–45.

60. He did so throughout his career. See Washington Gladden, *Working People and Their Employers* (Boston: Lockwood, Brooks, 1876).

61. Franklin D. Roosevelt, *The Public Papers and Addresses of Franklin D. Roosevelt*, comp. Samual I. Rosenman, 13 vols. (New York: Random House and Harper, 1938–1950), 5: 235 and 233.

62. Martin Luther King in *Representative American Speeches: 1963–1964*, ed. Lester Thonssen (New York: H. W. Wilson, 1964), 44 and 47.

63. Albert Gallatin, "Peace with Mexico," in *The Writings of Albert Gallatin*, ed. Henry Adams, 3 vols. (New York: Antiquarian Press, 1960), 3: 582–83.

64. See Lincoln, *Speeches and Writings*, 1: 168–170; Ulysses S. Grant, *Personal Memoirs* (New York: Library of America, 1990), 41.

65. John L. O'Sullivan as quoted by Julius W. Pratt, *A History of United States Foreign Policy* (Englewood Cliffs, NJ: Prentice-Hall, 1955), 216. See also Pratt's "The Origin of 'Manifest Destiny,'" *American Historical Review* 32 (1927): 795–98; and "John L. O'Sullivan and Manifest Destiny," *New York History* 45 (1933): 213–34.

66. *Democratic Review* (October, 1847), as quoted by Pratt, *History of United States Foreign Policy*, 258.

67. Josiah Strong, *Our Country: Its Possible Future and Its Present Crisis*, rev. ed. (New York: Baker & Taylor, 1891), 222 and 263.

68. Albert J. Beveridge, *The Meaning of the Times and Other Speeches* (Indianapolis, IN: Bobbs-Merrill, 1908), 84 and 85.

69. Ibid., 124 and 128.

70. Woodrow Wilson, *The Papers of Woodrow Wilson*, ed. Arthur S. Link, 69 vols. (Princeton, NJ: Princeton University Press, 1966–1994), 42: 366.

71. As quoted in Conrad Cherry, ed., *God's New Israel: Religious Interpretations of American Destiny*, rev. ed. (Chapel Hill: University of North Carolina Press, 1998), 271.

72. Wilson, *Papers*, 40: 534.

73. Ibid., 61: 436.

74. George W. Bush, *"We Will Prevail": President George W. Bush on War, Terrorism, and Freedom* (New York: Continuum, 2003), 17.

75. John W. Dietrich, ed., *The George W. Bush Foreign Policy Reader: Presidential Speeches and Commentary* (Armonk, NY: M. E. Sharpe, 2005), 63 and 89.

76. *We Will Prevail*, 71–72. See also Dietrich, *Bush Foreign Policy Reader*, 54.

77. Dietrich, *Bush Foreign Policy Reader*, 106.

78. Ibid., 259.

79. Ibid., 106.

80. Ibid., 89.

81. Donald H. Akenson, *God's People: Covenant and Land in South Africa, Israel, and Ulster* (Ithaca, NY: Cornell University Press, 1992); William R. Hutchinson and Hartmut Lehmann, eds., *Many Are Chosen: Divine Election and Western Nationalism* (Minneapolis, MN: Fortress Press, 1994); and Conor Cruise O'Brien, *God Land: Reflections on Religion and Nationalism* (Cambridge, MA: Harvard University Press, 1988).

82. Michael Walzer, *Obligations: Essays on Disobedience, War, and Citizenship* (Cambridge, MA: Harvard University Press, 1970), examines these matters at length.

CHAPTER 7: THE MARKET

1. This is the abbreviated title. The full citation is Adam Smith, *An Inquiry into the Nature and Causes of the Wealth of Nations*, ed. Edwin Cannan (New York: Modern Library, 1937).

2. Ibid., 651.

3. Cf. Charles E. Lindblom, *The Market System: What It Is, How It Works, and What to Make of It* (New Haven, CT: Yale University Press, 2001), 23; John McMillan, *Reinventing the Bazaar: A Natural History of Markets* (New York: Norton, 2002), 5–6; and Winifred Barr Rothenberg, *From Market-Places to a Market Economy: The Transformation of Rural Massachusetts, 1750–1850* (Chicago: University of Chicago Press, 1992), 242–43.

4. The image of the web is Lindblom's in *The Market*, 40.

5. John R. Freeman, *Democracy and Markets: The Politics of Mixed Economies* (Ithaca, NY: Cornell University Press, 1989).

6. As Robert L. Heilbroner emphasizes in his *The Making of Economic Society* (Englewood Cliffs, NJ: Prentice-Hall, 1962), 4–5.

7. Ibid., ch. 3; and Karl Polanyi, *The Great Transformation* (New York: Farrar & Rinehart, 1944), ch. 4, provide good, brief descriptions.

8. M. I. Finley, *Ancient Slavery and Modern Ideology* (New York: Viking, 1980), 80.

9. For a review of recent historiography on the ancient economy see Ian Morris's "Foreword" to M. I. Finley, *The Ancient Economy*, updated ed. (Berkeley: University of California Press, 1999), ix–xxxvi.

10. Compare the New Revised Standard Version.

11. See Leviticus 25:39–40 and 25:44–46; Deuteronomy 15:15; Exodus 21:7 and 21:21.

12. Genesis 9:25–27.

13. Exodus 21:2–11 and 20–27; Leviticus 25:42–46; Deuteronomy 15:12–18; and Proverbs 29:19, for example.

14. Ephesians 6:5–8; Colossians 3:22; 1 Timothy 6:1–5; Titus 2:9–10; and 1 Peter 2:18–19.

15. Matthew 8:5–13.

16. Exodus 22:25; Leviticus 25:35–37; Psalms 15:5; and Ezekiel 18:1–9, 13, 17 and 22:12.

17. Deuteronomy 23:19–20.

18. Matthew 6:19–34 and 19:23–24; and Luke 12:16–34 and 18:22–25.

19. Timothy 6:9.

20. Matthew 19:24.

21. Karl Marx, "The German Ideology: Part I," in *Marx-Engels Reader*, 150–61.

22. Smith, *Wealth of Nations*, 4–5.

23. Smith, *Wealth of Nations*, 734–35. See also Karl Marx, "Economic and Philosophic Manuscripts of 1844," in *Marx-Engels Reader*, 73; and Tocqueville, *Democracy in America*, 555–56.

24. I follow Lindblom, *The Market*, ch. 4, in identification of these conditions.

25. This is the contention in modified form of Max Weber, *The Protestant Ethic and the Spirit of Capitalism*, trans. Talcott Parsons (New York: Scribner's, 1930). See the commentary in Robert W. Green, *Protestantism and Capitalism: The Weber Thesis and Its Critics* (Boston: Heath, 1959), and that of Georgia Harkness, *John Calvin: The Man and His Ethics* (New York: Abingdon Press, 1958), ch. 9.

26. John Calvin, *Institutes of the Christian Religion*, trans. Henry Beveridge, 2 vols. (Grand Rapids, MI: Eerdmans, 1953), 1: 478–90.

27. Ibid., 2: 34–35.
28. Modern expression of this view can be found in W. Earl Waldrop, *What Makes America Great?* (St Louis: Bethany Press, 1957), 58.
29. Calvin, *Institutes*, 1: 36–97.
30. See the letter quoted by Harkness, *John Calvin*, 204–206.
31. Benjamin N. Nelson, *The Idea of Usury: From Tribal Brotherhood to Universal Otherhood* (Princeton, NJ: Princeton University Press, 1949), 74–77.
32. L. White, *Medieval Technology and Social Change* (Oxford: Oxford University Press, 1962), and B. H. Slicher van Bath, *The Agrarian History of Western Europe AD 500–1850* (London: Edward Arnold, 1963).
33. Mercantilism prescribed the promotion of exports and the accumulation of precious metals.
34. Polanyi, *Great Transformation*, ch. 5 and 278–79.
35. Heilbroner, *Making of Economic Society*, 71.
36. William J. Novak, *The People's Welfare: Law and Regulation in Nineteenth-Century America* (Chapel Hill: University of North Carolina Press, 1996).
37. William G. Roy, *Socializing Capital: The Rise of the Large Industrial Corporation in America* (Princeton, NJ: Princeton University Press, 1997).
38. Charles Perrow, *Organizing America: Wealth, Power, and the Origins of the Corporate Capitalism* (Princeton, NJ: Princeton University Press, 2002), 197–216.
39. *County of Santa Clara v. Southern Pacific Railroad Company* 118 U.S. 394 (1886).
40. Institute for Policy Studies, www.ips-dc.org/global_econ/top100 (accessed mid-2006). Current ranking of corporate sales are available at www.forbes.com/lists/2008/18/biz 2000global08 The-Global-2000 Sales.html and of national GDP at www.cia.gov/library/publications/the-world-factbook/rankorder/2001rank.html.
41. John Sperling et al., *The Great Divide: Retro vs. Metro America* (Sausalito, CA: Polipoint Press, 2004), ch. 5, and David C. Johnston, *Free Lunch: How the Wealthiest Americans Enrich Themselves (and Stick You with the Bill)* (New York: Portfolio, 2008).
42. Smith, *Wealth of Nations*, 14.
43. Ibid., 423.
44. Lindblom, *The Market*, 132–39; and Smith, *Wealth of Nations*, 55–63.
45. Naomi Lamoreaux, *The Great Merger Movement in American Business, 1895–1904* (New York: Cambridge University Press, 1985); and F. M. Scherer, *Industrial Market Structure and Economic Performance*, 2nd ed. (Boston: Houghton Miflin, 1980).
46. Louis Galambos, "The Triumph of Oligopoly," in *American Economic Development in Historical Perspective*, eds. Thomas Weiss and Donald Schaefer (Stanford, CA: Stanford University Press, 1994), 244–53.
47. Alfred Eichner, *The Emergence of Oligopoly: Sugar Refining as a Case Study* (Baltimore: Johns Hopkins University Press, 1969), 291–331; and Scherer, *Industrial Market Structure*, 151–266, 407–38, 459–74.
48. Fred Block, *Postindustrial Possibilities: A Critique of Economic Discourse* (Berkeley: University of California Press, 1990), ch. 3, examines this and other nonmarket restraints on the system.

49. The classic case was made by Friedrich A. von Hayek, *The Road to Serfdom* (Chicago: University of Chicago Press, 1944).

50. Merritt Roe Smith, "Army Ordinance and the 'American System' of Manufacturing, 1815–1861," in *Military Enterprise and Technological Change: Perspectives on the American Experience*, ed. Merritt Roe Smith (Cambridge, MA: MIT Press, 1985), 64.

51. Merritt Roe Smith, "Introduction," in ibid., 8–9.

52. Harry Dowling, *Medicines for Man: The Development, Regulation, and Use of Prescription Drugs* (New York: Knopf, 1971), 42–44.

53. Thomas Misa, "Military Needs, Commercial Realities, and the Development of the Transistor, 1948–1958," in Smith, *Military Enterprise*, 253–87; Kenneth Flamm, *Creating the Computer: Government, Industry, and High Techology* (Washington, DC: Brookings Institution, 1988); and Janet Abbate, *Inventing the Internet* (Cambridge, MA: MIT Press, 1999).

54. See www.nsf.gov about the work of the National Science Foundation; U.S. Congress, Joint Economic Committee, *Benefits of Medical Research and the Role of the NIH*, 106th Cong., 2nd sess., May 2000, Committee Print, 20; and U.S. Department of Agriculture, Agricultural Research Service, "Ethanol Feedstock from Citrus Peel Waste," *Agricultural Research* 54 (April 2006): 19.

55. Karl Marx, "The German Ideology," in *Marx-Engels Reader*, 160.

56. Karl Marx, "The Manifesto of the Communist Party," in *Marx-Engels Reader*, 477.

57. Jody Heymann, *The Widening Gap: Why America's Working Families Are in Jeopardy and What Can Be Done about It* (New York: Basic Books, 2000), ch. 7; Donald Tomaskovic-Devey, *Gender and Racial Inequality at Work: The Sources and Consequences of Job Segregation* (Ithaca, NY: ILR Press, 1993); and Judy Goldberg Dey and Catherine Hill, *Behind the Pay Gap* (Washington, DC: AAUW Educational Foundation, April 2007).

58. Smith, *Wealth of Nations*, 15–16.

59. U.S. General Accounting Office, *Report GAO-04-35* (Washington, DC: Government Printing Office, 2004); but see also Warren Farrell, *Why Men Earn More: The Startling Truth about the Pay Gap—and What Women Can Do about It* (New York: AMACOM, 2005); and Daniel E. Hecker, "Earnings of College Graduates: Women Compared with Men," *Monthly Labor Review*, March 1998, 62–71.

60. David Milstead, "That's a Lot of Clams," *Rocky Mountain News*, May 6, 2006.

61. "CEOs and Their Indian Rope Trick," *The Economist*, December 11, 2004, 61, and "Too Many Turkeys," November 26, 2005, 75. See also the annual survey of compensation at the 365 largest corporations in *Business Week*, the periodic reports from the Institute of Policy Studies and the Economic Policy Institute, and Graef S. Crystal, *In Search of Excess: The Overcompensation of American Executives* (New York: Norton, 1992). CEO pay includes bonuses, stock options, and perquisites like the use of cars, houses, and airplanes. *The Economist*, December 11, 2004, 60–61, looks at the link between CEO pay and performance.

62. Smith, *Wealth of Nations*, 388–89.

63. See the impressionistic studies done by Studs Terkel, *Working* (New York:

Avon Books, 1972); and Kenneth Lasson, *The Workers: Portraits of Nine American Jobholders* (New York: Bantam Books, 1971).

64. Joseph S. Zeisel, "The Workweek in American Industry 1850–1956," *Monthly Labor Review* 81 (January 1958): 23–29.

65. E. P. Thompson, "Time, Work-Discipline, and Industrial Capitalism," *Past & Present* 38 (December 1967): 56–97; but see also Eric Hopkins, "Working Hours and Conditions During the Industrial Revolution: A Re-Appraisal," *Economic History Review* 35 (February 1982): 52–66.

66. Joel Rogers and Wolfgang Streeck, "Workplace Representation Overseas: The Works Councils Story," in *Working Under Different Rules*, ed. Richard B. Freeman (New York: Russell Sage, 1994), 97–156; Joel Rogers and Wolfgang Streeck, eds., *Works Councils: Consultation, Representation, Cooperation in Industrial Relations* (Chicago: University of Chicago Press, 1994); and Raymond L. Hogler and Guillermo J. Grenier, *Employee Participation and Labor Law in the American Workplace* (New York: Quorum Books, 1992).

67. Rebecca Blank reviews the evidence in "Does a Larger Social Safety Net Mean Less Economic Flexibility?" in *Working Under Different Rules*, 157–88. *The Economist* undertook a brief review, "Economics Focus: Intricate Workings" (June 17, 2006), 84. See also Vincent A. Mahlen and Claudio J. Katz, "Social Benefits in Advanced Capitalist Countries: A Cross-National Assessment," *Comparative Politics* 21 (October 1988): 37–51.

68. This is Lindblom's contention in *Market System*, 162–64 and elaborated in ch. 12.

69. See chapter 5 of this book and the references there.

70. Smith, *Wealth of Nations*, 14.

71. The classic study is Michael Harrington, *The Other America: Poverty in the United States* (New York: Macmillan, 1962). See also Samuel Bowles and Herbert Gintis, *Schooling in Capitalist America: Educational Reform and the Contradictions of Economic Life* (New York: Basic Books, 1976). Jonathan Kozol has done several studies among them: *Savage Inequalities: Children in America's Schools* (New York: Crown, 1991) and *Amazing Grace: The Lives of Children and the Conscience of a Nation* (New York: Crown, 1995). For more recent data see Mark Nord, Margaret Andrews, and Steven Carlson, "Household Food Security in the United States, 2003," U.S. Department of Agriculture, Food and Nutrition Services, *Economic Research Report No. 11* (October 2005); and Mathematica Policy Research, *Hunger in America, 2006: National Report* (Princeton, NJ: Mathematica Policy Research for America's Second Harvest, 2006), chs. 5, 6, 8, and 9; Susan Starr Sered and Rushika Fernandopulle, *Uninsured in America: Life and Death in the Land of Opportunity* (Berkeley: University of California Press, 2005).

72. John Cassidy, "Relatively Deprived," *The New Yorker*, April 3, 2006, 42–47.

73. Paul Krugman, "For Richer: How the Permissive Capitalism of the Boom Destroyed American Equality," *New York Times Magazine*, October 20, 2002, 65.

74. "Wealth Inequality," *Dollars & Sense* 251 (January–February 2004): 65; Edward N. Wolff, *Top Heavy* (New York: New Press, 2002); and Robert J. Lampman, *The Share of Top Wealth Holders in National Wealth, 1922–56* (Princeton, NJ: National Bureau of Economics Research, 1962).

75. U.S. Census Bureau, *Statistical Abstract of the United States: 2002* (Washington, DC: Government Printing Office, 2002), Table 560: 367.

76. Ibid., Table 599: 390.

77. Ibid., Table 587: 380.

78. For research on this matter, see the bibliography in William P. Faunce, *Work, Status, and Self-Esteem: A Theory of Selective Self-Investment* (Lanham, MD: University Press of America, 2003), 209–51.

79. Pope John Paul II, Address to the Participants in the Fifth General Assembly of the Pontifical Academy of Social Science, March 6, 1999. Text at www.vatican.va/holy_father/john_paul_ii/speeches/1999.

80. Pope John Paul II, *Laborem exercens*, September 14, 1981, www.vatican.va/edocs/ENG0217/_INDEX.HTM.

81. David Braybrooke, *Three Tests for Democracy: Personal Rights, Human Welfare, Collective Preference* (New York: Random House, 1968), 74–81.

82. Angus Maddison, *Phases of Capitalist Development* (Oxford: Oxford University Press, 1982), 43.

83. Mun-Heng Toh, "External Liberalization and Economic Growth: The Case of Singapore," in *External Liberalization in Asia, Post-Socialist Europe, and Brazil*, ed. Lance Taylor (Oxford: Oxford University Press, 2006), 368–87.

84. Neither the Soviet economy under Stalin nor the Chinese economy under Mao was a pure command system, but they came close enough to show us in practice what such a system might look like. See Alec Nove, *An Economic History of the U.S.S.R.* (London: Allen Lane, 1969); and Andrew Walder, *Communist Neo-Traditionalism: Work and Authority in Chinese Industry* (Berkeley: University of California Press, 1986).

85. Gregory Grossman, *Economic Systems*, 2nd ed. (Englewood Cliffs, NJ: Prentice-Hall, 1974), 155.

86. *China in the World Economy: The Domestic Policy Challenge* (Paris: Organization for Economic Cooperation and Development, 2002), ch. 9.

87. Istvan Abel and Istvan P. Szekely, "Changing Structures of Household Portfolios in Emerging Market Economies: The Case of Hungary," in *Hungary: An Economy in Transition*, eds. Istvan P. Szekely and David M. G. Newbery (Cambridge: Camb-ridge University Press, 1993), 163–80; and Raphael Shen, *The Polish Economy: Legacies from the Past, Prospects for the Future* (New York: Praeger, 1992), 25–28.

88. Jerzy Wilkin, "The Role of Peasants in the Systemic Transformation of the Polish Economy, 1944–1990," in *The Economic Transformation of Eastern Europe: Views from Within*, eds. Bernard S. Katz and Libby Rittenberg (Westport, CT: Praeger, 1992), ch. 11; Maciej Iwanek, "Poland's Property Rights Problem in the Transition," 28 in the same volume; and Grossman, *Economic Systems*, 153.

89. Contrary to Hayek, *Road to Serfdom*, Robert A. Dahl argues that democracy is incompatible with a "strictly free market economy" in "Why All Democratic Countries Have Mixed Economies," in *Democratic Community*, eds. John W. Chapman and Ian Shapiro (New York: New York University Press, 1993), 259–82.

BIBLIOGRAPHICAL ESSAY

In the comments that follow I identify books that I found particularly helpful in responding to the questions that inform this book. The endnotes, I shall assume, provide sufficient direction as to where to look for the record of the American experience. The works below suggest what to look for. I devote a paragraph to each chapter and confine myself to a handful of titles in each case.

Clinton Rossiter, *1787: The Grand Convention* (1966), is a first-rate account of the Constitutional Convention. He is thorough in his coverage and balanced in his judgments. Thomas J. Curry in *The First Freedoms: Church and State in America to the Passage of the First Amendment* (1986) does real groundbreaking work, particularly on the use of language in colonial and revolutionary America. Mark A. Noll, ed., *Religion and American Politics: From the Colonial Period to the 1980s* (1990), brings together useful essays by Harry Stout, John Murrin, and Noll himself. Michael J. Malbin, *Religion and Politics: The Intentions of the Authors of the First Amendment* (1978) shows that First Amendment "free exercise" does not seem to have been intended to permit, on the grounds of religious principle, disobedience of an otherwise constitutional law. His interpretation of the "establishment" clause is unpersuasive. Michael Novak, *On Two Wings: Humble Faith and Common Sense at the American Founding* (2002) argues that the Framers must have had a millennial view of history solely on the grounds that almost all of them were (at least nominally) Christians.

There are two very competent books on original intent: Jack N. Rakove, *Original Meanings: Politics and Ideas in the Making of the Constitution* (1996) and Leonard Levy, *Original Intent and the Framers' Constitution* (1988). Both point out the formidable difficulties in the path of any effort to recover original intent. Rakove also edited a useful collection of contending views on the subject titled *Interpreting the Constitution: The Debate over Original Intent* (1970) that includes James Hutson's "Creation of the Constitution: The Integrity of the Documentary Record." Richard Hofstadter, *America at 1750: A Social Portrait* (1971), Jackson Turner Main, *The Social Structure of Revolutionary America* (1965), and Edwin J. Perkins, *American Public Finance and Financial Services, 1700–1815* (1994) are all worth consulting about the social and economic conditions in which Americans lived their lives at the time of the Founding.

The rationale for Madison's support for separation of powers and checks and balances is a much controverted question among students of the Founding. Chapter 1 of Robert A. Dahl, *A Preface to Democratic Theory* (1956), is the classic statement of interpretations that emphasize the significance of interest and of distrust of popular majorities in Madison's thinking. Garry Wills, who always has interesting things to say, sets out the boldest and most original response to that position in *Explaining America: The Federalist* (1981). He emphasizes the importance of civic virtue in Madison's politics. David F. Epstein, *The Political Theory of the Federalist* (1984) is a careful and thorough analysis. Bradford Wilson and Peter W. Schramm compiled a collection of essays entitled *Separation of Powers and Good Government* (1994) that takes a much more benign view of separation of powers and checks and balances than does this book.

Much of the literature on democracy is relevant to a study of tyranny of the majority. And, most explications of the thought of Madison, Tocqueville, and J. S. Mill devote attention to the problem. The place to start, however, is with Robert A. Dahl, *Democracy and Its Critics* (1989). This work reflects a lifetime of hard thinking about democracy and its ills, real and alleged. He regards tyranny of the majority as a real problem but prescribes increased democratization as the remedy. In the course of his attack on the reigning theories of political legitimacy, James S. Fishkin, *Tyranny and Legitimacy: A Critique of Political Theories* (1979), contributes much to sorting out conceptual issues involved in coming to grips with the idea of tyranny. Lani Guinier, *The Tyranny of the Majority: Fundamental Fairness in Representative Democracy* (1994), focuses on African-Americans whom she regards as a "permanent minority."

In *American Exceptionalism: A Double-Edged Sword* (1996), Seymour Martin Lipset presents the case for American exceptionalism at considerable length. He is concerned wholly with empirical matters. He succeeds in showing that the United States is unique in many respects. He is not successful in showing that the United States is exceptional. Byron E. Shafer, ed., *Is America Different? A New Look at American Exceptionalism* (1991) is an excellent collection of essays on the empirical question. Particularly valuable is Richard Rose's essay, which attacks head-on the notion that America is qualitatively different as Lipset maintains. Alexis de Tocqueville, *Democracy in America* (1835 and 1840) remains the major source of insight into the distinguishing qualities of American society. Many editions are available. The J. P. Mayer edition with translation by George Lawrence (1969) is competent and inexpensive.

The Puritans first gave expression to the idea of an American world-historical mission. Perry Miller in *The New England Mind: The Seventeenth Century* (1939), *The New England Mind: From Colony to Province* (1952), and *Errand into the Wilderness* (1956) displays a keen eye and a sure hand in his critical examination of Puritan thinking. Miller argues that the Puritans departed from Calvinism in their conviction that men and women could hasten the coming of Christ's kingdom. Nathan O. Hatch, *The Sacred Cause of Liberty: Republican Thought and the Millennium in Revolutionary New England* (1977), describes how the understanding of the mission changed in the eighteenth century: civil liberty supplanted the millennium and religious reformation as the goal. Frederick Merk, *Manifest Destiny and Mission in American History* (1963); Ernest Lee Turveson, *Redeemer Nation: The Idea of America's Millennial Role* (1968); and Robert D. Linder and Richard V. Pierard, *Twilight of the Saints: Biblical Christianity and Civil Religion in America* (1978) follow the career of the American mission down to modern times.

One could hardly find better guides to the role of the market in ordering society or to the role of the corporations as the major players in and apologists for the market than Charles E. Lindblom, *The Market System: What It Is, How It Works, and What to Make of It* (2001), and Robert L. Heilbroner, *The Making of Economic Society* (1963). Karl Polanyi, *The Great Transformation* (1944), describes the rise of capitalism and decries many of its consequences. Friedrich A. von Hayek sees *The Road to Serfdom* (1944) in the efforts of government to mitigate some of the consequences of capitalism. Charles Perrow, *Organizing America: Wealth, Power, and the Origins of Corporate Capitalism* (2002), is well worth consulting on the corporations' role. Finally, mention must be made of the great apologist for the market, Adam Smith, and its most profound critic, Karl Marx. Their works are available in many editions. Readily accessible are Richard F. Teichgraeber's abridged edition of *Wealth of Nations* (1985) and the second edition of Robert C. Tucker's *The Marx-Engels Reader* (1978).

INDEX

Adams, Abigail, 39
Adams, John, 12, 39
African Americans (blacks), 52, 75, 92, 94, 105, 109–10, 131; discrimination against, 76, 84–86, 158; violence against, 111. *See also* slavery; Three-Fifths Compromise; Tuskegee syphilis experiment
American Exceptionalism (Lipset), 97
American Federation of Labor (AFL), 114–15
American Indians (Native Americans), 47, 110–11, 125, 133
American mission, secular theory of, 127–29, 137–38
Anti-Federalists, 14, 22, 39, 47, 50; objections to Constitution, 5–6, 28

Baldwin, Abraham, 10
Baldwin, Ebenezer, 125
Bassett, Richard, 6, 7, 32
Bedford, Gunning, 42–43
Beecher, Lyman, 129–30
Beveridge, Albert J., 133
Bible, the, 6, 87, 127; in covenant theology, 120, 122; on materialism, 145; as referent at the Founding, 10, 14; on slavery, 144–45; on usury, 145, 149. *See also* millennialism
bicameralism: in the Constitution, 42, 53–54; in Madisonian system, 58–59, 61, 63; as remedy for tyranny of the majority, 91
Biddle, Francis, 88
Bill of Rights, 1, 29–30, 98, 110, 169; to allay popular suspicions, 5, 20, 25, 28, 65

Bork, Robert, 28
Bradford, William, 126
Bush, George W., 87, 95, 134, 135
Butler, Pierce, 8, 35, 41

Calvinism, 3, 7; and rise of the market, 148–50; tenets, 2
capitalism (free enterprise), 131, 136, 139–41, 150–56, 170–72; in Marxism, 107, 112. *See also* division of labor; economic efficiency; economic growth; freedom
Chauncy, Charles, 126
checks and balances, 41, 50, 69, 71, 73–74, 79, 97, 100, 202; consequences, 91–92, 98; description of, 53–54; in Madisonian system, 58–68
chief executive officers (CEOs), 151–52, 158–59
Christian fundamentalism, 3, 25; definition of, 6
City of God, The (St. Augustine), 123–24
civic virtue, 130, 202; definition of, 9, 66
civil unions, 89–90
class consciousness, 107, 113–14
Cohen, Roger, 128
Colbert, Jean-Baptiste, 151
command, economic system of, 140–41, 158; as alternative to market, 142–44; in Bible, 144–45; compared to market, 155–57, 165–70; in corporations, 151–52; flaws of, 146–48
Compleat Body of Divinity, A (Willard), 119
Congregational Church, 6, 23–24, 100, 119, 121, 123, 128, 132; affiliation among Framers, 7; amended theory of exceptionalism, 129–30; established

ABOUT THE AUTHOR

John T. Bookman is professor emeritus of political science at the University of Northern Colorado. He has published articles on political philosophy and American politics in academic journals, and he taught those subjects to undergraduates and graduate students for thirty-four years. He is also the coauthor with Stephen Powers of *The March to Victory* (Harper & Row, 1986, and University Press of Colorado, 1994). Both editions were History Book Club selections. He received his PhD from the University of Cincinnati. Since retirement, his days have been filled with sculpture, fly-fishing, and hiking, in addition to his writing. He lives in Greeley, Colorado.